THE COMPLETE ZAHA HADID

Thames & Hudson

THE COMPLETE ZAHA HADID

This is a revised and expanded edition of *Zaha Hadid: The Complete Buildings and Projects*, originally published in 1998 by Thames & Hudson Ltd, 181A High Holborn, London WC1V 7QX
www.thamesandhudson.com

British Library Cataloguing-in-Publication Data
A catalogue record for this book is available from the British Library

ISBN 978-0-500-34250-3

Printed and bound in China by Hing Yip Printing Co Ltd

The film, on the one hand, extends our comprehension of the necessities which rule our lives; on the other hand, it manages to assure us of an immense and unexpected field of action. Our taverns and our metropolitan streets, our offices and furnished rooms, our railroad stations and our factories appeared to have us locked up hopelessly. Then came the film and burst this prison-world asunder by the dynamite of the tenth of a second, so that now, in the midst of its far-flung ruins and debris, we calmly and adventurously go travelling. With the close-up, space expands; with slow motion, movement is extended. The enlargement of a snapshot does not simply render more precise what in any case was visible, though unclear: it reveals entirely new structural formations of the subject. So, too, slow motion not only presents familiar qualities of movement but reveals in them entirely unknown ones 'which, far from looking like retarded rapid movements, give the effect of singularly gliding, floating, supernatural motions'. Evidently a different nature opens itself to the camera than opens to the naked eye – if only because an unconsciously penetrated space is substituted for a space consciously explored by men.[1]

THE EXPLOSION OF A TENTH OF A SECOND

Zaha Hadid is a great cinematographer. She sees like a camera. She perceives the city in slow motion, in pans, swoops and close-ups, in jump-cuts and narrative rhythms. As she draws the world around her, she draws out its unconscious spaces. She finds what is latent in the constructions of our modern world and storyboards them into utopias. She boldly explores, she slows down and accelerates the rhythms of everyday life, and she subjects her environment to the surgical exposition of architecture as a form of representation. She builds the explosion of a tenth of a second.

This does not mean that she is not an architect. Hadid aims to build, and her images are part of the process that moves towards construction. She does not, however, propose inserting an autonomous object into a blank site. Instead, her buildings are intensifications that lead to extensions. She compresses all the energies that cause the building to appear, from its programme to its technological infrastructure. Her buildings are free to reach out from this density to create spaces that are free of encumbrances. Where there was once (the potential for) private activity, walls and pipes, there are now shards and planes that slice through the landscape to open up a space we did not know could exist.

Hadid has constructed her career in architecture in a similar manner. She has folded the memories of a youth spent on woven carpets into a training at London's Architectural Association. She has used the forms of early 20th-century artists as the building blocks out of which she has erected her palaces of abstracted memories. She has drawn the energies of the city and the heavy contours of the landscape around her like a cloak, and then used that force as the starting point for explorations into an unknown territory towards which her angular forms point.

One might say that Zaha Hadid is a Modernist, designing lofts tied to technological cores as a celebration of the new.[2] Hadid has no truck with typologies, applied orders, implied assumptions or gravity: she believes that we could and should build a better world, one marked by freedom, above all else. We would be liberated from the past, from the constraints of social convention, from physical laws, and free of our bodies. Architecture, for Modernists such as Hadid, is the always fragmentary construction of such a world.

THE THREE MODES OF MODERNISM

Traditionally, there are three aspects to such modernism. First, its adherents believe in new structures. By harnessing technology, a good Modernist posits, we can use our resources (including ourselves) more efficiently to create the maximum amount of surplus, whether of space or of value. This 'too much' is that which is the heroic reality of the always new, the future, the utopian. It is that which has no shape and comes about by reducing form to its minimum. Second, the Modernist believes in new ways of seeing. Perhaps the world is already new, but we just don't recognize it as such. We see only what we have been trained to perceive. If only we can look in fresh ways, we can change the world by just that act. We need to open our eyes, our ears and our minds to the realities of our existence. Then we will already be free. Third, the Modernist wishes to represent the reality of modernity. Fusing the first two aspects, she or he transforms our new perceptions into representations for the forms we have created. Such shapes are the prototypes for a reality in which things have become rearranged and dissolved to the point that all but the new disappears. By representing new things in new ways, we can build a new world and inhabit it, if only with our eyes.

It is this third aspect that characterizes the work of Zaha Hadid. She does not invent new forms of construction or technology; she shows us a world in new ways by representing it in a radical manner. She finds

the roots of Modernism in the dissolution of both subject and object, and draws them out onto the stage of the modern landscape, which she reshapes as a place in which we can boldly go wandering.

The models for such modernism go back at least to the Baroque, when subject and object first lost their unquestioned authority. Instead of the human body, which stood before God in a world of sin, there was only the continuity of the real into which the self became folded:

> Matter thus offers an infinitely porous, spongy, or cavernous texture without emptiness, caverns endlessly contained in other caverns: no matter how small, each body contains a world pierced with irregular passages, surrounded and penetrated by an increasingly vaporous fluid, the totality of the universe resembling a 'pond of matter in which there exists different flows and waves'.[3]

Architecture attempts to make this flow of energy present, to catch it in its myriad forms:

> The Baroque invents the infinite work or process. The problem is not how to finish a fold, but how to continue it, to have it go through the ceiling, how to bring it to infinity . . . [the fold] determines and materializes Form. It produces a form of expression, a *Gestaltung*, the genetic element or infinite line of inflection, the curve with a unique variable.[4]

The industrial revolution, of course, built such a world of chaos, removing meaning or value from each object or individual and folding it into the flow of capital. As a result, architecture increasingly dissolved into fields of glass, steel and concrete, flowing around the last vestiges of form and burying them behind the accumulations of consumer goods. It is these flows that Zaha Hadid builds.

BRINGING THE OUTSIDE(R) IN

Yet Hadid's work does not have only the Western roots associated with modernity. Born in Iraq, she speaks of her fascination with the Persian carpets of her youth, the intricate patterns that defeated comprehension and embodied the collaborative efforts of hands transforming reality into a sensuous surface, simple spaces into lush ones. Note, coincidentally, that was also women's work.[5]

In the narrative unfolding of Hadid's work, one can also draw a comparison to Chinese and Japanese scroll paintings. Modernism proposes that we construct sense out of the accretion of everyday activities that continually change our reality, rather than fixing a particular order onto things. This is a method of working that the painters of scrolls knew well. They slithered in and out of their works, focusing on small details, showing scenes several times from different angles, stringing together landscapes out of isolated elements. The sweeps of echoing lines folded into a vision that altered and returned a world, transformed, back to the viewer.

All of these traditions were available to the artists of the early 20th century, and their art provides clues to Hadid's pictorial building blocks. Whether in Cubism, Expressionism or Suprematism, abstract fragments were assembled into a narrative structure. These artists blew up their world – Duchamp's *Nude Descending a Staircase* is Zaha Hadid's grandmother.

Hadid's most immediate parentage is that of the Architectural Association in London. She studied there during a period when the school was at its peak as the world's centre of architectural experimentation. Building on the legacy of Archigram, students and teachers such as Peter Cook, Rem Koolhaas, Bernard Tschumi and Nigel Coates transcribed the convulsions of the modern world into the subject and the form of their work. Daring to be Modernist all over again, they sought to capture the energy of all our changing activities by telling stories about them, and in so doing added a narrative viewpoint to the attempt to give shape to modernity. Whether the works were anecdotal and convoluted (Tschumi), or represented a mythical collage (Koolhaas) or a manifesto (Cook), they all incorporated multiple perspectives, sweeping and expressive forms, and technological frameworks into images whose representation described rather than defined.

Grand Buildings, Trafalgar Square

CONDENSED COLLAGES

It is in this context that Zaha Hadid's work took shape. Her first notable project, her thesis design for a bridge over the River Thames [Malevich's Tektonik, 1976–77; p. 18] is undoubtedly indebted to her association with Rem Koolhaas – she collaborated with the Office of Metropolitan Architecture for three years – in the way in which it foregrounds a geometry reduced to its essence, literally evoking the Suprematist work of Malevich. Her painting of the bridge looks like the Malevich aeroplanes that could also be sculptures or homes. The neutrality of the image is intentional, as she saw the building as a 'social condenser', to use a phrase then popular at the Architectural Association. The building itself is a Modernist loft that folds back on itself to bring different programme elements (which she does not actually show) into close contact with each other. What astounds us as viewers, however, are not the project's functional aspirations or its quotations of the past, but the image itself: it holds the page and eye with a resolute statement of the new.

In several projects after her graduation, Hadid continued to develop her narrative stance more fully into a spatial language. The forms of 59 Eaton Place [1981–82; p. 21], an apartment design for her brother, directly evoke an IRA bomb that had exploded nearby. The drawing itself is an explosion, and the elements it places on the page are fragments from this most modern release of energy. In what was to become a central theme in Hadid's architecture, the objects condense and the city's forms turn into furniture. These interior pieces then move back out to take their place as Pop Art elements, a stage set for the reoccupation of a modern city.

Hadid developed the 59 Eaton Place drawings further into her vision of Halkin Place [1985; p. 28]. In a rooftop view, the viewer soars above the eaves of the city's row houses to have a Peter Pan view of a city coming apart at the seams, a perspective that lets Hadid's fragments of a Modernist utopia reinhabit their historical forms.

Hadid's proposal for the new residence for the Irish Prime Minister [1979–80; p. 20] introduced collage into her work. Representational elements (tiles, globes, bricks) populate a simple cube through which a long, curving wall cuts to open up the project's narrative. Instead of telling us about the programme or the site, Hadid evokes the cosmopolitan nature of the residence; rather than give us the plot, she sets the scene.

Her proposal for the Grand Buildings project in London's Trafalgar Square [1985; p. 25] summarizes many of her achievements and shows her ability to reimagine the urban landscape. The painting is a diptych that depicts the building from at least five perspectives. It also shows the city peeling away from itself in both a right-side-up and a bottom-up view, creating the unsettling effect of not knowing what is the reflection and what is the preferred ground of the painting. By combining the cleverness of an Escher drawing with the aspirations of a Constructivist composition, Hadid delaminates the city.

Hadid has a programmatic rationale for this manner of representation: the Grand Buildings project was something that would put the activities and forms of Trafalgar Square into a dense composition that would free up layers of open spaces to allow the city to breathe into the building, while its aggressive shapes moved out into the urban terrain. Opening up the city at the seams, where the reality we experience and the fantasy of a new projection or building meet, became a recurrent subject of her paintings. In this instance, she accomplished this within the image itself, leaving Trafalgar Square to its over-touristed reality and her building in the utopian realm of unfulfilled fantasies.

The summation of these early works took two forms. The first was a painting that presented all of her projects to that point, *The World (89 Degrees)* [1983; p. 24]. In it, Hadid imagines our global reality as a collection of her designs as we might see them from a helicopter or a missile shooting off into space. As the world turns, its landscape heaves up into fragments of new geometries. The real world becomes Hadid-land, where gravity disappears, perspective warps, lines converge, and there is no definition of scale or activity. This is not a specific scene of functions and forms, but a constellation of possible compositions that together form a veritable landscape: a space shaped by human hands into an artificial depiction of the physical environment in which we live.

The second summation made Hadid famous. Her winning entry for the Hong Kong Peak competition [1982–83; p. 22] proved to thousands of architects and design students (including this author) that the techniques she had been developing were a new form of architecture. Situated at the highest point of the then colony, the project was itself a summation of the site as well as of all those programmes that jettisoned the mundane demands of existence in favour of a purely hedonistic collection of forms. The building was a facility that aimed to delight and discipline the body in a form that appeared socially acceptable.

Hadid's architecture embodied this programme and site in tubes that stacked up on top of each other like a pile of wooden beams on a construction site. They extended the verticality of the site in cantilevers and stratified spaces. The interstices of the forms articulated the Peak's function as a social club where activities intersected, while the beams' movement seemed to capture and solidify the trajectory of bodies in motion. It was a building that brought human and mountain together to test each other. It did not just 'crown the brow', it pulled the very Peak apart so that we, like latter-day Titans, could do battle with it.

Hadid laid out this vision in a set of very large paintings that seemed to aspire to the scale of the Peak itself. Although the architect emphasized the rational nature of her construction, the drawings pulled the parts and pieces apart, exploding its site and its programme. In one painting Hadid showed elements of the club becoming part of downtown Hong Kong, while the metropolis's skyscrapers below became abstract planes that rotated, flew off and actually turned into the building blocks for the Peak. In these instances Hadid put forward an architecture that represented the artificial landscape of that or any metropolis as an assembly of abstract geometric forms. These shards of the new pointed towards a more open, intense and unstable arrangement of space.

SETTING SAIL ON A SEA OF GESTURES

In the following decade Hadid expanded these themes in buildings, designs and proposals around the world, a number of which were in Germany. These included two of her most ambitious projects to date, the IBA-Block 2 in Berlin [1986–93; p. 33] and the Vitra Fire Station in Weil am Rhein [1990–94; p. 50]. While the former built the basic forms used in the Grand Buildings design, the latter pointed the direction to a new phase of her work.

The projects for the Victoria City Areal [1988; p. 40] in Berlin, the Hafenstraße Development in Hamburg [1989; p. 44] and the Zollhof 3 Media Park in Düsseldorf's Rheinhafen [1989–93; p. 54] had in common what had by now become Hadid's signature prow shapes, loft-like spaces around eccentric cores, public spaces brought into the building and shapes extending out into the city. Over the years, these forms took on an almost stylistic cast, yet they also changed character. They became lighter, more transparent and more layered. To some degree, this was the result of larger and, in most cases, more conventional programmes. These office buildings and apartment blocks had few hybrid elements, so it was perhaps difficult to develop a narrative representation of them.

One also sensed a shift in focus. Where Hadid's earlier buildings were collages assembled out of disparate elements, her forms now seemed to evolve as singular gestures. To Hadid this was the result of seeing her work as a form of landscape, or shaping of the land. While the Victoria City Areal still followed the recipe of intensification and extrusion Hadid had first proposed in the Grand Buildings scheme, the large complexes in Düsseldorf and Weil am Rhein read like fragments of a Modernist iceberg, whose clefts leave the edges as openings. These fissures reveal the partial nature of each building. In the Düsseldorf project, the complex's various functions accrue similar forms, which are sheared off into bridges, walkways and public buildings that are unified in their free exploration of space. Whether in the public realm or in the office towers, everything is part of the same universe of forms.

Vitra Fire Station

9

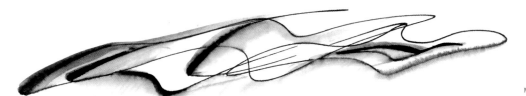

Museum of Islamic Arts

Hadid's use of colour also began to change. After the hot image of *Metropolis* [1988; p. 38] and the colour-coded fragments that still haunted both Berlin buildings, the other German designs were remarkably soft in their colourations. This was partially because glass now predominated, and perhaps also because of the relatively grey environment of German cities. It also, however, seemed to mark a cooling down of Hadid's palette: tones and tonalities, folds of continual forms and modulated volumes displaced collages of shards.

These developments culminated in the Vitra Fire Station. When one sees it from Frank Gehry's celebrated all-white museum, one is most aware of the prow-like shape of the building. In reality – and Hadid's drawings make this clear – the fire station has been conceptually sheared off from the factory blocks next to it and shot through with a curving walkway that leads back to the museum and around the complex. It is an eruption out of its place that freezes the muteness of the factory walls as tilting enclosures. The building opens up views along the fire station's contours, rather than standing against them. This geological formation continues on the inside, where the larger spaces for the fire trucks curve into the shower and lounge areas, and the stairs step up with the volumes towards the second floor.

Hadid proved with Vitra that she could build a landscape. Although the forms may appear familiar, they are a long way from the constructed assemblages of her early work. Instead of building on the land, opening up new spaces and inserting forms that reared up with aggressive challenges to their surroundings, she now drew her forms out from the site, moulded them out of functions and used spatial logic to create monumental built facts. Her architecture became reminiscent of how fields rise up over hills and caves open up below them, of how rivers move through undulating landscapes and peaks provide a sense of orientation. Perhaps Hadid realized that the 'explosion of a tenth of a second' revealed not so much the construction of the human psyche as it did the nature of the built environment as a sedimentation of human habitation that follows rules analogous to those in inorganic nature.[6] She found free spaces not in the fragments of a utopia, but in the exploration of what already exists.

SPIRALLING INTO CONTROL

After Vitra, spirals begin to appear in Hadid's work, in the folded metal plate that enclosed the Blueprint Pavilion for Interbuild 95, in Birmingham [1995; p. 76], the curling up of the 'urban jewels' in the Cardiff Bay Opera House [1994–96; p. 80] and the tight sequence of spaces at the Victoria & Albert Museum's Boilerhouse Extension [1996; p. 84]. After wandering in the landscape, Hadid's buildings seem to want to make the landscape their own by wrapping it around the programmes and then using the surroundings to shelter or contain space. In the V&A project, the gallery spaces reach up beyond the rooftops in the same way they did in Halkin Place. At the Cardiff Bay Opera House, spirals enclose the grand space of the main hall; in the Blueprint Pavilion, they created an aedicular presence for the fair stand.

Although most of her recent works are large buildings, Hadid draws them as transparent volumes. Instead of the weighty presence of tectonic plates, she now suggests that the manipulation of geometry and structure could liberate a space from its confines. The preoccupation with continuity of a landscape becomes recast as open reaches and interior volumes. Many of the drawings associated with these projects have white lines on black surfaces, as if they were but sketches of possibilities open to interpretation. The certainties of her early projects have given way to the gestural exploration of abstract openness.

This translucent, gem-like quality reached a culmination in Hadid's proposals for the Hackney Empire theatre in London [1997; p. 96] and the Lois & Richard Rosenthal Center for Contemporary Art in Cincinnati [1997–2003; p. 104]. Here the skins dissolve into nothing more than the interface between the energy of the city and the interior. These forces become more and more localized in ramps and spiralling volumes. Folding and interlocking, positive forms (walls, floors and ceilings) and negative spaces (inhabitable spaces) turn into eels slithering around each other in ever more dense, and yet fully lucid, spatial organizations.

At the same time, the tubular forms of her earlier projects turn into dominant features. They are bundled together to form the Spittelau Viaducts in Vienna [1994–2005; p. 70] and the Habitable Bridge project in London [1996; p. 86]. Though to some extent the beams recall the slabs of the Peak in Hong Kong, they are now much denser and more tightly packed; circulation and usable space become virtually indistinguishable. They also emphasize the horizontal movement through space over the vertical build-up of form. In the Landesgartenschau 1999 project in Germany [1996–99; p. 90], they merged with Hadid's previous interests in the making of a landscape to create a great curved plane.

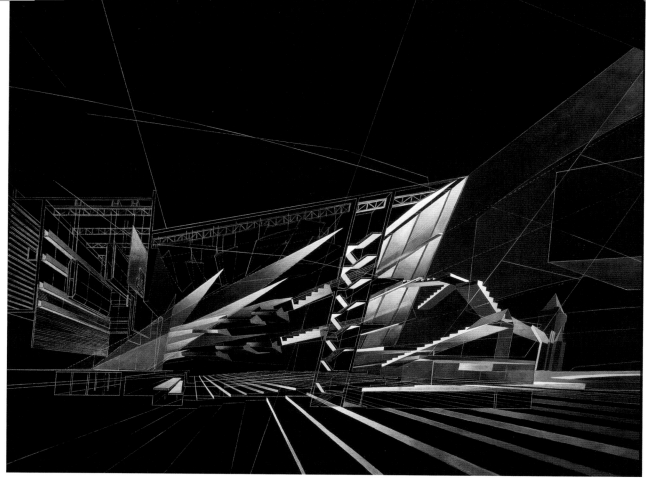

TOWARDS A NEW LANDSCAPE

Landscape has become a dominant preoccupation in Hadid's work. If the volumes of her designs are increasingly fluid, so are their exteriors. In projects like the Museum of Islamic Arts in Qatar [1997; p. 94], the building becomes no more or less than a ripple undulating out of the site, moving up to encompass spaces and then dying back down into the ground. Courtyard slots weave space and solid together like a Persian carpet, but also like rivers or lakes, and move in and out of land. Like ripples in clothing or the forms of the Verner Panton chairs she adores, these buildings are moulds of the programme that rise up only as far as they must to accommodate use, but then reveal the beauty of the body inherent in the movement itself.

Inside this new world, however, there is a different reality. It is one Hadid has most fully explored in such recent projects as her scheme for the Mind Zone exhibit in London's Millennium Dome [1998–2000; p. 98]. The complex interweaving of spaces and forms is smoothed over by the landscape-like skins, but with a flip of a wall, the contours of landscape become overhanging prows. Hadid has not forgotten her desire to gesture beyond the limitations of site and programme to create structures that seem larger and more open than we expect from a confined building.

Most of Hadid's recent projects thus appear to have replaced slabs, prows and blocks with spirals and tubes. Motion and gesture have replaced form as dominant elements, and the work is more open, tentative and lyrical. Opening up the urban landscape, unfolding the energies of the modern metropolis and creating a visionary world, Hadid explores the spatial possibilities of such an architecture in forms that have their own typology, structure and – dare one say it – stylistic properties.

The manner in which she presents this work parallels its intentions. Over the years, Hadid has involved herself less and less with the execution of her paintings and drawings. She now prefers to work, like a Renaissance master, as the head of an atelier. She sketches and does 'all the precise lines' that indicate her design objectives;[7] her co-workers render the work at a larger scale and fill in the spaces between her gestures. There is less detail in the work, less differentiation and less colour. Having moved from multi-coloured and heavily painted collages to monochrome washes, she now produces paintings that are only white lines on black paper, ghosts of a future city.

SCREEN GEMS

Despite her continuing painterly approach, Hadid now also makes use of the computer to advance her aims. The latest software allows her to take the existing landscape and unfold it, to pan, swoop, swerve, cut, slow down and speed up. In many ways, the computer fulfils Walter Benjamin's promise, especially as the separation between perception, representation and realization dissolves. The computer is a way of registering facts about our environments. It makes visible forces that are otherwise too abstract to see, it allows us to form and reform those facts however we choose, and it can then quantify these critical representations into buildable qualities. Thus the new comes out of a manipulation of the representation of what already exists.

What disappears in the process is the hand of the maker. This Benjamin also predicted, but it would seem particularly ironic in this case because of Hadid's heroic stance as a maker of outrageous structures. To a certain extent, this is not something that she can avoid. The latest computer programs can render what Hadid had constructed with such care in the 1970s and 1980s into a common mode of presentation. Everyone today sees their buildings from swooping helicopters, and many designers follow the stress points of metal and stone to create undulating, attenuated and prow-like structures. At the same time, Hadid is responsible for engendering a style that now forms office buildings, homes and fast-food franchises from Seattle to Singapore.

MAXXI: National Museum of XXI Century Arts

Instead of the framed image, the critical painting or the film, the model for her work is now the screen that collects the flows of data into moments of light and dark. The reflection of her own face is barely visible on that screen. Most of the space is dark, and the lines point not out of the cadaster of the space of representation, but in towards the flows of information. The question Hadid now faces is whether she can solidify these flows into form. Can she find the landscape beyond the physical metropolis? Can she form the spaces that open up not as Modernist lofts, but as the fragments of tuned and wired environments suspended in global relationships? Can she make something real and free out of what is hard to grasp and constrained by the logic of technology and capital?

When Hadid summed up her and our world together in 1983, she had confidence in the power of her painting to reassemble the disparate pieces of our reality into a new one. She is poised to realize many of her dreams, and her ability to do so owes a great deal to the tremendous freedom computers have given us to not only imagine new worlds, but also to construct them. Even if we miss the visionary painter of the early 1980s, we must recognize that the visible evidence of her signature on paper or canvas has disappeared exactly because her vision can now take concrete shape. As paintings disappear into computer drawings, their imagined world begins to appear.

By the turn of the millennium, Hadid was moving beyond landscape into a new kind of space. It is one that is at once dense and open, defined and indefinite, real and virtual, beyond 89 degrees, beyond right angles and skewed geometries, and beyond the event horizon in which human activities solidify into form.

BUILDING FLUID FORM

Since 2000, Zaha Hadid has become one of the most successful, recognized and prolific architects working today. In 2004, she won the Pritzker Architecture Prize, considered by many to be the discipline's highest honour. Her face has become familiar to millions on the pages of fashion magazines as well as on those of the more specialized publications on architecture. This recognition is not insignificant. It means that she can sell herself and thus her work: her signature on a building plan will raise its profile, the client's prestige and ability to sell or rent the apartments or office space she has created. This status in turn has allowed her to obtain many commissions. Now what was once a small atelier hidden away in an obscure corner of London has become a sprawling complex of studios, a design factory employing several hundred employees. More and more, Hadid relies on the immense possibilities opened up by the computer and on her collaboration with Patrik Schumacher and her most trusted designers, and more and more her buildings have developed a signature.

In some instances, this is literally the case. One might identify in some of her works of the last decade the letter 'Z', which one could also read as a logical development of the snakes slithering through some of the earlier forms, here becoming a more tightly bundled way of defining space within confined circumstances. At both the National Museum of XXI Century Arts in Rome [1998–2009; p. 156], known as MAXXI, and the BMW Plant in Leipzig [2001–05; p. 128], the serpentine shape meanders through constraints. In Rome, these consist of existing historic buildings Hadid is renovating as part of the overall complex of what will be the largest modern art museum on continental Europe. The shape is most evident in the giant beams that zig-zag from the opening projecting into an interior court, past the slightly overwhelmed historic structures, and out into the rear area where future expansions will take place. Underneath this strong form, galleries open up in

Eli & Edythe Broad Art Museum

cascades rising up towards light which Hadid admits between structural roof members. The expansion of space along terraced galleries and the movement of circulation around angled corners, up and down stairs and escalators, and through a complex arrangement of spaces that is the result of this simple gesture, all help to create the sense of endless development, of always more rooms waiting to unfold around the next bend. What ties all of this together is the roof, which is in actuality what makes possible and shelters the new space. A continuity of structure enables a continuity of space, but the two are not equivalent, and it is out of the contrast between these two that the character of the institution emerges.

The zig-zag shape is even clearer in Leipzig, where Hadid had to work around the giant production halls for the automobiles, which had already been designed by others. Her task was to create the communal as well as the office spaces, the public exposition

of how the car was made and the provision of worker amenities, and she interpreted this as one job. The trajectory here also shelters and defines the entrances, and wend its way past the public reception area and rising terraces for workers' cubicles that shelter the cafeterias underneath, to the rear area where a gym and more prosaic facilities fill out the gesture's final nooks. The roof trusses here again create the continuity that ties all of these elements together. In this case, they are a bundle of super high-strength concrete beams capable of spanning large distances, leaving the spaces beneath open to each other. Against this grand gesture, the conveyor belt along which the partially assembled and painted cars move from one production hall to the next seems almost trivial, though it does give both a programmatic and a propagandist meaning to what might otherwise remain just a gesture.

These spaces are magnificent, but they also appear – along with their vertical and concrete embodiment, the Bergisel Ski Jump in Innsbruck [1999–2002; p. 112] – to be among the last of the forms which unfold out of any kind of geometry that one might recognize from traditional building practices. But the diagonal motif does reappear in the Glasgow Museum of Transport Riverside Project [2004–10; p. 162]. It also has become a façade element that slices open and brings down the scale of what would otherwise be rather massive and closed blocks, such as the Pierres Vives building in Montpellier [2002–11; p. 158] and the Eli & Edythe Broad Art Museum at Michigan State University [2007–; p. 176].

In some recent projects, the whole building becomes a mound of triangular forms that do not so much develop as snakes of spaces as pile up, as in the Guangzhou Opera House in China [2003–09; p. 160] into an artificial mountain sponsoring its own pebbles for entrance and service functions. The opera house and other related projects rely on space frames and cladding to contain a complexity of spaces that seem to be bursting at the buildings' confines.

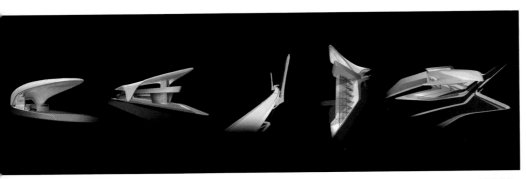

and give one the hope that someday soon Hadid's alternative to 1983's *The World (89 Degrees)* may not so much unfold out of her past work and our planet as float out into the sky as the promise of freer space.

In the meantime, Hadid is keeping busy with the production of many and massive buildings, including several skyscrapers in sites as far afield as Dubai and Warsaw. There she is taking her twisting fluidity out into the sky, trying to open up the closed and too often phallic shaft into snakes that have been charmed up into the air, into shapes she likens to flowers unfolding, and into bulbous blocks cut open with atria and large openings that slash away at what are otherwise hermetic, air conditioned and secured blocks divorced from their surroundings. Whether or not she can pull these behemoths apart sufficiently remains to be seen.

At the opposite end of the spectrum in terms of scale, Hadid is developing the building blocks for such a post-object reality. Her furniture, in which she has a great deal of structural and formal freedom, is dissolving more and more from slashing and twisting blocks into webs that reach out into space and barely contain the human body. Her urban designs, by contrast, are turning into schools of rounded shapes that together create an overall pattern. In the masterplans for Kartal-Pendik in Istanbul [2006–; p. 183], Zorrozaurre in Bilbao [2003–; p. 204], and one-north in Singapore [2002; p. 126], she has made the argument that the designed landscape consists of a collection of elements, some of them spatial, some of them no more than undulations in the landscapes or streets, that have to be entrained to create a reality that one can inhabit beyond the confines of one structure, one function or one site. To Hadid and her office, these are crystallizations of what architecture does in abstracting, opening up, reshaping and then fixing in fluid form the world in which they operate.

There is obviously a method behind this amazing proliferation of forms at all scales. What started as an unfolding and a liberating of at first only notional planes from gravity has turned into something both more ancient and more modern. One might say that Hadid has become a weaver. Her plans look more and more like intricate patterns that come out of the threading of strands, rather than like parallel slithering snakes. One wonders whether there is a connection with the carpets that covered every surface of the homes in which Hadid grew up, but the tendency towards this all-over pattern made out of distinct threads also comes out of the computer's tendency to translate flows of both people and static forces into continuous forms. While some architects might abstract these diagrams, Hadid and Schumacher go with the flow, exploiting it to create fluid forms.

Nordpark Cable Railway

They also exhibit the firm's reliance on the computer to create integrated, large-scale buildings that finally accomplish the intertwining of structure and space of which Hadid has dreamt since her student years. Schumacher proclaims the primacy of the computer, arguing that it is the technologies that rely on its power that are allowing us to create what he considers to be truly modern structures.

Hadid has come to rely more completely on the ability of the computer to unfold continuous spaces under and through an undulating fabric that at times rises up into bulbous masses or towers. In projects such as the E.ON Energy Research Department in Aachen [2006–10; p. 202] and, most notably, the Abu Dhabi Performing Arts Centre [2008–; p. 187], the snaking forms reappear, coiling over and around each other. They then change, at their collective heads, into a mass of structure and circulation elements that surround a bulbous central space with a web of ramps, beams and rooms. This device both allows the building to exist as a physical entity and lets one explore the complexities of its interstices. These buildings appear almost impossible in their fluidity, but they let Hadid prove that her vision of unfolding and reweaving reality can in fact be accomplished with the help of the most advanced computer modelling equipment. One might add, however, that many of these projects also exist in what are tabula rasa landscapes, in which all they unfold is new construction and facilities, rather than existing as a revealing of a latent reality.

Out of the snaking roofs and bending shapes, Hadid has recently also developed forms that billow out into what appear to be lighter-than-air structures barely tethered to the ground. The most poetic of these is the Nordpark Cable Railway in Innsbruck [2004–07; p. 150]. It is no more than a canopy, and is made possible by an intricate web of steel, but all one sees is a gleaming white cloud of painted metal panels tied down along a few tips around the escalators and stairs. The architecture gestures and opens, defines and reveals the landscape without ever constraining either interpretation or space. In the designs for the Nuragic and Contemporary Art Museum in Cagliari, Italy [2006–; p. 185] and the London Aquatic Centre [2003–12; p. 163], proposed for the 2012 Olympics but not to be built as designed, these clouds become containers of space that inflate to huge heights

14

INTRODUCTION: BEYOND 89 DEGREES

What emerges out of this computer-generated carpet is at first only an undulation of the landscape, as in the large-scale urban projects and in particular in the scheme for the Kartal-Pendik masterplan. The landscape develops a palimpsest that then takes on a life of its own, tending towards moments of intensity around infrastructural intersections. As strands articulate themselves vertically and extend into the landscape, they can become containers of space, whether as towers in Dubai or in the structural tubes in Leipzig or Rome. In other projects, their intersections become the heart of the project, again both vertically and horizontally. Both the projects for a proposed museum in Vilnius, Lithuania [2007–11; p. 206] and the Nuragic and Contemporary Art Museum in Cagliari develop out of X-shapes that mark the site, but also leave it open to circulation through and underneath the structures, and then extend out into long galleries. The skyscrapers in Dubai and Warsaw become intersections of tubes extending almost indefinitely.

In some structures, such movement reaches a crescendo, as in the Abu Dhabi Performing Arts Centre, which opens itself to the sea and gives one the sense that the continual implication of space is the whole (non-)point of the building. In many buildings, however, the promise is always deferred as the structures flow and slither, bulge and cantilever, and weave a dense intersection of smooth shapes that leave functional issues sliding away into often unresolved details.

What remains is a strong sense of form, one that grows out of both the site and design process, rather than being the imposition of an abstraction. As Hadid and her team of designers are able to increasingly control such forms at different scales, learning from their experiments in furniture and, paradoxically, from their reading of the landscape at an urban scale, and to extend their successful designs from intersections and jumping off points as at Innsbruck or Leipzig, one anticipates the development of the spaces hidden inside Hadid's magic carpets.

NOTES

1   Walter Benjamin, 'The Work of Art in the Age of Mechanical Reproduction', in *Illuminations*, trans. Harry Zorn (New York: Schocken Books, 1969), p. 236.

2   The loft is the Modernist space par excellence, as it is an industrial, open and functional space that frees us from the distinctions between programmes, both private and public, and decoration. It is the building block not only of Hadid's work, but also of such other late Modernists as Coop Himmelb(l)au. I discuss the significance of the loft in greater detail in *Coop Himmelb(l)au* (London: Architectural Review Press, 1998).

3   Gilles Deleuze, *The Fold: Leibniz and the Baroque*, trans. Tom Conley (Minneapolis: University of Minnesota Press, 1993), p. 5.

4   Ibid., pp. 34–35.

5   Conversation with the author, 14 December 1997.

6   See Manuel De Landa, 'Nonorganic Form', in *Zone 6: Incorporations* (New York: Zone Press, 1992), pp. 128–67.

7   Conversation with the author, 16 December 1997.

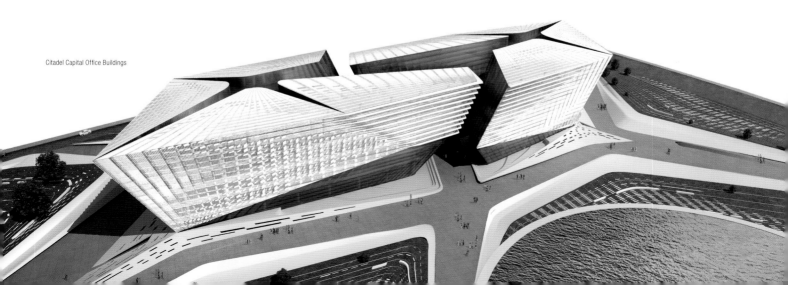

Citadel Capital Office Buildings

BUILDINGS AND PROJECTS

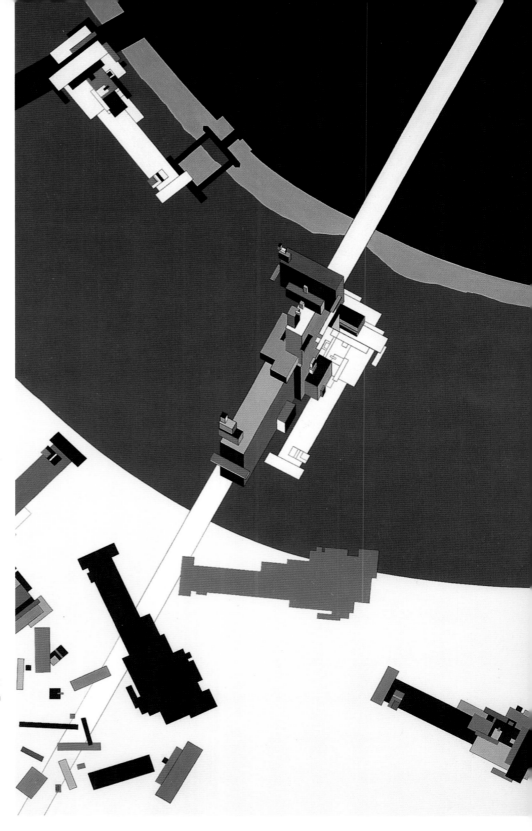

p. 16: Nassim Villas

→ For my graduation project from London's Architectural Association, I wanted to explore the 'mutation' factor for the programme requirements of a hotel on the Hungerford Bridge over the Thames. The horizontal 'tektonik' conforms to and makes use of the apparently random composition of Suprematist forms to meet the demands of the programme and the site.

The bridge links the 19th-century side of the river with the South Bank, which is dominated by the Brutalist forms of a 1950s arts complex. The structure's fourteen levels systematically adhere to the tektonik, turning all conceivable constraints into new possibilities for space.

The project has particular resonance with my later projects: first, in 'The Great Utopia' show at New York's Guggenheim Museum [p. 63], in which I was able to realize some of these tektoniks in concrete form, and second, in the Habitable Bridge project [p. 86], which considered the possibilities of a mixed-use development, also on the Thames.

MALEVICH'S TEKTONIK
London, England 1976–77

→ Situated within a rectangular 'fortress' in the centre of The Hague, the politically distinct branches of the Dutch parliament and government were housed in a single complex called the Binnenhof. To separate these two politically opposing branches, a triangular site was acquired to allow for an expansion of parliamentary accommodation. The programme therefore involved working within existing structures, while making the parliament spatially autonomous. This was achieved by creating a gap in the Binnenhof that is occupied by two slabs: a horizontal element (a glass-brick podium that contains a variety of functions and acts as a covered forum for political activity), and a small skyscraper of oval rooms. The two structures are unified by an assembly space that bridges the general public and government officials; an ambulatory running through one slab allows circulation.

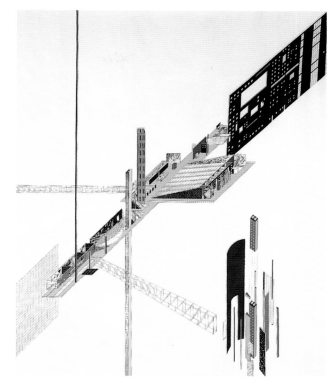

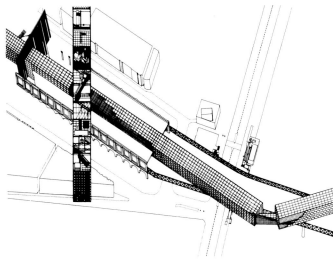

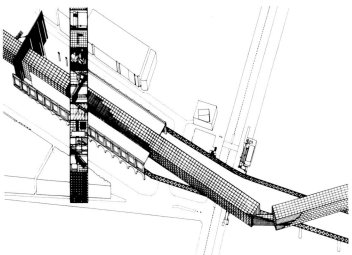

← ↑ One of my first ideological and conjectural projects, in which I sought to establish principles for the role that architecture should play in cities at the end of the 20th century. I was particularly interested in the problems of historical and cultural context. The archetype of the 19th-century museum was thus explored in two ways: through the elaboration of the precise social scenario of the metropolitan location, and through the display of a symbolic sensitivity, an aspect that appeared to be absent in the work of the contextualist architects at that time.

19

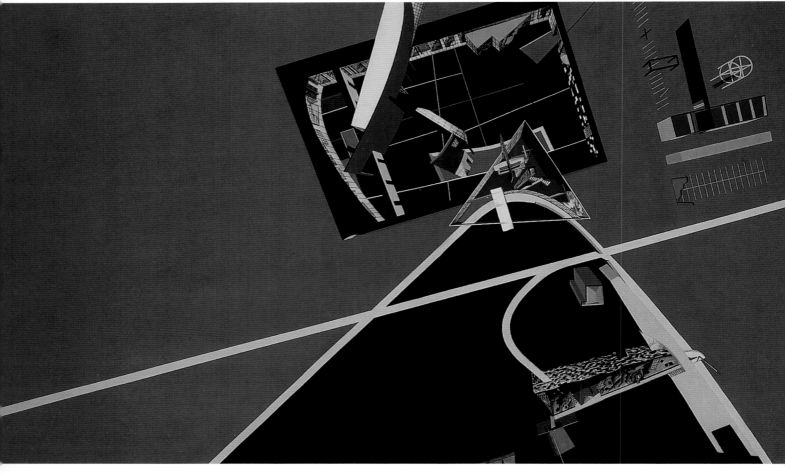

IRISH PRIME MINISTER'S RESIDENCE
Dublin, Ireland 1979–80

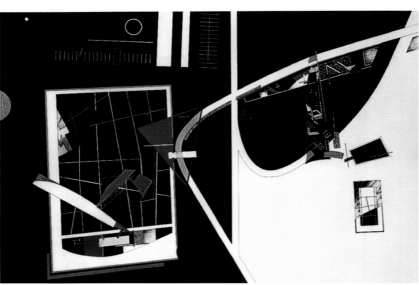

← ↑ For my first major project, a new residence and state function room for the Irish prime minister (or 'Taoiseach'), the objective was to create a weightlessness, a freedom from the stress of public life. Both buildings, though connected by a road and walkway, needed to retain their privacy. Placed within the existing walled garden, the new guesthouse is screened from the Taoiseach's residence by the main reception rooms. The guesthouse rooms are located around its perimeter, apart from the reception block and master suite, which 'float' over the garden.

→ For a competition to design the plan and elements of a park devoted to science, located outside central Paris's most visited areas, we created floating pieces that would move across the site's flat terrain. The green plateaux in a field form a new type of garden, suspended rather than hanging. Together, these pieces function like calligraphy on the land, which is dictated by mechanical systems that are at once controlled (human activity) and random (nature). Picnic areas, fast-food restaurants and information kiosks orbit within their own galaxy, in contrast to a long, monochrome 'planetary strip'. Appropriate to a project conceived for the future, there is a 'discovery garden', which condenses all the park's functions and landscapes.

CONCOURS INTERNATIONAL . PARC DE LA VILLETTE PARIS N°

← A gas explosion at the Italian Consulate at 38 Eaton Place provided the main inspiration for our renovation of an elegant turn-of-the-century townhouse on a sterile, white-washed street in Belgravia. The apartment is contained on three floors, which we inverted conceptually as three vertical zones. Our intervention in these spaces was intended to provide a certain newness, which we achieved by introducing materials such as silk and stone on the ground and top floors, as well as by inserting a new staircase in the lobby and dining area to open the public domain up into the middle level.

PARC DE LA VILLETTE
Paris, France 1982–83

59 EATON PLACE
London, England 1981–82

21

A Suprematist geology (materials that are impacted vertically and horizontally) characterizes this clifftop resort, loftily located above the congested city. The architecture is like a knife slicing through the site, cutting through traditional principles of organization and constructing new ones, defying nature and taking care not to destroy it.

Like the mountain itself, the building is stratified, with each layer defining a function: the first and second levels contain apartments; the third layer – a 13-metre-high void suspended between the second and penthouse storeys – features the club. The void becomes a new architectural landscape within which elements such as exercise platforms, a snack bar and a library are suspended like planets. The fourth and fifth levels contain penthouse apartments.

Offering and symbolizing the pinnacle of the high life, the Peak's beams and voids are a gentle seismic shift on an immovable mass.

THE PEAK
Hong Kong 1982–83

22

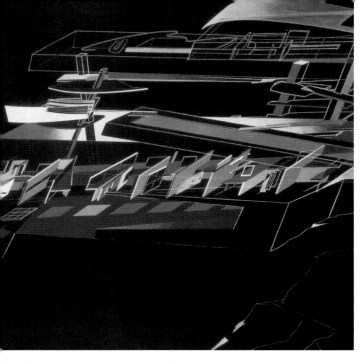

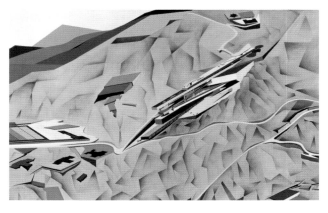

THE WORLD (89 DEGREES)
1983

→ This painting represents the culmination of a seven-year exploration into architecture's uncharted territories that began with my work as a student at the Architectural Association. Technology's rapid development and our ever-changing lifestyles created a fundamentally new and exhilarating backdrop for building, and in this new world context I felt we must reinvestigate the aborted and untested experiments of Modernism – not to resurrect them, but to unveil new fields of building. Here, projects that I had carried out over the last seven years have been compressed and expanded.

MELBURY COURT
London, England 1985

→ This design aimed to explode the rigid box rooms of the small post-war, purpose-built flat. Two curved glass walls were stretched across the existing apartment, occasionally overlapping, to create a generously fluid space around the central light well. Furniture is placed on tracks or pivots to allow spatial and functional flexibility in the living areas.

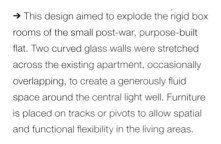

← ↑ Schemes to recapture London's most famous square continue to this day. In the hope that outdated planning restraints might be abandoned, we presented a proposal that celebrated the dynamic possibilities of the urban landscape by extending the public realm into professional offices, thereby pushing forward the frontier where modern architecture can contribute to the quality of city life. A public podium, slabs of offices and towers are the central characteristics of the buildings. Beneath the towers, which are topped by penthouses, are subterranean lobbies. A shopping concourse peels up, gently curving around the site's perimeter and enclosing a new public domain as it winds up to the roof, which features a public terrace that overlooks the mire of cars below. As one's vantage point moves around the square, the towers appear to mutate from shards that penetrate the square's surface into a single solid mass.

GRAND BUILDINGS, TRAFALGAR SQUARE
London, England 1985

HALKIN PLACE
London, England 1985

→ This study considers London at various levels, from small housing sites to larger urban schemes. We envisaged a roofscape that would relate to the sky and its immediate urban condition – some roofs are habitable, others not. (This idea anticipates our concept for La Fenice [p. 88]). In a metropolis where land is scarce and planning restrictions are severe, these elevated areas are considered sites in themselves, with spaces divided vertically into indoor and outdoor zones. In the scenario of Halkin Place, the penthouse's spaces are sandwiched between the existing and new roofs.

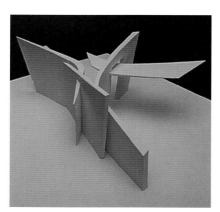

KYOTO INSTALLATIONS
Kyoto, Japan 1985

↑ This installation is a fragment of the ideas that would reach fruition in the 24 Cathcart Road project [opposite], just as the Osaka Folly [p. 48] served as a test for design principles later employed at the Vitra Fire Station [p. 50]. Seeking new ways to articulate space within a confined context, we used curved walls to warp or bend space (as at the Melbury Court project [p. 24]) and canopies to mark the entrance.

← This exhibition gave us the opportunity to create a modern contrast to the Victorian notion of tents, which so often characterized the interiors of the period. Our scheme inserts a plastic structure within a pre-existing space. Intended to be viewed from above, the structure's plan embraces the space by means of its exclusion – the opposite effect of the enclosure created by the Victorians' tents and curtains.

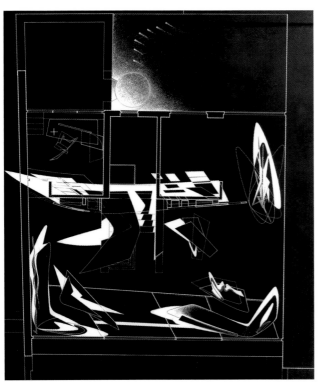

← ↑ This International Style residence provided the backdrop for the first material display of my 'Suprematist geology', an extension of my exploration at 59 Eaton Place [p. 21]. The ensemble included our Bitar furniture, which created a dynamic space of their own, rather than acting as sculptural objects in a neutral container. Pivoting, sliding and swivelling, a storage wall further animated the space with the actual physical movements of its doors and cabinets.

↓ → During the late 1980s, there was tremendous interest in revitalizing waterfront areas in numerous cities across Europe and America. As part of two workshops set up in Hamburg to explore the possible reuses of these districts, we were asked to consider ways in which the city's historic harbour area, particularly the former warehouse district of Speicherstadt, could be masterplanned to regenerate the area and accommodate a wide range of mixed uses.

The openness and large scale of the harbourfront, as well as its integration into the city centre, raised a number of interesting problems that we addressed in various ways in the Hafenstraße Development [p. 44], also in Hamburg, and in Cologne's Rheinauhafen project [p. 66]. By pushing the city's urban context into the harbour to capitalize on the spaces particular to it – views, openness, ever-present water – we sought new geometries and zones for redevelopment that would create not only a new style of urban living, but an entirely new dynamic within the city's fabric.

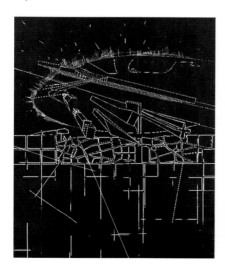

HAMBURG DOCKLANDS
Hamburg, Germany 1986

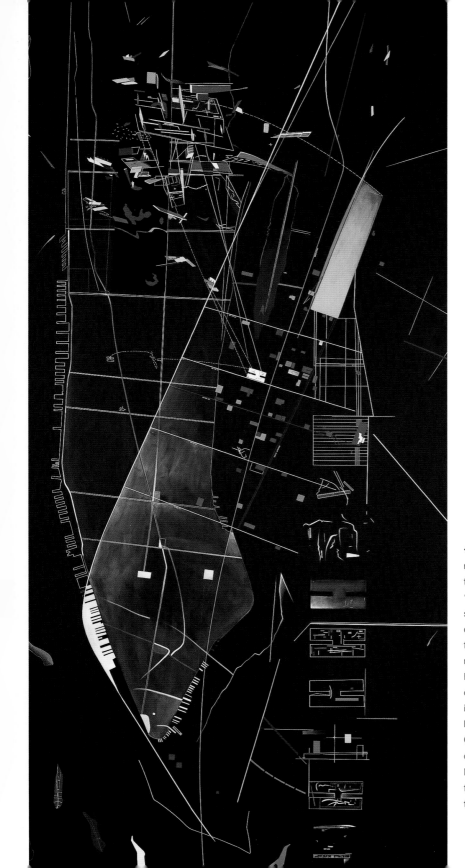

← Relating to a proposal for the reconstruction of a hotel, this sketch outlines the possibilities and variations for redefining 'hotel' and 'metropolitan living' as a specific series of confined explosions. The point of departure was Le Corbusier's Ville Radieuse for Manhattan, which I believe fundamentally misjudges New York's urban conditions. Because Manhattan is a multilayered city, intensified by its urban density, built interventions should be considered to be like condensed explosions. Whereas Le Corbusier's vision was to dissolve the city, only to replace it with a carpet of bland Modernism, I believe it is possible to sustain the intensity of the metropolis without eroding the grid that holds it together.

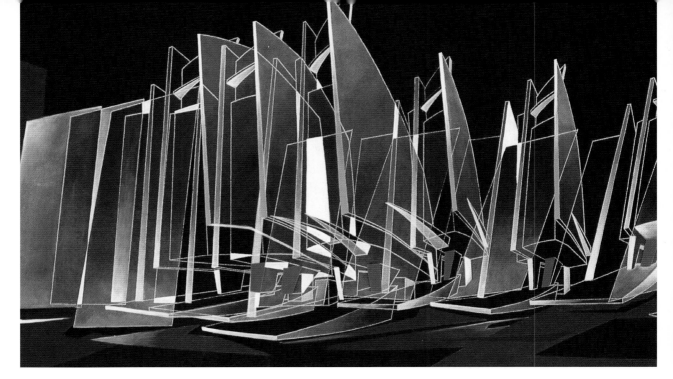

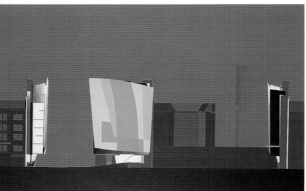

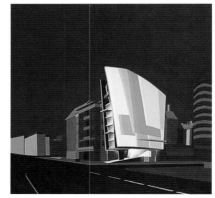

↑ ↗ → The constraints of an extremely narrow site (2.7 × 16 metres) gave rise to our design of a compressed 'sandwich' structure that comprised a series of planes, spaces and uses. The horizontal planes of the sandwich are the basis for the floor plan, which establishes the separation of circulation and movement from the office spaces. Vertically, the sandwich of spaces differentiates between the ground-floor plan for the public entrance and the cantilevered building above, which houses offices and a double-height office at the top. The lobby and entrance are raised above the ground and reached by a ramp, liberating the plan from the ground, a nod to the Russian Suprematists. The structure above is pulled away from a new back wall, and the gap above this ramp reveals the main entrance.

The plan is gently bowed and moves out towards the corner; thus, the floor area reaches its maximum at the top and creates a dynamism that rejects the usual office-block repetition. The long street elevation has a transparent surface – a structural mesh of aluminium extrusions suspended from the top – that becomes an illuminated glass box through which the interior's activities can be detected.

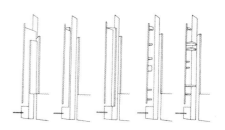

Sectional sequence [above]

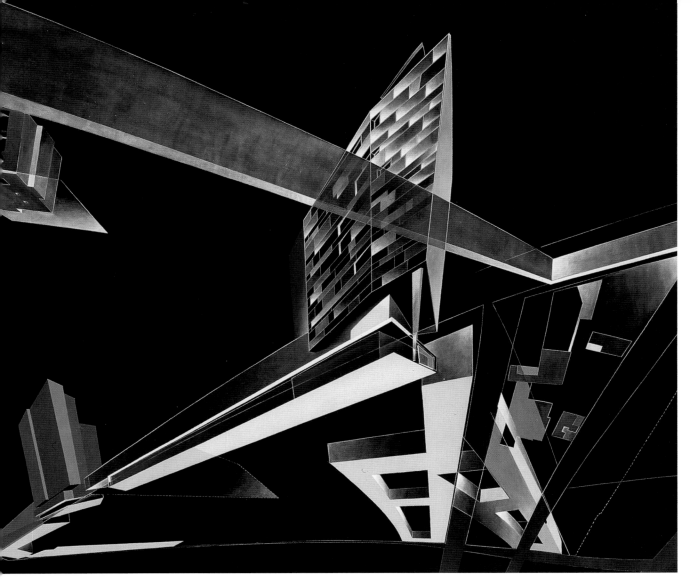

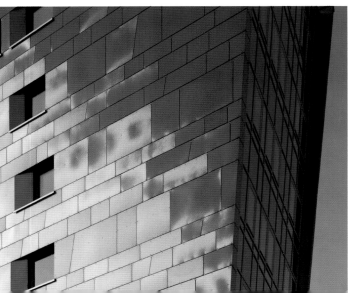

← ↑ Right from the beginning we had to confront two fundamental issues: the IBA strategy of infill and repair, and the tight building regulations for social housing, which contradict modern open-plan layouts. In addition to these constraints were the surrounding buildings, which represented a wide range of different types and periods, so despite guidelines stipulating that new developments in the area must contain an average of five storeys, a seamless insertion into this erratic context would have been virtually impossible.

We therefore interpreted the five-storey planning restriction by creating a long three-storey block that terminated in an eight-storey tower at the corner. The longer block's lower floors contain commercial premises with standardized dwellings above; on top is a roof garden with a children's playground. The sculpted tower, clad in anodized sheet metal, contains three wedge-shaped lofts on each floor.

IBA-BLOCK 2
Berlin, Germany 1986–93

33

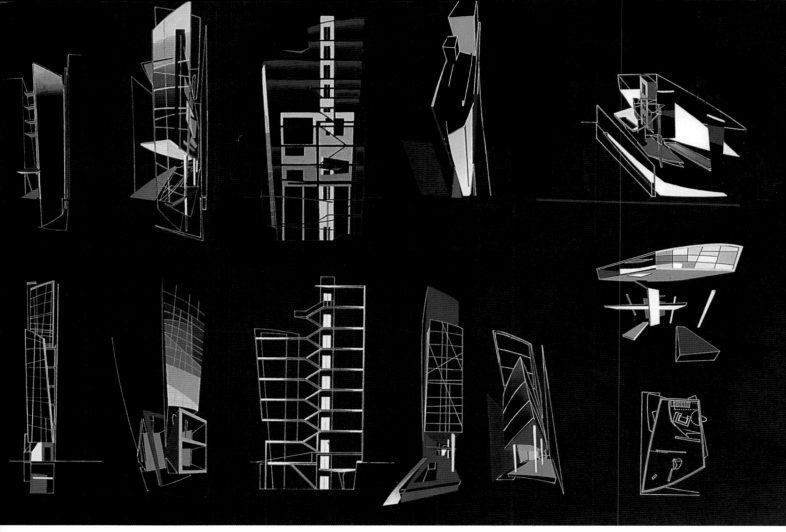

Combined plans and sections for Azabu-Jyuban and Tomigaya

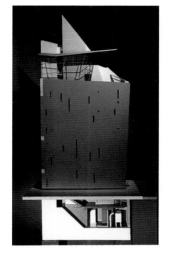

AZABU-JYUBAN
Tokyo, Japan 1986

↑ → Drawing on the experiences of the Ku'Damm project in 1986 [p. 32], we realized the great potential for releasing space. In Tokyo – *Blade Runner* territory – most sites are beyond the boundaries of space, and many buildings only increase the city's stifling congestion.

Slicing into the landscape and piercing the earth, the building exaggerates the pressure of its narrow site in a canyon of random buildings near the Roppongi district. The pristine glass structure is compressed between a tall metal wall and a reinforced concrete wall punctured by jewel-like windows. Between the walls are two curtain walls – one of blue glass, the other clear – that tilt out, rising to the terrace's parapet walls. Inside, the full impact of the released space is immediately apparent in the three-storey entrance space. A vertical stairway runs from the building's heart all the way up to the top, exploding into dramatic balconies.

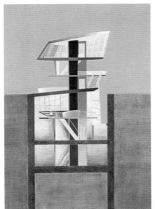

Section

← ↑ This small, mixed-use project in a cluttered residential area is related in several respects to Azabu-Jyuban [opposite], but the concept here is inverted. Composed as a series of suspended horizontal spaces and vertical elements that are interlocked by the spiralling motion of stairs and platforms, it is a building in which the volume becomes the void, rather than compressing the void out, as at Azabu-Jyuban. The centrepiece of the design is a delicate elevated glass pavilion, open on three sides, that hovers above open ground. Most of the building is below the curving ground floor, which is pulled back from the edges and holds a tall glass wall that allows light into the lower space, whose generous proportions make them flexible for retail and office activities.

In such a dense city, light and air are valuable commodities. We must release these spaces from their constricted sites and breathe light and air into the urban condition.

TOMIGAYA *Tokyo, Japan 1986*

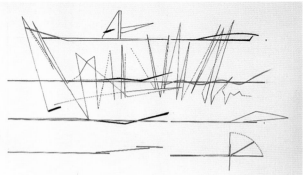

↓ → There were several interesting challenges in the brief for this design. The first was the relatively young and progressive municipality that sought to make its mark within the patchwork of Los Angeles's complex urban layout. The second was the area's fertile creative resources: West Hollywood has one of the highest concentrations of interior and graphic designers in the country, a fact symbolized by Cesar Pelli's 'Blue Whale', one of the city's most recognizable architectural landmarks; the site for the civic centre was adjacent to it.

The relatively context-free environment brought about one of my earliest explorations of the building as landscape, while the area's flat terrain allowed us to consider the site as a geometric topography, an approach foreshadowed by projects like the Parc de la Villette [p. 21]. On this urban geometric canvas, objects float and interact in a way that is only possible in wide-open spaces.

WEST HOLLYWOOD CIVIC CENTER
Los Angeles, California, USA 1987

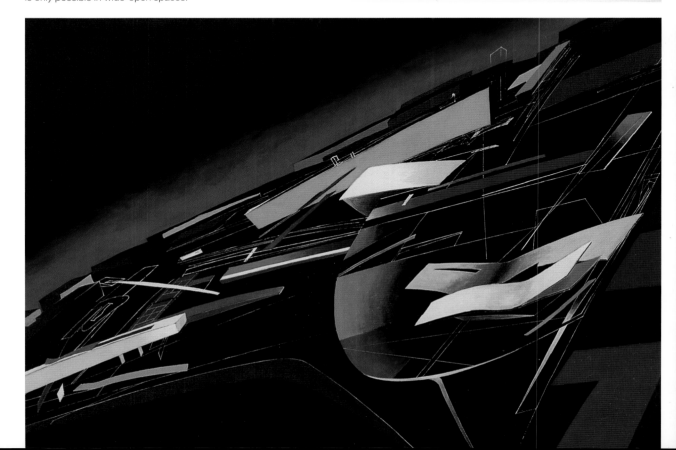

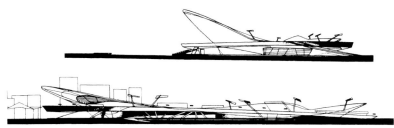

Elevations [above]

← ↑ In stark contrast to the dense urban projects executed for sites in Berlin and Tokyo [pp. 32–35], the setting for this sports complex allowed us to expand into, rather than compress, the setting. The structure therefore became a large-scale landscape relief, mirroring and settling into the land's contours. To some extent, this project marks an early exploration into the landscape. It comprises three main elements: a podium, conceived as a suspended park that provides access to the stadium and viewing platforms; a new ground plane, which ascends from street level and slips underneath the podium; and the stadium, which rises out of the shifting ground plane and podium, and permits various seating arrangements and uses.

AL WAHDA SPORTS CENTRE
Abu Dhabi, UAE 1988

→ The screaming redness of this painting, commissioned for an exhibition at London's Institute of Contemporary Arts that explored facets of the metropolis, is meant to express an exasperation with the city's sprawling mess. On one level, the painting shows London as a patchwork of villages. But rather than promoting an even distribution of this urban merging – which has been evolving for centuries – we articulated the city as polycentric, where a number of metropolitan centres condense at different focal points. In this context, the red represents the fires of London, where new settlements and new centres need to be invented to replace an exhausted and overworked heart.

↓ Before the collapse of the Berlin Wall in 1989, we were invited to speculate about the city's future. As part of an overall scheme between the axes of Mehringplatz to Bahnhof Friedrichstraße and Brandenburger Tor to Alexanderplatz, the falling of the Wall offered new possibilities for regeneration. We considered both the expansion and the repair of the city, ranging from corridors of development to 'Wall-zone' building programmes.

The focus of our vision was the Alexanderplatz. Because it represents one of the few attempts to go beyond typical 19th-century urbanism, we decided to leave it free of homogeneous commercial development, to stand in poignant contrast to the vulnerable line that used to demarcate Berlin's division. A series of diagrams shows possible development of these newly released territories. Corridor cities project into the landscape, and new geometries inhabit the former 'dead zone' (seen below), sometimes rectilinear yet slightly out of sync with the existing order.

In our eyes, the Wall zone could become a linear park. Where were once a concrete ribbon wall and no-go zone, we would lay down a strip of park, decorated with buildings.

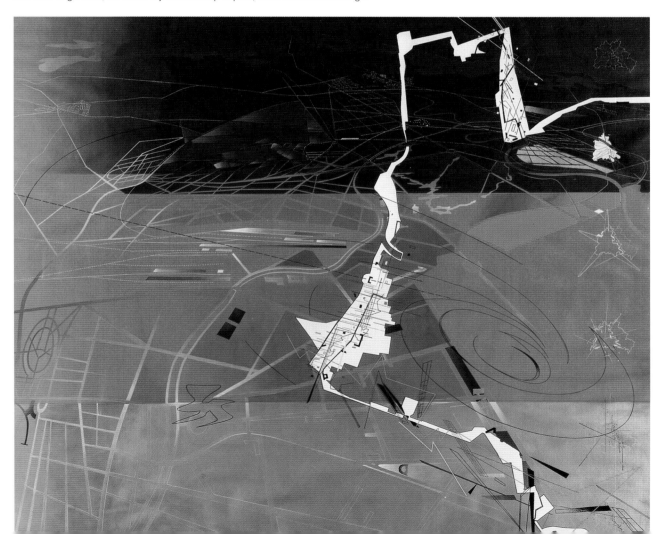

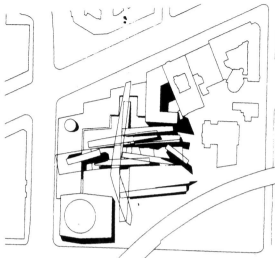

Before the Berlin Wall came down, this site epitomized the city's state as an urban island. The site is on a major axis, the Kurfürstendamm, but completely enclosed and virtually inaccessible. To create a building in such a fortified context suggested that we should intensify the urban density horizontally. The site was thus divided into new air corridors with three distinct zones that contain the three major functions: shopping facilities, offices and a hotel.

Because the cruciform site would be the new focus of several major thoroughfares – streets and rail lines – a new shopping area is terraced in concentric relation to the shops on the fringe of the site. This enclosed space is glass-floored and is suspended over further public facilities, which include more shops, the hotel lobby, a multipurpose assembly hall, a conference centre and a restaurant. Above, an extendible system of office beams – each of which might maintain a distinct corporate identity – is superimposed on the shopping facilities. On top of this floats a bent slab containing the hotel.

VICTORIA CITY AREAL
Berlin, Germany 1988

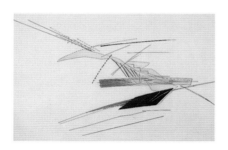

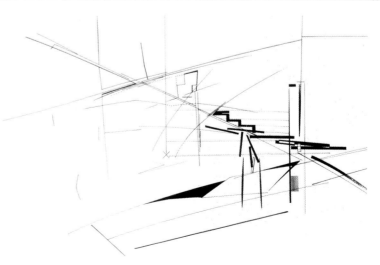
↑ ↗ → The diagonal axes of Ildefons Cerdà's 19th-century plan for the city's expansion is the pivotal element for our reconstruction of it. Our new urban geometry is based on a subtle twisting of the diagonal into skewed, interlocking fragments. As this field traverses urban contexts, it is constantly intersected by an 'elastic corridor' of local conditions – irregular (village), gridded (housing zones) or strips (railways and waterfront) – that triggers an urban response and multiplies street activity in each neighbourhood.

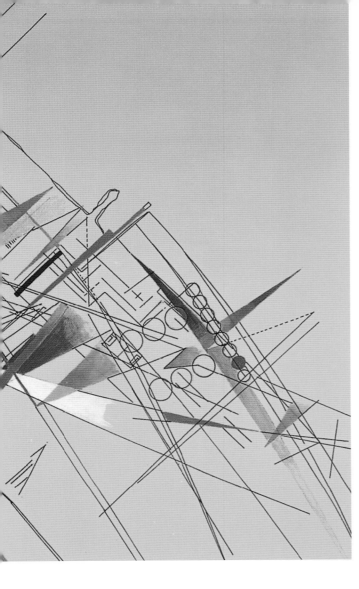

→ Similar to the principles employed in the Azabu-Jyuban and Tomigaya projects [pp. 34, 35], this design aims to counteract the congestion of Tokyo. The central form is a void – a glass container – out of which smaller voids are dramatically hollowed and which house the building's cultural and conference areas.

Within a labyrinth of closely knit rooms – like the plan of Pompeii – these conference areas are clustered and separated by variable partitions. At ground level, the spaces can be glimpsed through sharply cut slits in the glass floor. Upper levels contain exhibition spaces, studios, restaurants and public areas. On the roof is a landscaped garden with a diagonal cut that allows light and ventilation into the lower floors.

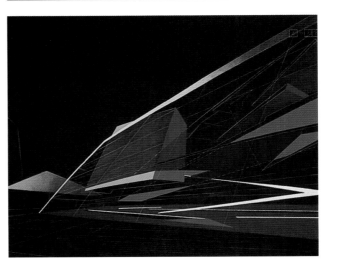

TOKYO FORUM
Tokyo, Japan 1989

In the old harbour street containing traditional four- and five-storey houses were two sites – or rather, gaps – slated for redevelopment. The street and its row houses are part of a series of parallel strips – a small park, the new street and the embankment being the other elements – that step down to the River Elbe. Our objective was to create links running across the strips and transform the embankment into a recreation area.

One site is located on an acute corner. A slab building leans forward and twists back, opening to the riverfront. The vertical organization is a sequence of commercial and residential layers, with a public space on the first two levels. Sliding sections of the glass curtain wall enable parts of each floor to become outdoor terraces. The elevation facing the river is a continuous curtain wall that wraps over to become the penthouse roof.

The second site was a gap in the 19th-century block. We envisioned a series of compressed slabs that, despite being a dense agglomeration, allowed for a degree of transparency. As one passes the building, gaps open and close between the structure's interstices, defying the notion of a flat façade. The ground floor contains retail spaces; residential units are above, and some connect horizontally across the slabs. Many aspects of this project anticipate the underlying principles of the Zollhof 3 Media Park in Düsseldorf [p. 54].

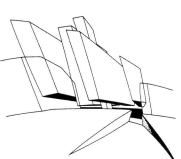

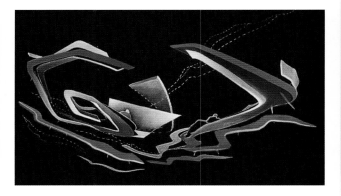

For a two-fold programme of formal eating and relaxed lounging, we wanted to create an opposition of moods. The result is two synthetic and strange worlds: fire and ice. Inspired by the seasonal ice buildings of Sapporo, the ground floor features cool greys materialized in glass and metal. Tables are sharp fragments of ice; a raised floor level drifts like an iceberg across the space. Above the ice chamber whirls a furnace of fire, rendered in searing reds, brilliant yellows and exuberant oranges. A spiral above the bar tears through the ground-floor ceiling, curling up to the underside of the upper-level dome like a fiery tornado bursting through a pressure vessel. A plasma of biomorphic sofas accommodates eating and lounging, and allows an infinite configuration of seating types with movable trays and plug-in sofa backs.

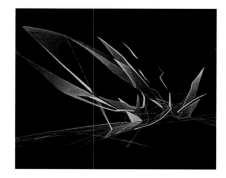

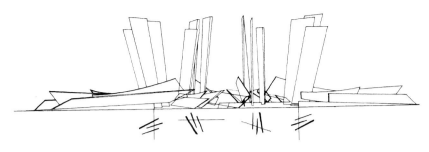

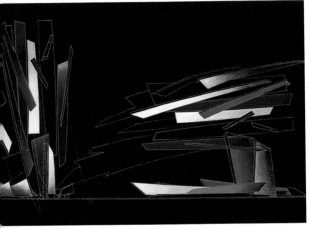

Plans/elevations [above]

OSAKA FOLLY, EXPO 90
Osaka, Japan 1989–90

↑ ↗ → Our site at the International Expo in Osaka was located on an open plaza at the junction of several paths. We designed a series of compressed and fused elements to expand in the landscape and refract pedestrian movement. From afar, two vertically extruded planes signal the folly to approaching visitors, while up close, horizontal planes define the structure's perimeters and create a series of canyons. Contrasting with the flying planes, five ramps of varying size stretch along the ground plane. The unexpected junctions of these dynamic horizontal and vertical elements create a number of coves, where visitors may seek temporary refuge from the arduous exercise of walking and sightseeing.

With its bundled and twisting walls, we were also able to treat the Osaka project as a half-scale experiment for the Vitra Fire Station [p. 50].

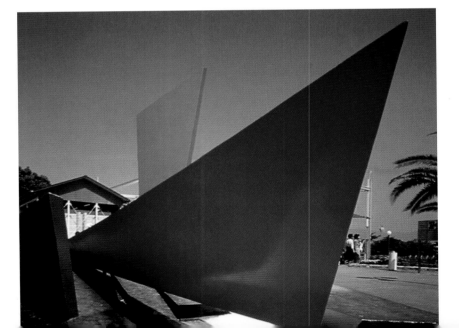

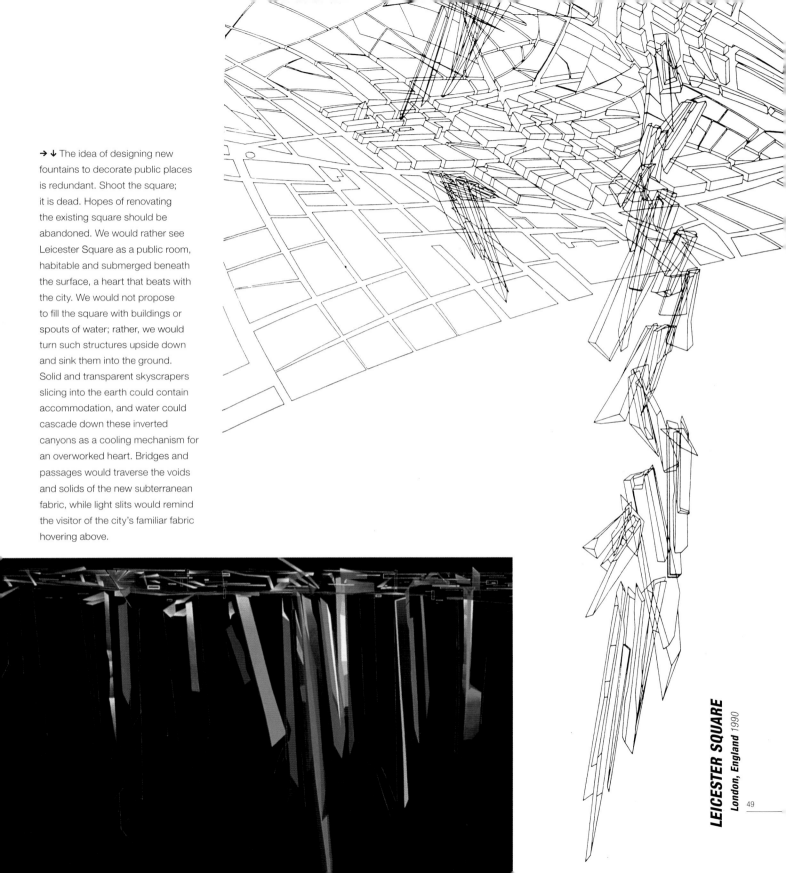

→ ↓ The idea of designing new fountains to decorate public places is redundant. Shoot the square; it is dead. Hopes of renovating the existing square should be abandoned. We would rather see Leicester Square as a public room, habitable and submerged beneath the surface, a heart that beats with the city. We would not propose to fill the square with buildings or spouts of water; rather, we would turn such structures upside down and sink them into the ground. Solid and transparent skyscrapers slicing into the earth could contain accommodation, and water could cascade down these inverted canyons as a cooling mechanism for an overworked heart. Bridges and passages would traverse the voids and solids of the new subterranean fabric, while light slits would remind the visitor of the city's familiar fabric hovering above.

LEICESTER SQUARE
London, England 1990

49

This project began as a commission to build a fire station in the northeast section of the vast Vitra factory complex in Weil am Rhein. The brief was then extended to cover the design of the boundary walls, a bicycle shed, and an exercise ground for the fire brigade.

The design was initiated by a study of the entire factory site. The intention was to place the few elements so that they would not be lost between the enormous factory sheds, and to use them to structure the whole site, giving identity and rhythm to the main street running through the complex. This street was envisaged as a linear landscaped zone, an artificial extension of the linear patterns of the adjacent agricultural fields. Rather than the fire station being an isolated object, it was developed as the outer edge, defining space rather than occupying it. This was achieved by stretching the design into a long, narrow building alongside the street, allowing it to function as a screening device against the bordering buildings.

The fire station is located where the street previously made an abrupt parallel shift, and still reflects this shift of direction, cutting into the street at an angle and bending within itself, leading the street around. The geometry of the building derives from the collision of the two main organizing geometries of this area, and the direction of the surrounding fields and factory complex is cut by a second directional movement that slices off the corner of the otherwise

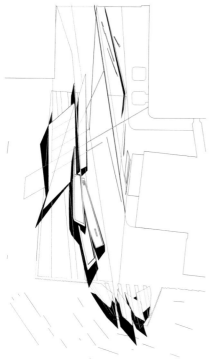

rectilinear site, itself the repercussion of the large field of railways that follow the direction of the river.

The space-defining and screening functions of the building were the point of departure for the development of the architectural concept: a linear, layered series of walls. The station inhabits the spaces between these walls, which puncture, tilt and break according to functional requirements.

The building itself reveals its interiors only from a perpendicular viewpoint. As one passes across the spaces of the fire station, one catches glimpses of the large, red fire engines. Their lines of movement are inscribed into the asphalt, a series of choreographic notations. The whole building is movement, frozen. It expresses the tension

of being on the alert, and the potential to explode into action at any moment. The walls appear to slide past each other, while the large sliding doors literally form a moving wall.

The whole building is constructed of exposed, reinforced in-situ concrete. Special attention was given to the sharpness of all edges; attachments such as roof edgings or claddings were avoided as they distracted from the simplicity of the prismatic form. This same absence of detail informed the frameless glazing, the sliding planes enclosing the garage, and the treatment of the interior spaces, including the lighting scheme. The lines of light direct the necessarily precise and fast movement through the building, which is now a chair museum.

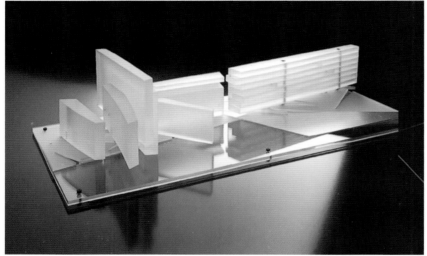

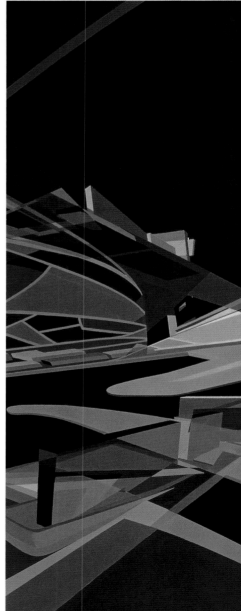

ZOLLHOF 3 MEDIA PARK
Düsseldorf, Germany 1989–93

For the redevelopment of Düsseldorf's prominent harbour into an enterprise zone containing offices for an advertising agency and studios interspersed with shops, restaurants and leisure facilities, we created an artificial landscape that faced the river and became an extension of the water's activities and functions. This landscape is protected by a 90-metre-long wall-like building that both contains the offices and blocks out traffic noise. From the river, an enormous metallic triangle cuts into the site, piercing the wall to form an entrance ramp. The adjoining ground planes crack open to reveal technical studios to the north, and shops and restaurants. Below ground, a wall of technical services is compressed, so that part of the wall rises above ground and curves around to create a 320-seat cinema.

The wall's street side has tiny linear incisions in its concrete; on the river side, levels are articulated by varying depths of cantilever on each floor. A glazed 'finger' building is a fragmented series of slabs set perpendicular to the street like glass splinters that have broken free from the wall. Where the slabs converge, a void is carved out for conference rooms and exhibition areas. The entrance lobby, a minimalist glass box surrounded by a family of sculpted feet and heavy triangular structures, is at the intersection of the wall and the finger building. From here, the street and riverscape are visually connected. A ribbon-like grand stairway leads up to the conference rooms through the underbelly of a heavy slab suspended above.

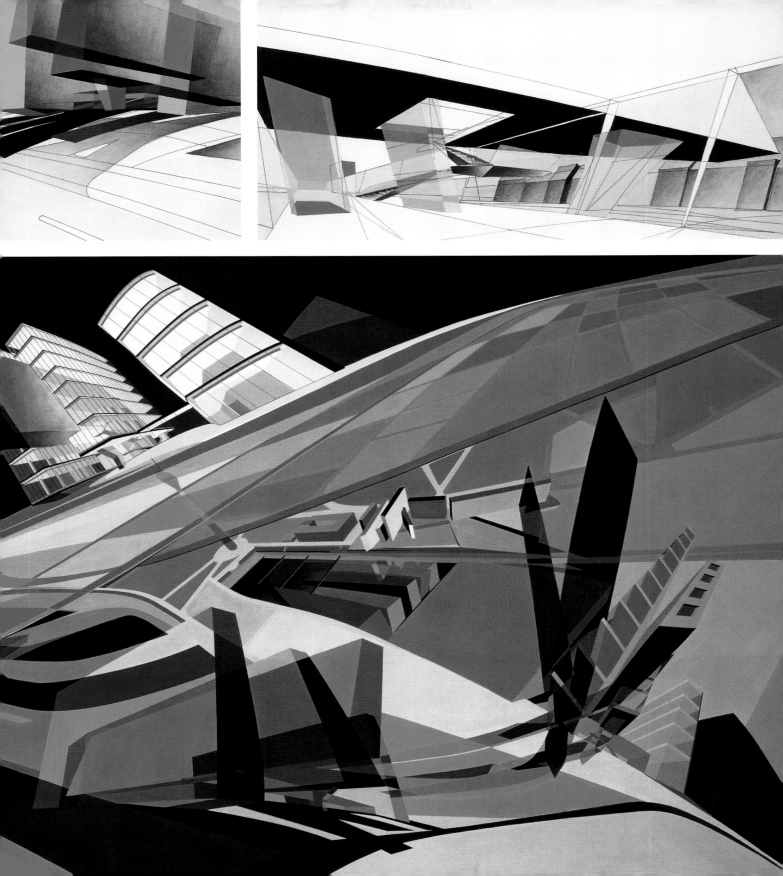

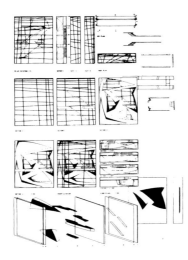

The intention for our music-video pavilion was to make a playful place in what was for me the most challenging location in the city: the gap between the monumental A-kerk and the Korenbeurs buildings in the Vismarkt district. Like the 'monitor' houses of New York's Fire Island – clapboard houses with huge plate-glass windows facing the ocean, revealing lofty interiors at night – the design for this pavilion provides a window to the world in which people can be seen moving amid video imagery, becoming part of the performance.

Trapped between two walls set one metre apart are decks which protrude into the glazed enclosure. Images are projected from the upper decks onto the mid-deck, onto translucent panels set into the glazed façade, and onto the raised-ground finish beneath. It takes a lot of money and effort to produce short video slices of message and song, but the videos are insufficient on their own. We wanted film-makers, performers and producers to have a structure with which they could experiment.

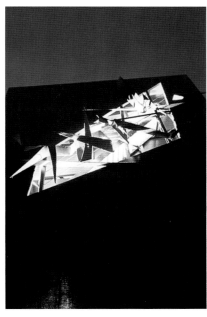

Alternative proposal: plans, elevations, sections and
structural frames [opposite, far left]

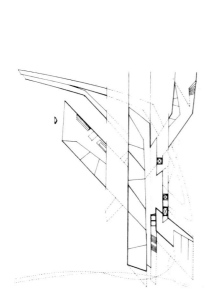
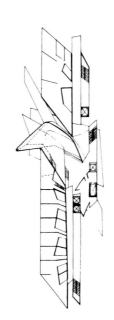
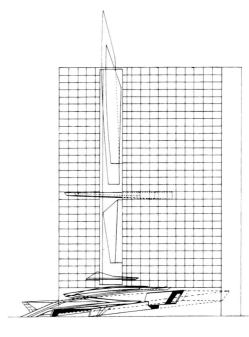

HOTEL AND RESIDENTIAL COMPLEX
Abu Dhabi, UAE *1990*

↑ ↗ → Like many American cities, Abu Dhabi is organized on a grid. As a uniform structure, the grid serves as the basis against which special architectural 'events' are placed. For a hotel complex located on a prime site in the city centre, we flipped up this horizontal urban grid to become a vertical plane, a slab of apartments and hotel rooms that become a backdrop for hotel-related spaces like conference rooms, restaurants and a health club. Where the slab splits apart, these spaces are suspended and sculpted in a 'vertical courtyard'. At ground level a four-storey beam cuts across the site and through the slab, providing spaces for a shopping mall below and offices above. On the beam's fourth floor, with views over the gulf, is the hotel lobby, whose vehicle access is via a curved ramp that swoops from one corner of the site, around the slab and into the vertical courtyard.

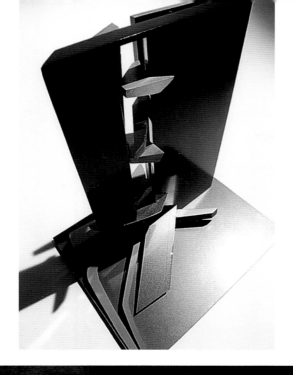

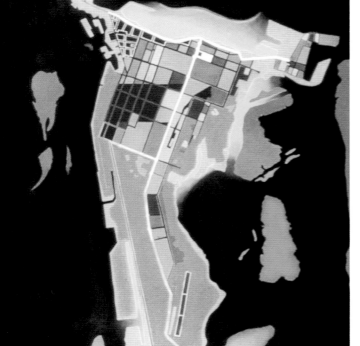

↑ We were asked by a German timber manufacturer to create an exhibition stand on which to display their products for the biannual Interzum trade show. The primary intention of our design was to create a separate environment that could be experienced on several levels. Within the backdrop of a large and sterile trade show, we wanted to induce the sense of an insolated landscape within an enclosed structure. Inside, a central pathway (which, like the trunk of a tree, had branches that ran off it) led to product exhibits and ambient surroundings.

INTERZUM 91
Gluzendorf, Germany 1990

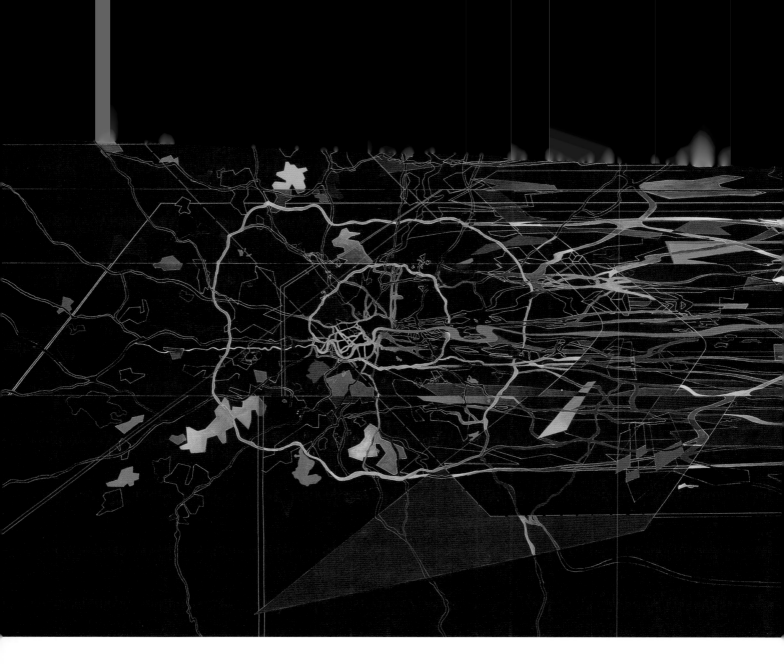

LONDON 2066
1991

This large-scale painting for British *Vogue* continues our exploration of views into London's urban character that began with the Grand Buildings [p. 25], Metropolis [p. 38] and Leicester Square [p. 49] schemes. The work presents our most radical shake-up of the metropolis in both diagrammatic and pictorial terms within a single painting – and it should be judged by this radicalness. We studied the open spaces, rail, road, water and air routes and borough layout, and restructured the entire plan. As the brush moves over London from the west, strands converge, stretch and continue towards the east. These strokes cut new section-lines of air and area for what we believe could be new sites for buildings, for it is the very intersection of vertical structures to the ground where public activities would be intensified in this new plan.

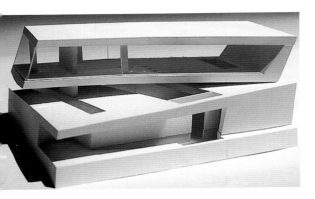

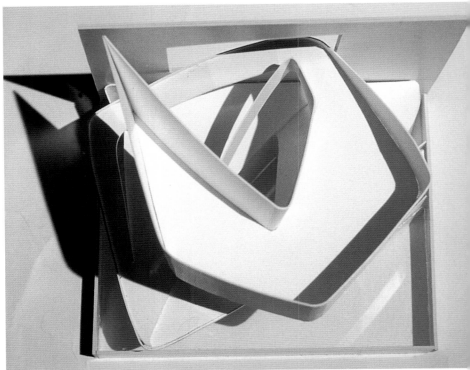

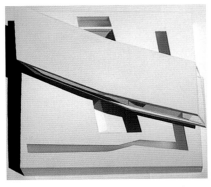

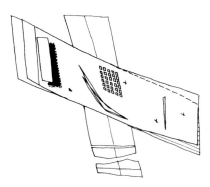

Cross-house sketch [below, left]; spiral-house section [below, right]

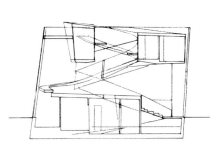

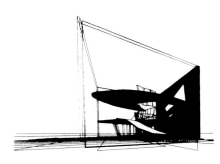

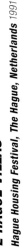
↑ ↗ Two designs, to be constructed of reinforced concrete, were presented as part of a 'field' of eight villas to be located in a suburb of The Hague. The villas abstract the conventional configuration of domestic spaces to create unexpected spatial and social interactions. The first design – the 'cross' house – is formed from a ground-level podium that is intersected by two 'beams', which enclose most of the residence. The lower beam is cut into the podium level, a 'negative' space that forms a courtyard. The upper beam is 'positive', housing an open living and studio space that floats above the podium and crosses the courtyard. The 'spiral' house is essentially a cube through which a floor plate revolves from the entrance level up through the living areas to a studio, occasionally poking through the exterior. Glazed façades follow the floor's spiral, describing a rotation that is alternately solid, louvred, translucent and, finally, transparent. Residual spaces and gaps between the interstices of the exterior and internal spiral afford surprising views and channels of communication and interaction.

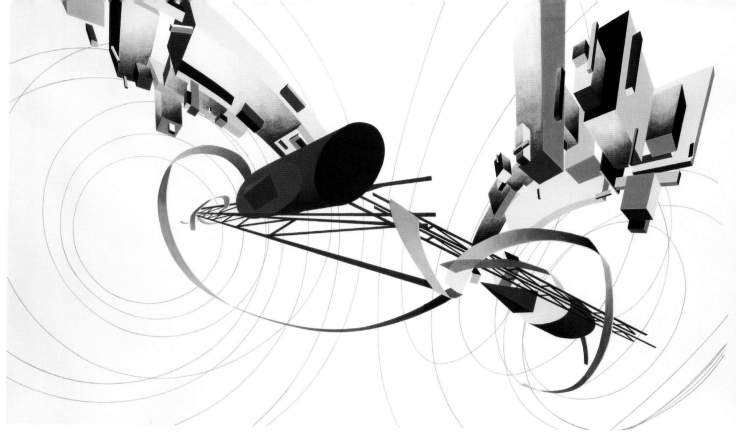

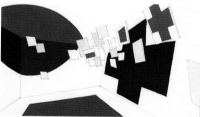

← ↑ The design for an exhibition on Russian Suprematism and Constructivism offered the opportunity to revisit my student explorations of the three-dimensional qualities of Malevich's Tektonik [p. 18]. Our proposal for the Guggenheim show featured two large-scale installations of the Tatlin Tower and Malevich's Tektonik, which both engaged in their own ways with Frank Lloyd Wright's spiralling form, and were in turn distorted by the space. For the first time, the tektonik was habitable: visitors had to pass through it to reach the upper galleries.

Our design features interventions that actively engage with the displayed objects. The tower and tektonik, for example, set up the opposition between Malevich's *Red Square* and Vladimir Tatlin's *Corner Relief*. For the space containing work from the original '0.10' exhibition, one of Malevich's compositions has been extruded from the floor; in the Black Room, which shows objects from the 1921 exhibition '5 × 5 = 25', paintings displayed on Perspex stands appear to dematerialize and float above the floor.

THE GREAT UTOPIA
Solomon R. Guggenheim Museum, New York, New York, USA 1992

VISION FOR MADRID
Madrid, Spain 1992

↑ → Historically, the growth of Madrid could be described as a successive bursting of shells: the circular medieval city, the 19th-century grid, and, in the 20th century, the linear development now defined by a highway in the form of an ellipse. Framed in the west by the Río Manzanares, the city is now growing mainly eastwards. Suburbs of housing blocks have mushroomed beyond the M30 highway, and are about to engulf the nearby villages.

Our objective was to prevent the city from collapsing into formlessness, to channel and organize this anarchic spread of development. To that end, we proposed four specific areas of redevelopment and regeneration. To the south, the former industrial fabric around the city's railways would be transformed into lively parks and leisure-landscapes; new commercial development would be concentrated along the strip-corridor leading to the airport; the north–south axis, Paseo de Castellana, would be intensified by inserting buildings into existing slivers and public spaces into open pockets; and, finally, the remaining gaps in the suburbs would be preserved.

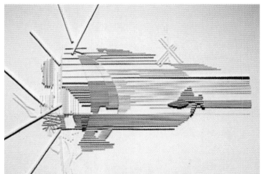

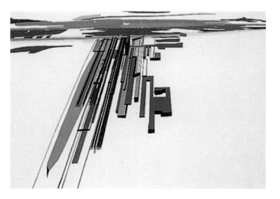

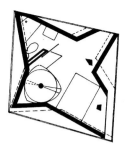
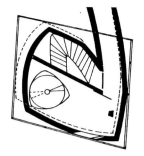

Plans for the first (star), second (spiral) and third (cross) floors [left to right]

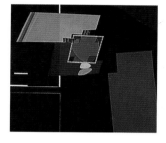

← ↙ The context for this art-hotel addition was an interesting one: a half-timbered farmhouse and stable, which the clients wanted to augment with a challenging new structure that would have a sculptural presence. The heart of the design is a 'blobby', an elliptical space that mediates between the old building and the new one. Partly set into the foundation, the space can be used for performances or exhibitions. In the tower above this lively pivot point are three levels of rooms based on the cross and star, each of which has a completely self-contained environment with built-in furniture and fittings. A third motif, the spiral, is shared by the two other spaces as they connect back to the main building. In a village of strong local character, the ensemble sets up a striking contrast, one that is intended to encourage debate and creativity.

ARTHOTEL BILLIE STRAUSS
Nabern, Germany 1992

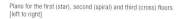

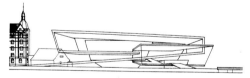

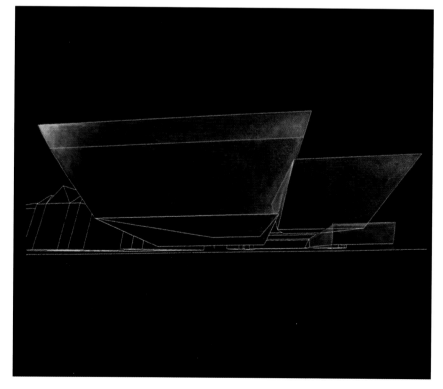

← ↑ This large structure achieves both compactness and openness by striking deep cuts of light, land and water through a solid volume that occupies a compact site. These sharp cuts are open to the sky, and show the full relief of the hall. A curved diagonal cut cleaves off the public-square component, bringing the promenade slowly up into the building. Sculpturally expressive volumes of the structure, articulated by different colours of granite, compress space between them. The structures are made from cast-in-place reinforced concrete to allow irregularly shaped flat slabs to be formed.

CONCERT HALL
Copenhagen, Denmark 1992–93
In collaboration with Patrik Schumacher

To connect this former industrial zone to the city we used three distinct formal devices – trapezoid, wedge and spiral – to define and adapt the multipurpose site to its heterogeneous surroundings. The shapes are massive, ambiguous entities that are scaled somewhere between buildings and land forms. Working together, the sections form a coherent area with a high density of cultural, leisure, housing and commercial facilities, as well as incorporating old buildings with converted uses and new structures.

The trapezoidal area embraces the entire harbour basin, with two quayside buildings that contain boating facilities and a check-in centre for the riverboat; an area to the north includes a conference centre. Between the trapezoid and wedge areas rise slanting office towers. The wedge section itself cuts from the banks of the Rhine into the Ubierring, connecting the riverfront with the Severins residential quarter. Housing is organized in long, horizontal blocks on stilts, like the former warehouses, as if they have been lifted to allow unobstructed views of the river. The spiral links the Römerpark with the quayside, spanning part of the riverside road. Throughout the site, new cultural centres were envisioned as scattered jewels that would reflect the water's movement as it flows by and changes with the seasons.

Site plan [below]

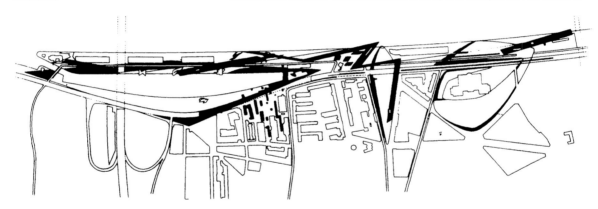

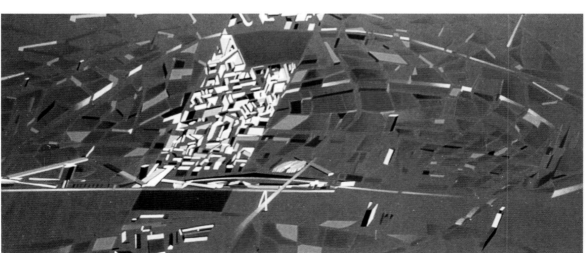

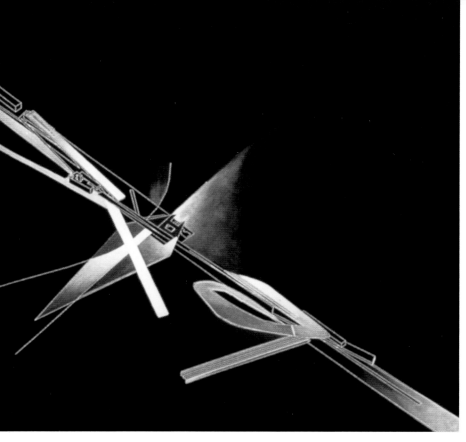

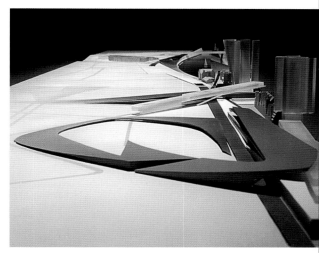

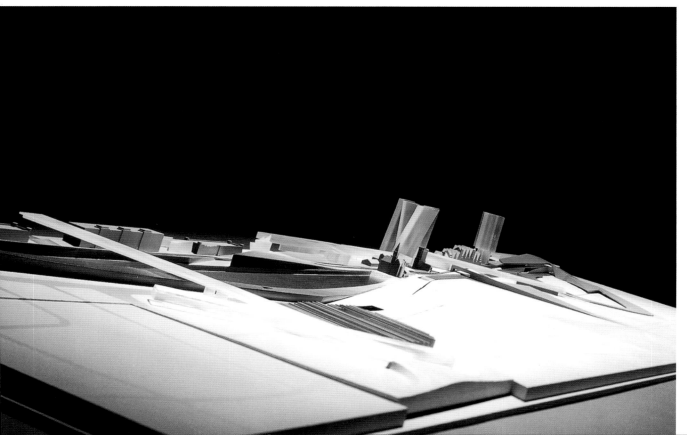

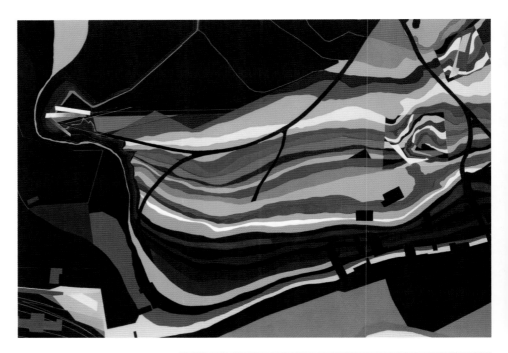

One of the fascinations of archaeological sites is the way in which the remains of human civilization have merged into the landscape and seem at one with nature. In this vein, we wanted the architecture of this mountainside cultural park – a geological centre, outdoor theatre, belvedere and museum – to become another man-made extension of the landscape. The buildings are the first fragments of a new culture that over time will inhabit the surrounding quarry, fragments that suggest an archaeology in reverse.

The geological centre is housed in the history of the mountain itself, cutting into the strata like a blade, revealing the bedrock and becoming part of the exhibition. Floors slant against each other like faulted planes; one cuts slices into the mountain, the other follows its slope. The outdoor theatre is conceived as a Greek amphitheatre, a 'found object' in the quarry that follows the earth's contours. Out of this negative, carved space emerges a positive projection, cantilevering over the slope and crystallizing itself over time out of the site's plateau. The museum represents the intersection of the concepts explored in the other three projects. The ground plane erupts and thrusts large slabs up into the air, like geological outcroppings.

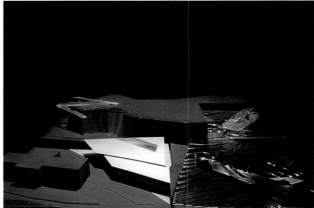

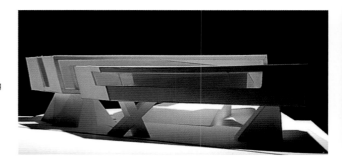

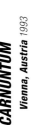

CARNUNTUM
Vienna, Austria 1993

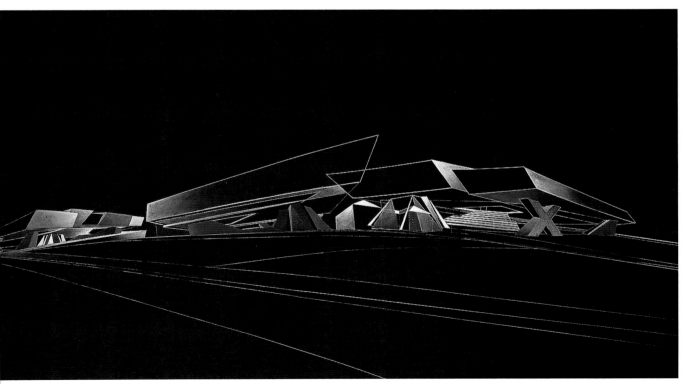

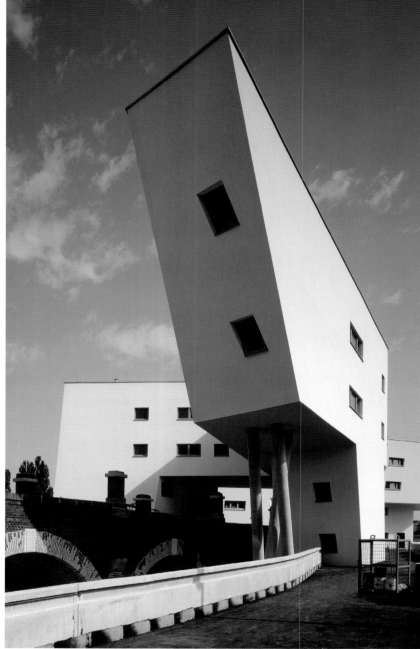

SPITTELAU VIADUCTS
Vienna, Austria 1994–2005

Part of a revitalization initiative undertaken by the City of Vienna for the Wiener Gürtel, a ring-formed slice through the urban fabric, the site is marked by densely overlapping infrastructure, including one of Vienna's most highly travelled roadways, the Donaukanal and the busy bike path that runs along its banks, and historical fragments of the Viennese railway system, in particular a protected viaduct designed by Otto Wagner. A series of apartments, offices and artists' studios playfully weaves like a ribbon through, around and over the arched bays of the viaduct, generating different indoor and outdoor spatial relationships. Rooftops are private retreats and add to the visual activity along the busy canal.

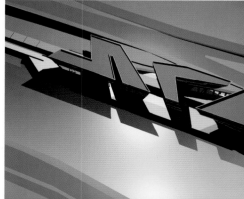

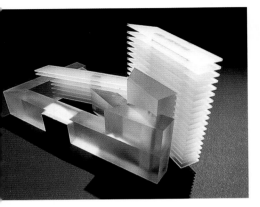

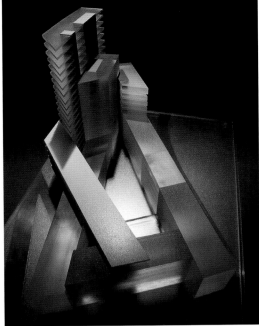

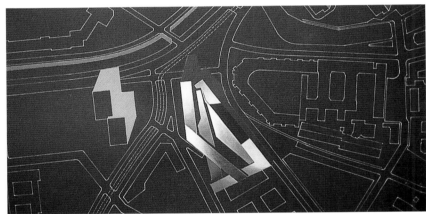

SPITTALMARKT
Berlin, Germany 1995
In collaboration with Patrik Schumacher

Site plan [above]

← ↙ ↓ The centre of the former East Berlin's Mitte district is one of the biggest and busiest redevelopment sites in Europe. We were asked to design an office development along one of the area's busiest thoroughfares, the Leipzigerstraße, at a major junction – not unlike the scenario presented to us in the city's Victoria City Areal development [p. 40]. The building would contain both the headquarters of a major financial institution and private office spaces. Our design attempts to mediate between the 19th-century buildings and the characterless post-war structures that dominated the skyline before the Wall's collapse. Using an iteration of L-shapes that are collided and woven together, the building consists of three primary slabs. Like the swarming traffic intersection at which they stand, these monolithic structures mirror their surroundings while picking up and accentuating the dynamism of the passing cars.

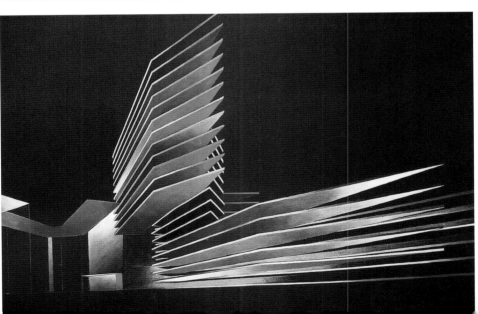

← ↑ The owners of a lycée in South Kensington requested a gatehouse and porter's quarters to mark the entrance to the small existing building and its courtyard. We decided to rotate the traditional vertical gate so that it could be merged with the house on a floating horizontal plane. One passes freely through this building via a forest of column systems, just as one would pass through a gate. The raised horizontal plane is then shattered into puzzle-like segments, each of which is supported by its own structural system of columns, fins and podia, transforming the ground level into a playground of structural elements. In addition to living quarters for the porter and his family, the building contains four classrooms.

↗ → Because of the historic context of London's financial district, designing an office development on a tight site came with a number of planning and building restrictions. The most pertinent was that the ground-floor level must include a public area off the street that would function as a kind of interior park. We resolved this issue by creating a building that wraps its structure around an area to create an 'outdoor room'. Within the permitted envelope of the site, the 'snake' establishes a balance between indoor and outside space, private office and public plaza, while introducing a dynamic interaction into the traditional architecture of the City.

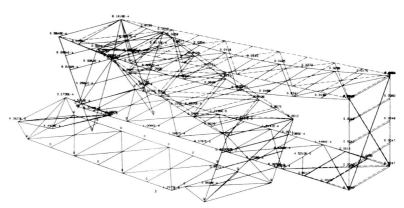

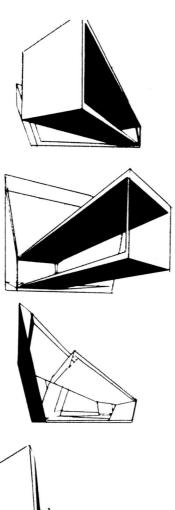

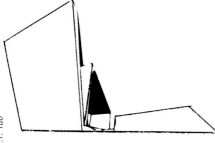

↑ ↗ → The pavilion's form was designed as a continuous and unified space that would express the circulation of visitors while unifying the products on display. The structure is defined by a continuous plate that folds onto itself to create two interlocking beams, so that the inside of the plate becomes the exhibition area. The plate comprises a chassis of steel beams sandwiched between an external cladding material (sheet aluminium or industrial siding) and an internal cladding material (MDF, industrial flooring, or other finish). With this arrangement, finishes can flow uninterrupted from the floor and around the walls. Lighting is recessed into the plate or suspended from it.

As a whole, the Möbius strip-like plate functions as a completely integrated exhibition space. Each exhibitor has a specific location within the 'object', while displayed surface materials move seamlessly across one space and into another.

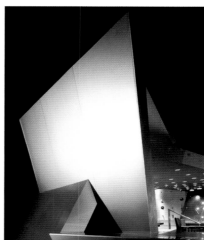

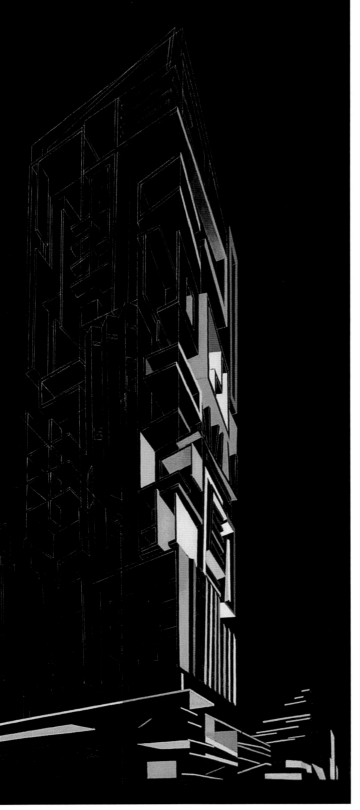

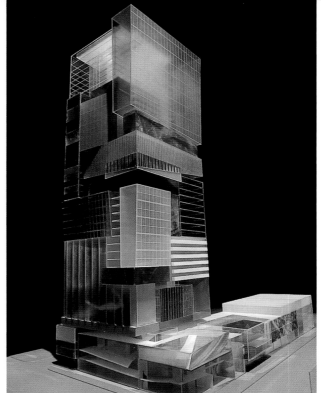

← ↑ Our design for a hotel complex at 8th Avenue and 42nd Street was motivated by a desire to create a microcosm of urbanity that asserted the intricacy and magic of a global city. The proposed complex comprises two three-level commercial podia and two hotels, forty-five floors on the north side and twenty-two floors on the south. Circulation systems, kinetic signage, lighting schemes and the synergy of related entertainment and retail activities unify the complex. The hotel is a vertical street – a tower of towers containing 950 rooms. A void through the main tower's centre is interrupted by elements of the second. Where the hotel tower connects to the commercial podium, the vertical street spills out into the horizontal plane – a network of retail shops, restaurants and public facilities – integrating itself into the city and down to the subway concourse below.

42ND STREET HOTEL
New York, New York, USA 1995

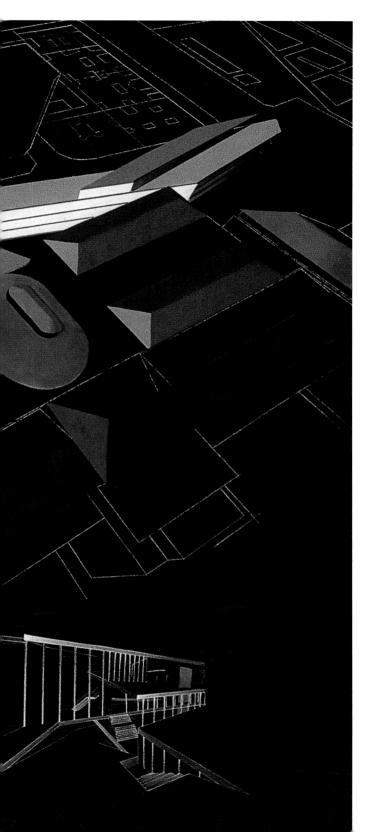

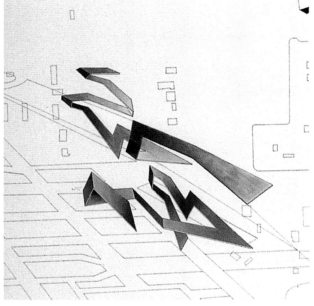

The various museums that constitute the Prado are interwoven by an urban calligraphy, architectural inscriptions in the form of embankments, staircases and walls – a twisted ribbon of cultural events in the city. Our addition to the Prado occurs at the focus and crossing point of the movements through the museum complex, the point at which this ribbon compresses and curls into a tight wedge behind the Villanueva building. As a natural extension of this ribbon, the new building turns upon itself, generating a continuous flow of interlocking spaces. A wide ramp carves deep into the ground and establishes a new main entrance at basement level. New foyer spaces and ancillary zones are illuminated by light wells that articulate the structure. As the ribbon penetrates the end of the site's wedge, it flips into a vertical strip containing offices, ateliers and conservation studios.

PRADO MUSEUM EXTENSION
Madrid, Spain 1996

CARDIFF BAY OPERA HOUSE
Cardiff, Wales 1994–96

The proposed design aims to embody two often mutually exclusive paradigms of urban design: monumentality and space. The project is part of the continuous mass of buildings that forms the Oval Basin Piazza, but in itself becomes a strong landmark against the waterfront. The dichotomy of the typical perimeter block externally shaping a larger public urban space, while enclosing a secluded internal space, is dissolved into a continuum between those two types of space. This is achieved through three complementary tactics: the raising of the perimeter; the opening-up of the perimeter at the corner pointing at the pier head to reveal the volume of the auditorium as the main solid figure within the delineated site; and finally, the continuation of the public space by extending the piazza with a gentle slope into the site, establishing a new ground plane over the main foyer areas. Thus the project provides a raised piazza suitable for outdoor performances and allowing a view back to the Inner Harbour and the bay.

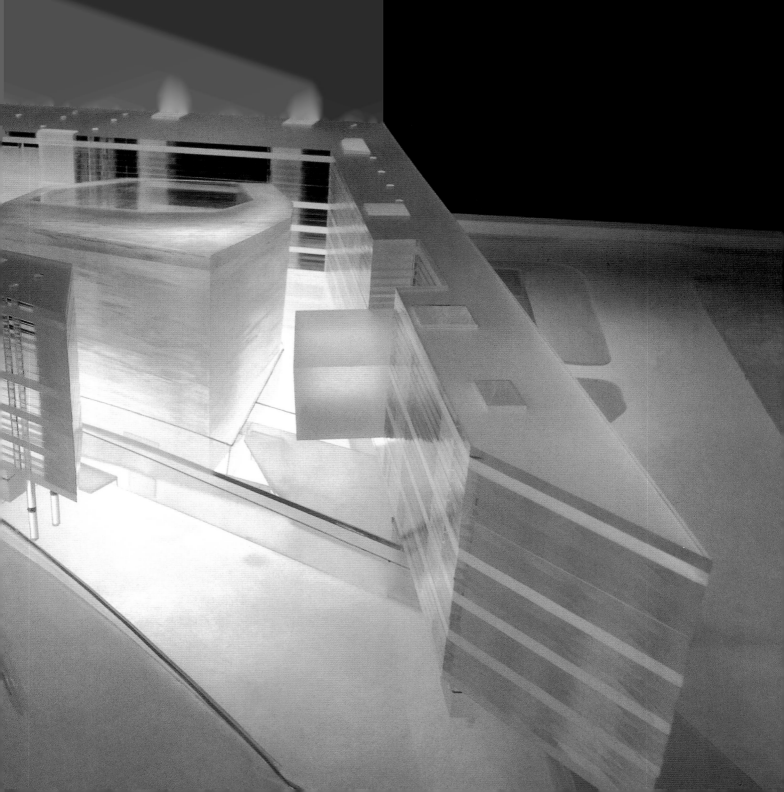

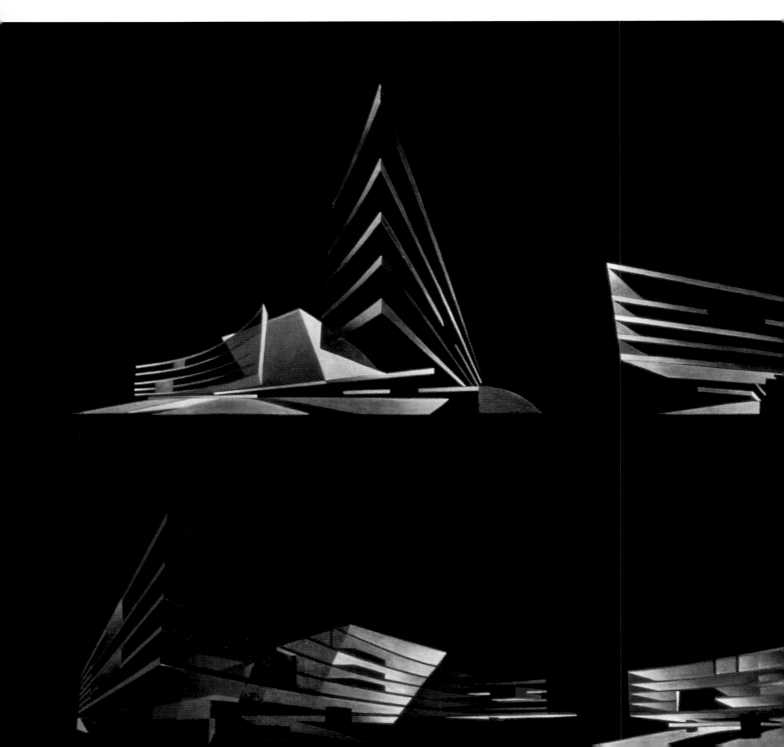

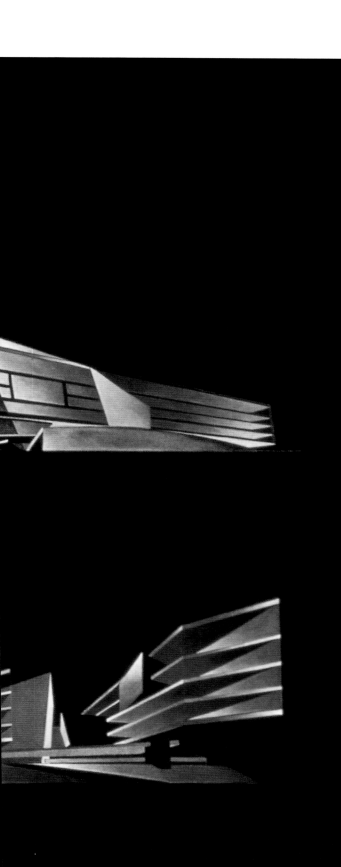

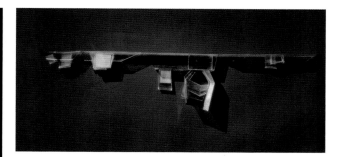

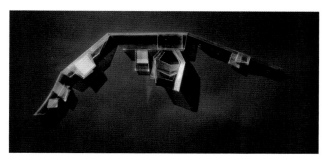

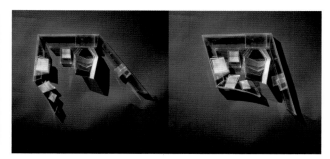

The building concept is based on the architectural expression of the hierarchy between serviced and servicing spaces; the auditorium and the other public and semi-public performance and rehearsal spaces spring like jewels from a band of rationally aligned support structures. This band is then wrapped around the perimeter of the site like an inverted necklace, with all its 'jewels' turning towards each other to create a concentrated public space that is accessible from the centre, while being serviced from the back around the perimeter. This central space is experienced from the open-air courtyard, as well as from the foyer areas under the ground floor. The auditorium and the main rehearsal studios penetrate this raised ground floor. Cuts in this plane mark the two axes that cross the space from the two main entrances: the pedestrian entrance from the Oval Basin Piazza and the concourse entrance from Pierhead Street.

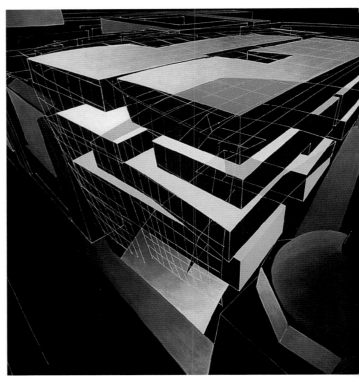

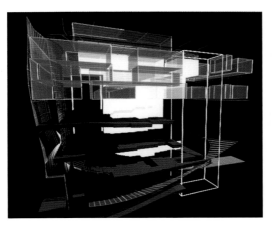

↗ → The V&A is a rich patchwork of period buildings that has grown over the last 150 years. After a process of outward expansion, the museum had decided to look inward, and make use of its remaining empty spaces. Our design for the former boilerhouse reflects the V&A's role as an agent of change in architecture. We used the pixel as the medium for configuration, whether on the scale of a display panel or an exhibition space. The top three floors are interlocking volumes that house administration facilities, an educational and events centre and plant rooms, and connect to the museum's existing wings. Between these solids, voids are cut into the roof and elevations to bring in daylight, and inserted into the areas between the existing façades and the new building allowing Aston Webb's elevations to still be seen. The façade is made of two skins that serve specific functions, but also weave and sometimes merge with each other to form floors, walls and windows. The undulating outer skin is a rain-screen made of flat panels in glass and metal; the inner skin incorporates blinds for solar protection and blackouts for exhibitions.

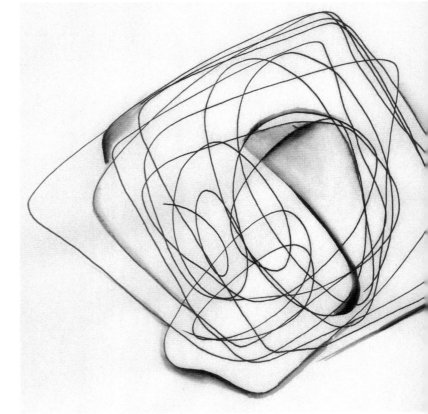

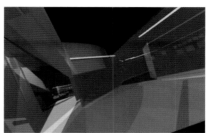

←↙↓ The architectural interpretation of humanity's tangle of fact and fiction cannot be reduced to ideal, Platonic forms. Nothing is conceived a priori. The exhibition spaces here are thus ambiguous perspectival effects of a bundle of walls. The walls emerge at the point of entry and traverse the box, which can barely contain them, in all directions. Without a prescribed route, surprises are inevitable.

WISH MACHINE: WORLD INVENTION
Kunsthalle, Vienna, Austria 1996

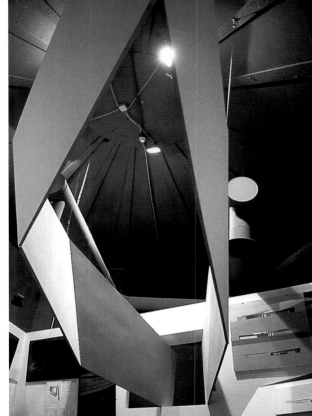

↑ → This gallery space in the Palazzo Grassi comprised an elliptical room and a small adjacent terrace. Because all four sides of the room were connected to the major circulation routes, we emphasized the space's volume, but did not interfere with visitor traffic by emancipating the wall display area from the floor and suspending it two metres high. The manner in which paintings, drawings, models and reliefs were composed on the walls created a 'super-image'.

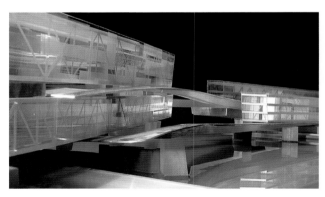

↘ → With its potential for becoming a dominant feature of a cityscape, a bridge can take the form of a horizontal skyscraper. Drawing on a city's cultural diversity, a bridge can weave together a variety of activities and functions – retail, cultural and recreational – into a living structure. Our proposal for such a bridge in London is characterized by beams that are bundled together to mirror the urban density of the riverfront. The bundle splinters apart as it reaches together, forming a series of volumes and routes that veer towards the river bank. The splintering is emphasized by an interruption in the bridge that allows views down the east–west axis, permitting a vista from Richmond in the southwest all the way to St Paul's in the east. The programme is organized vertically, with free-flow public-access 'streets' – a mixture of commercial and cultural spaces – on the lower levels and private, loft-like areas in the volumes above. The spaces and routes function as a fluid whole, maximizing the presence of the river.

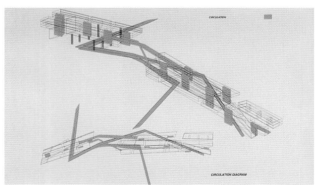

↑ We were commissioned by London newspaper *The Daily Telegraph* to offer a response to the fire in January 1996 that had devastated one of Italy's most revered opera houses. Venice is a city of towers, its roofscape punctuated by chimneys and spires, and we wanted to contribute to this fabric with an elevated opera house that would be incorporated into the city's roofscape. Because Venice is already a theatre in itself, we proposed to invert the plan to expose performances to the outside, creating an outdoor stage and seating that faced the square and canal. The canalside would be adapted to become a stage in itself, and the houses' façades behind it a kind of projection screen. As in our design for the Cardiff Bay Opera House [p. 80], foyers on different levels look down from the auditorium to the square below. The public ascend the walls to open balconies to get a better view of ground-level activities, or further up to balconies within the auditorium.

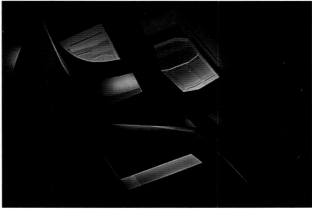

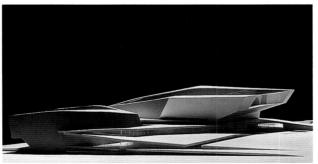

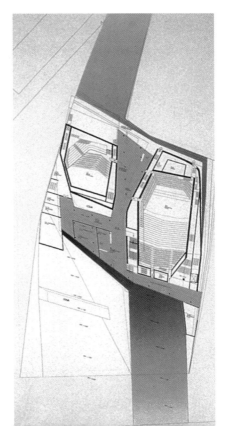

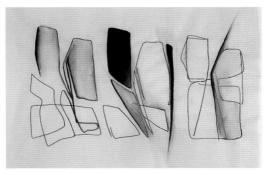

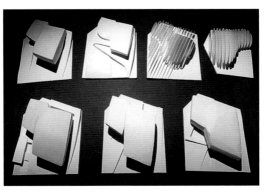

← ↖ ↑ The steep hill facing the old city provided the inspiration behind the concept that drives our scheme: landscape. We developed the idea of an artificially contoured site through a series of tiered, stepped and ramped floors, roofs and levels. Out of this 'landscape' emerged a grand auditorium and chamber hall. Visitors enter the building via a gently rising ramp that leads to the lobbies at the front and to the balconies and foyers. These slopes and ramps are like a continuous undulating landscape, with courtyards inserted at strategic positions to admit light to the activities at ground level. The interiors extend the landscape, with contours that define circulation.

PHILHARMONIC HALL
Luxembourg 1997

In collaboration with Patrik Schumacher

89

This exhibition hall for an international gardening show is part of a sequence of projects that try to elicit fluid spatialities from the study of natural landscape formations, such as river deltas, mountain ranges, forests, deserts, canyons, ice flows and oceans. The most important characteristics of these landscape spaces, as distinct from urban and architectural spaces, are the subtle territorial definitions and the smoothness of transitions – traits that allow for a complex and nuanced order of spaces to emerge. Whereas architecture generally channels, segments and closes, landscape opens, offers and suggests.

The space-bundle of the pavilion embodies the most liberating aspects of landscape. The building is not contained, but literally 'bleeds out', gradually emerging from the tangle of paths, leaving it to the visitor to define its beginning and its end. The public path that sweeps over the building and the terrace carving into the ground make any definition of 'ground' ambiguous. Column rows are misaligned through level shifts in the floor, which are countered by shifts in the ceiling, continuous geometries cut against the façade. The result is a compressed space full of overlaps and visual oscillations, as alignments, rhythms and textures are played off against each other.

LANDESGARTENSCHAU 1999
Weil am Rhein, Germany 1996–99
In collaboration with Patrik Schumacher and Mayer Bährle

91

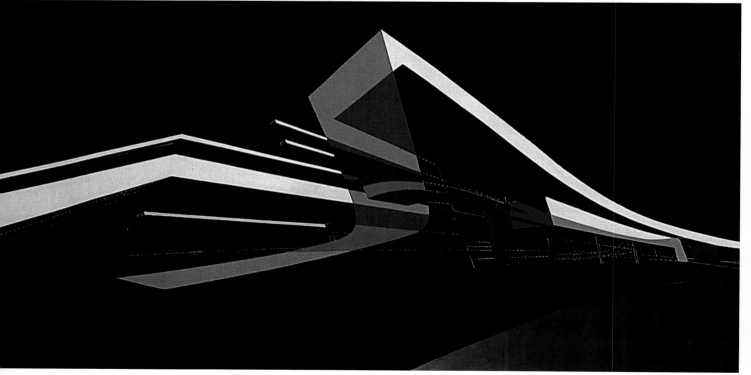

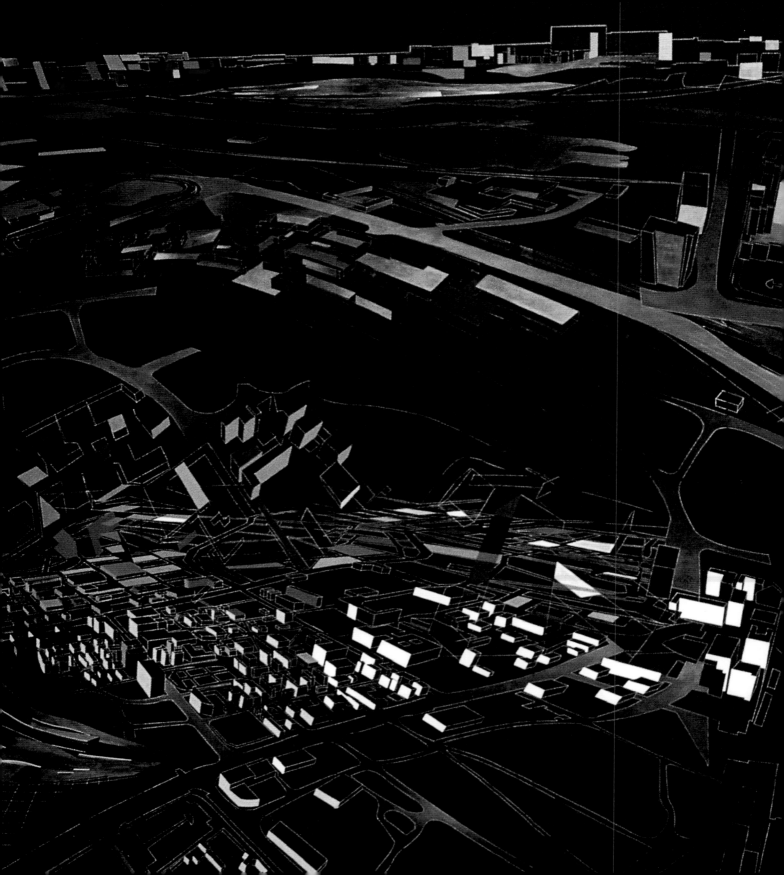

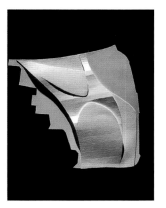

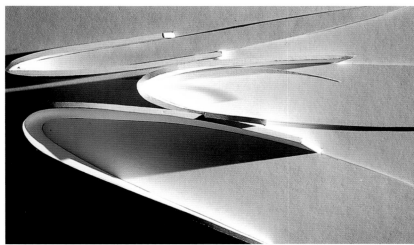

There is no strong precedent for a 19th-century-style museum in the Middle East, so we developed a typology rooted in the Islamic predilection for repetitive patterns punctuated by moments of difference. The building as a whole is a container for programmatic 'objects', an idea echoed in the gallery spaces: an extensive terracing of horizontal and sloped plates that house a broad spectrum of artefacts, from coins and manuscripts to glassware and carpets. Landscape plays a vital role in the building's conception, particularly in the attempt to fuse the context with architectonic elements as seamlessly as possible. The roof is the defining feature, articulating the building as a continuous but differentiated field of spaces while mediating between the landscape, sky and galleries. Courtyards slotted into the interior provide natural light and relate to the strong tradition of the *al-fina*, so integral to Islamic architecture and planning.

MUSEUM OF ISLAMIC ARTS
Doha, Qatar 1997

In collaboration with Patrik Schumacher and Woody K.T. Yao

95

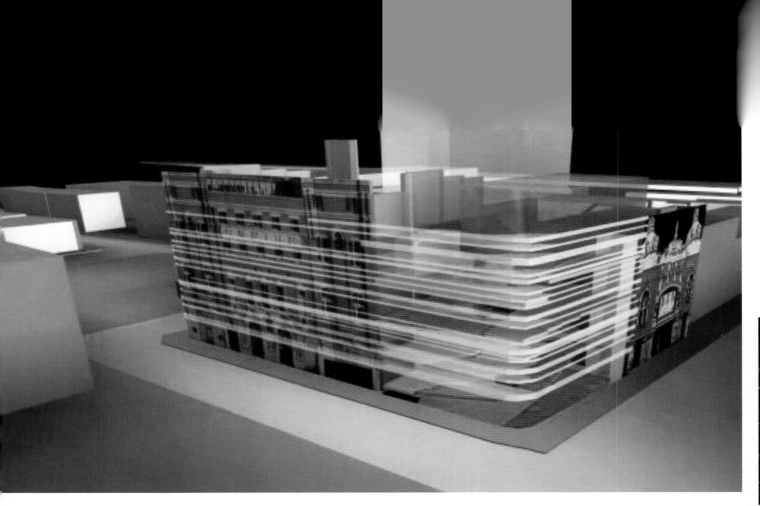

HACKNEY EMPIRE
London, England 1997

↑ → A corner in North London offered the prospect of commercial development centred around the activities of the old Hackney Empire. The design concept is a spiral that ascends from the basement to a new fourth-floor level and cabaret theatre. We allowed the building to be essentially transparent, so that the interior would be seen as a continuously moving spiral of people and activities. Inside the existing auditorium, we opted not for a faithful historical restoration, but for the use of four palettes: lighting, acoustics, texture and colour. Natural and artificial lighting would be enhanced; balustrades, walls, arches and ceiling would be embellished and the proscenium opening restored; seats and floor finishes would be revitalized; and an abstract expression of colour, fabric and finish would improve acoustic performance.

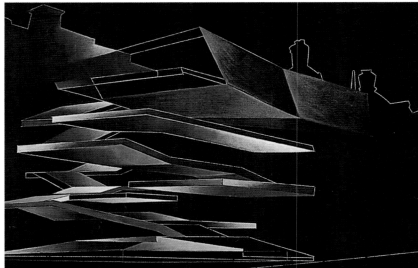

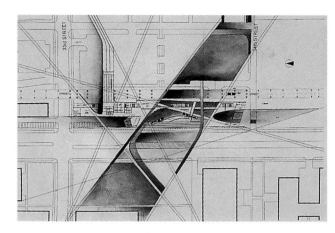

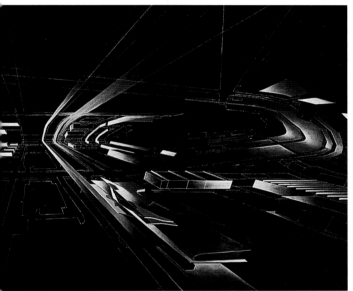

← ↑ ↗ The proposed insertion of a student centre into Mies van der Rohe's campus offered an opportunity to echo the multiple-use patterns of social groups within the university and the texture of Chicago itself. We opted for a fluid organizational system that blurred the areas of work and leisure, and aimed to fold the laterally distributed masterplan onto itself, ensuring that the campus's elements came together in a compact, multilayered volume. Approach to the building is through a play of graduating floor surfaces and curving ramps into a double-height vestibule that orients the visitor towards the auditorium, cafeteria and retail spaces. The second floor partly peels off from the first, leaving voids that peer downward, cut by stair ramps. Meeting rooms are a matrix of sliding panels that recede and protrude according to the needs of the student associations. All of these spaces lack clearly definable edges, encouraging cross-fertilization of events; this is enhanced by a modular system of tabletops, which allows for surprising configurations.

CAMPUS CENTER, ILLINOIS INSTITUTE OF TECHNOLOGY
Chicago, Illinois, USA 1998
In collaboration with Patrik Schumacher

THE MIND ZONE

Millennium Dome, London, England 1998–2000

→ The Mind Zone was one of fourteen individual exhibition spaces within the Millennium Dome. For this unique undertaking, we designed both the curatorial and the architectural scheme. The design engages the complex subject matter of the mind through a structure of three overlapping sections, unfolding to create a continuous surface that can be floor, wall or soffit and that allows for a fluid journey through the space. The continuous floor-wall is a unique lightweight transparent panel made of fibreglass skins with an aluminium honeycomb structure. Similarly, the steel base is layered with translucent materials, seeking to create an ephemeral quality that befits an exhibition whose lifespan was just one year.

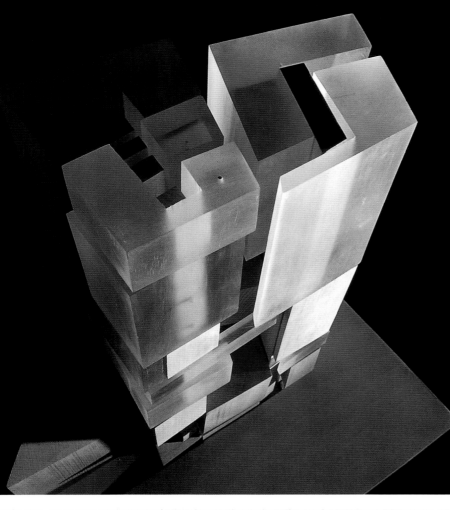

← The proposal for the Future TV Media Centre is to provide a new landmark on the Beirut skyline, making a clear statement and providing a focus for the city and beyond. Our intention is to bring employees and visitors across the breadth of the site, either into the refurbished presidential palace or beyond into the lobbies and upwards into the new tower building, whose most striking feature is the lightness of its structure. Visitors enter the new building by means of ascending ramps that peel off the ground. The space between the old and the new – the palace and the tower – becomes the lobby to the main studio, hovering over the gap or void. Voids and terraces above further enhance the theme, creating the potential for gardens and providing long-distance views northwards across the city.

FUTURE TV MEDIA CENTRE
Beirut, Lebanon 1998

← The University of North London campus is dispersed across an urban field that comprises Holloway Road, the railway and the underground. Within this city network is a secondary layer of routes that are part of the university's own internal circulation pattern. Our bridge design bundles and extends this internal network, attaching itself to existing building cores and routes. As it flows, the bridge adapts to meet new situations and the changing requirements of the university. Sky lobbies are located at the bridge's landing points, forming a network of cafés, libraries and seminar rooms. The structure is composed of steel trusses, whose arrangement, bracing and cladding give the impression of an interference pattern and provide a rhythm of light and shadow inside.

UNL/HOLLOWAY ROAD BRIDGE
London, England 1998

CAR PARK AND TERMINUS HOENHEIM-NORD
Strasbourg, France 1998–2001

To combat increasing congestion and pollution in the city centre, the city of Strasbourg developed a new tram service to encourage drivers to leave their cars in specially designed car parks and take a tram into the city. The concept for this 700-place car park and station, at the northern apex of the line, is one of overlapping 'fields' and lines that knit together to form a constantly shifting whole. Each field of movement – created by cars, trams, bicycles and pedestrians – has a trajectory and a trace, as though the transition between transport types (from car to tram, train to car) is rendered in the material and spatial transitions of the station, landscaping and context.

The station contains a basic programme of waiting space, bicycle storage, toilets and shop. The sense of three-dimensional vectors is enhanced in the treatment of space: the play of lines continues as light lines in the floor, furniture pieces or strip-lights in the ceiling. Viewed in plan, all the 'lines' coalesce to create a synchronous whole. The notion of the cars as ephemeral and constantly changing elements on site is manifested in the form of a 'magnetic field' of white lines on black tarmac, each delineating a parking space, that start off aligned north–south at the lowest part of the site, and then gently rotate according to the curvature of the site boundaries. The field of light posts for each space maintains a constant datum height that combines with the gradient of the floor slope. Again, the intention is to create reciprocal relationships between static and dynamic elements at all scales.

As an ensemble, the tram station and the car park create a synthesis between floor, light and space. By articulating the moments of transition between open landscape space and public interior space, a new notion of 'artificial nature' is created, one that blurs the boundaries between natural and artificial environments and improves civic life for Strasbourg.

CAR PARK AND TERMINUS HOENHEIM-NORD

The Center for Contemporary Art was founded in Cincinnati in 1939 as one of the first institutions in the United States dedicated to the contemporary visual arts. The aim of the new building is to draw in pedestrians and to create a dynamic public space. Starting at the corner of Sixth and Walnut Streets, the ground curves slowly upwards as it enters the building, rising to become the back wall, an 'urban carpet' that encourages visitors into the entrance and lobby. As the wall rises and turns, it leads visitors up a suspended mezzanine ramp

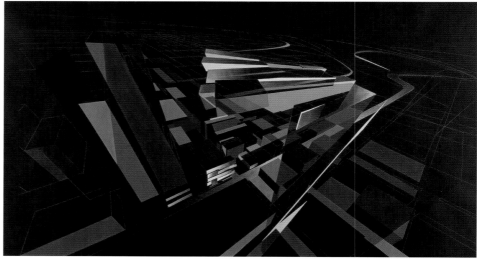

through the full length of the lobby, which functions during the day as an open, daylit 'landscape' or artificial park.

In contrast to the urban carpet and its series of polished, undulating surfaces, the galleries are expressed as if they had been carved from a single block of concrete and were floating above the lobby space. Exhibition spaces vary in size and shape to accommodate the great range of scales and materials in contemporary art. Views into the galleries from the circulation system are unpredictable, as the stair-ramp zig-zags upwards through a narrow slit at the back of the building. Together, these varying galleries interlock like a three-dimensional jigsaw puzzle, made up of solids and voids.

The building's corner situation led to the development of two different, but complementary, façades. The south façade, along Sixth Street, forms a translucent skin through which passers-by can see the activity inside the centre. The east façade, along Walnut Street, is expressed as a sculptural relief, a negative imprint of the gallery interiors.

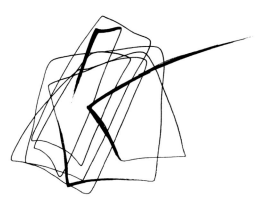

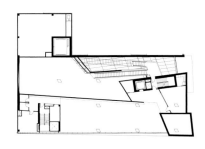

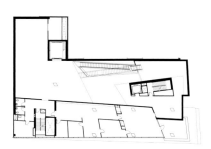

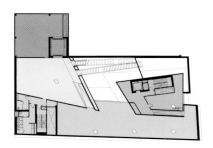

→ Architecture and musical performance
are not necessarily easy to fit together as
they are subject to very different sets of
rules. The stage set for the British pop duo
Pet Shop Boys, however, proved to be a
challenging and inspiring process that led
to a hybridization of both disciplines. Rather
than composing spatial sequences, a white
canvas was unfolded to contain and direct the
dynamics of the concert. A single, continuous
surface was thrown into relief as it bent and
split, creating background, structure and
floor. Other parts of this surface became
detachable mobile elements that acted as
choreographic tools in a three-dimensional
luminous landscape of projection and sound.

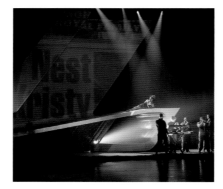

L.A. EYEWORKS STORE
Los Angeles, California, USA 1999

→ This interior design scheme was derived
from the concept of 'object and void', the
object sculpting the form of the walls. The
shop houses optical wear, which is stored and
displayed in different striation types within the
wall. The object serves as the counter space
and as a sculptural object in its own right.

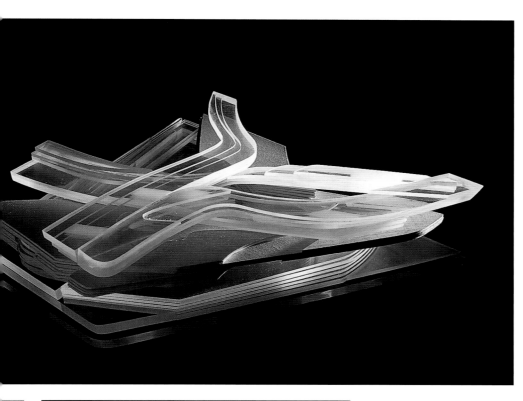

← Our primary intention was to create an instantly recognizable building for the museum that was vivid in its individuality, with flexibility being one of the key objectives. The galleries are linked by an immediately identifiable route that creates a unique journey and makes the most of each space. Natural overhead light is maximized through the use of interwoven layers that splay and split. Public access is via the east façade, dividing the building clearly into public and private zones and allowing the west façade to be used for deliveries.

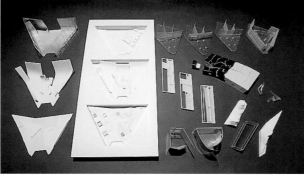

← ↙ The brief to design the interior of an entrance hall, complete with reception desk and display cabinet, for a new N.M. Rothschild bank headquarters in London was approached in three different ways. The first was to treat the entrance as a glass room within a room, standing independently from its surroundings; the second to sculpt the space as a continuous surface without differentiation between walls and floors; and the third to consider the space as an interior landscape from which the furniture pieces would emerge. Landscape studies were developed into specific furniture pieces, each an 'inverted landscape', which could be attached and detached from each other and from their context as objects. The inverted landscape pieces, the desk and the cabinet, are built up from layers of wood with a glass case. Like jigsaw puzzle pieces, the desk and chair units can be opened up and assembled into different configurations.

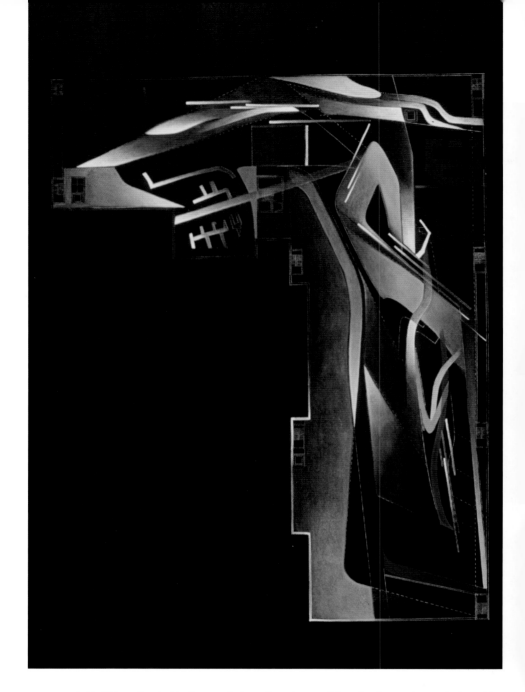

MUSEUM FOR THE ROYAL COLLECTION

Madrid, Spain 1999

In collaboration with Patrik Schumacher

↗ The architectural language for a new museum in Madrid was inspired by the morphology of erosion, so all figuration is negative, enclosing voids rather than solid shapes. The new building would occupy the space below the square between the Royal Palace and the Catedral de la Almudena, hidden underground and revealed only through slender incisions in the plaza and a slight bowing of the plaza surface. The plaza itself would be maintained and extended through the low sloping roof, which frames the space and is accessible to pedestrian visitors. The interior space is framed by a sweeping, three-dimensionally articulated wall, along which two spatial loops weave through the volume. The available volume of space is not segmented into levels, but remains integral throughout the gallery, with the two winding paths – in/down and up/out – intersecting visually while maintaining a strict linearity of sequence. The vertical movement through the spaces is achieved through terracing, allowing extensive horizontal surfaces. These terraces transform into smooth ramps along the central void to allow circulation through the space.

← Lugano's glacial topography has created a smooth, contoured landscape onto which the city has been grafted. Our site landscape pours from the hilltop, forming a lava flow that is partially captured by the façade of the hotel as it descends towards Lake Lugano. The lava flow is voluminous, housing the hotel and casino facilities, and pitted, providing pockets of light and air in open landscapes and courtyards. The hotel is placed within the existing façade, while the casino is situated away from it on the lower levels of the hill, allowing historic sight lines to the façade to be maintained.

← Frédéric Flamand's dance work for the Charleroi/Danses company evokes the rhythms of the city. The scenic structure is a woven topology of different layers in different materials, creating a fluid, hybrid space that coincides with the dancers' movements. Flamand's choreography follows and provokes the morphological transformations of the space, with the dancers wrapped into a spatial complexity that both captures and liberates them. The structure is constantly in transition through a process of compression and release. Three translucent bridges with a 10-metre span slide into different configurations as they are worn by the dancers. Costumes are seen as intermediate layers, flexible structures that extend the dance into four-dimensional patterns.

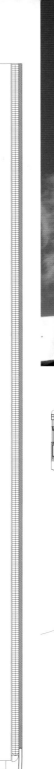

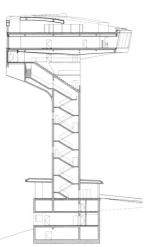

Part of a larger refurbishment project for the Olympic Arena, the ski jump on Bergisel Mountain in the Tyrol is a hybrid of a highly specialized sports facility and public spaces, including a café and viewing terrace. These different programmes are combined into a unified form that extends the topography of the slope into the sky. At a length of about 90 metres and a height of almost 50 metres, the building is a combination of a tower and a bridge. Structurally, it is divided into the vertical concrete tower and a green building that houses the ramp and the café. Two elevators take visitors to the café, where they can enjoy the surrounding Alpine landscape and watch the athletes below flying above the Innsbruck skyline.

The Phæno Science Centre, the first of its kind in Germany, is intended to confront visitors with a degree of complexity and strangeness. Located along a chain of culturally important buildings by Alvar Aalto, Hans Scharoun and Peter Schweger, the building is a connecting link to the VW Autostadt and echoes the grand scale of its surroundings, even if on the ground level its massiveness is made visually porous.

The project is based on an unusual volumetric structural logic. Floors are not piled above each other, or form a hall spanned by a large roof. Instead, a large volume is supported and structured by cones turned inside and out of the box above them. The interior of the box is accessible through some of these funnels, while others are used to lighten the interior space and house service equipment. The cones' arrangement was derived from the primary urban axes: one funnel is the main entrance, another forms the lecture hall, and three are fused to become an exhibition space underneath the main concourse level. The public bridge leads like a wormhole through the building's interior, causing the inside and outside to melt together and interpenetrate.

This strategy of strangeness and fusion is continued in the choice of materials. Smooth, porous, acoustically damped surfaces can be used for projection or for watching activity inside the centre. A carpet of light runs underneath, while reflected light catches the underside and sculpts the truncated volumes. Light and shadow provide a visual guidance system. Reinforced concrete was chosen for its easy application to the building's free-flowing forms. Floor and roof structures are two-way spanning waffle slabs, supported on shear walls around the workshops, auditorium, main entrance and administrative areas. To maximize the repetition of formwork and reinforcement, the parallelograms' waffles are on a regular grid, so that the concrete ribs in between intersect at an acute angle, following the visual axis of the building.

PHÆNO SCIENCE CENTRE
Wolfsburg, Germany *1999–2005*
In collaboration with Christos Passas

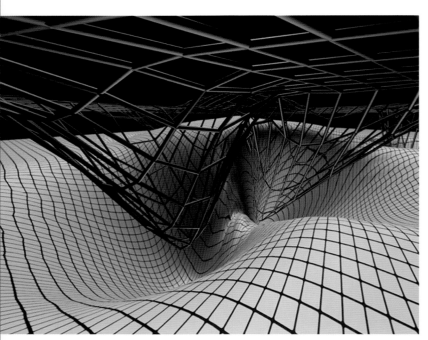

PHÆNO SCIENCE CENTRE

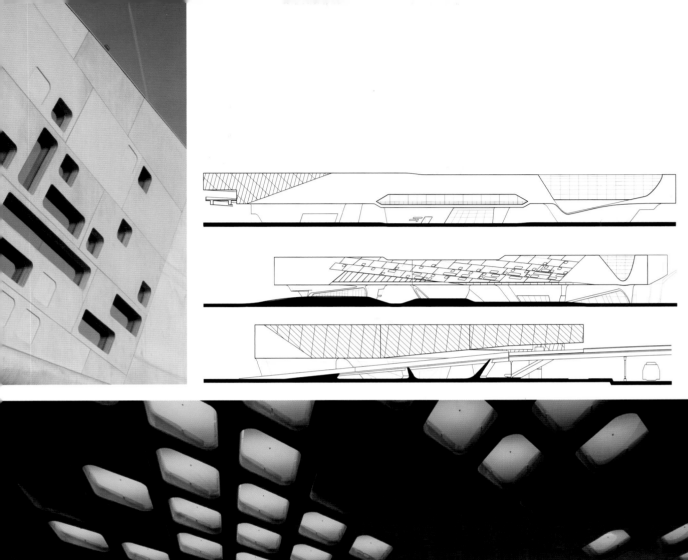

MESHWORKS
Villa Medici, Rome, Italy 2000

↑ ↗ → As part of a biennial cycle of exhibitions dedicated to contemporary art at the Villa Medici in Rome, we were asked, together with forty other architects and artists, to select a part of the villa's garden for an installation that would link it to the city. Meshworks projects the nine-kilometre ancient city wall of Rome into one of the typical Renaissance garden squares, thus creating a new experience for visitors.

← The Serpentine Gallery, located in London's Hyde Park, commissioned us to create a pavilion for its thirtieth anniversary gala event. Situated on the front lawn outside the gallery, the tent-like design used a triangulated roof to play with the traditional notion of a tensile fabric construction. The folded planes engage with the site by extending to the ground at different points, while undulating to create a variety of internal spaces. Inside is a field of specially designed tables whose colour graduates from white to black, reinforcing a sense of movement dissipating throughout the space. Although originally erected for only five days, the structure's life was extended by popular demand for two months. Today the pavilion is in Stratford upon Avon, in the service of the Royal Shakespeare Company.

SERPENTINE GALLERY PAVILION
London, England 2000

← Our British pavilion for the 2000 Venice Biennale featured a series of recent projects that worked with ribbons: folded, twisted, bundled or splintered. Three of the projects are bridges that funnel and distribute various trajectories; the fourth also foregrounds movement and trajectory, moving visitors through the story of 'The Mind'.

BRITISH PAVILION, VENICE BIENNALE
Venice, Italy 2000

121

PESCARA URBAN PLAN
Pescara, Italy *2000*
In collaboration with Patrik Schumacher

→ This project was conceived as an intense accumulation of diverse individual units into a dynamic swarm that sweeps across the southwestern edge of Pescara, between the built-up city core and the urban sprawl. Railway tracks are the dominant physical feature. A fresh gesture was needed to provide a strong new identity and focus, so the railway's linear force is taken up by the sweep of the urban field, which is organized around two new streets: a main street that unifies the field, and a parallel pedestrian alley that allows for more intimate interaction. Tenants will participate in the strong collective identity of the site while still being able to claim their individual pieces of architecture.

NATIONAL LIBRARY OF QUEBEC
Montreal, Quebec, Canada *2000*
In collaboration with Patrik Schumacher

→ The functions of this commission for a new library are diverse, from the handling of rare manuscripts to a 24-hour access zone. The design creates self-contained environments for these activities, which are connected contextually to the other parts. By differentiating these 'localities', the sense of institutional alienation that can befall large public buildings is subverted. The main architectural concept is based on a continuous navigation space that follows the logic of disciplinary differentiation – the tree of knowledge – and is expressed as the veins eroding the solid mass of the building. Visitors can follow the branching veins upwards, before choosing paths to the collections and the reading rooms. Major collections are shaped like terraced valleys, with books lining the perimeter and reading areas in the centre.

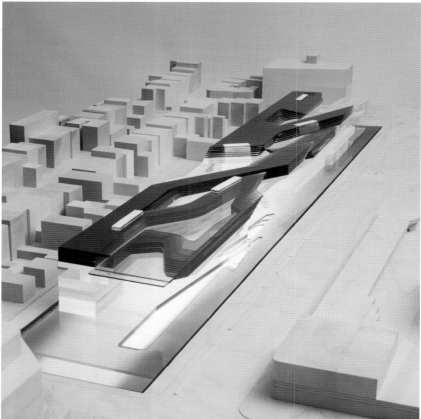

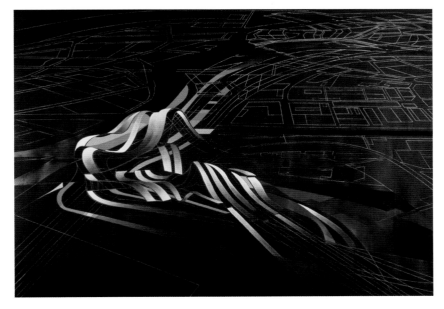

← ↙ Our concept for a new mosque is organized as a matrix established in one direction by the axis for prayer, or *qibla*, and the Rhine river's curvature in the other. Where the two axes intersect, they fractalize and generate volume; the focus of this directional field is the mosque. The project carefully separates the building's functions: secular spaces are at street level, and the mosque and courtyard are lifted above ground to float above the city. A central courtyard, a contemplative space, is reached from the lower, secular level and used as the entrance. Public spaces pay respect to the principles of traditional Islamic architecture, with prayer rows oriented towards Mecca, water channels drifting across the ground-floor level and in the courtyard, and geometric patterns to achieve harmony and proportion. Islamic calligraphy, too, is recalled in the structure's flowing lines.

LA GRANDE MOSQUÉE DE STRASBOURG
Strasbourg, France 2000
In collaboration with Patrik Schumacher

← The Centro JVC site in Guadalajara is a fascinating setting of ten interrelated buildings, including a convention centre, museum, office, entertainment and shopping complex and a university. Our scheme for the location of a future five-star hotel, which would lie on an artificial lake on the site's northern perimeter, would create a strong and directly accessible icon for the centre. Vistas and other site-specific relationships would create the shape of a system grid based on the room module. The hotel room is the spatial sub-entity that makes up the overall fabric of the hotel, with a layer of 'hotel-particles' directly at the lake's perimeter, starting at water level before rising into a more vertical pattern. By opening and raising the built structure from the ground, the building becomes part of the landscape.

CENTRO JVC HOTEL
Guadalajara, Mexico 2000

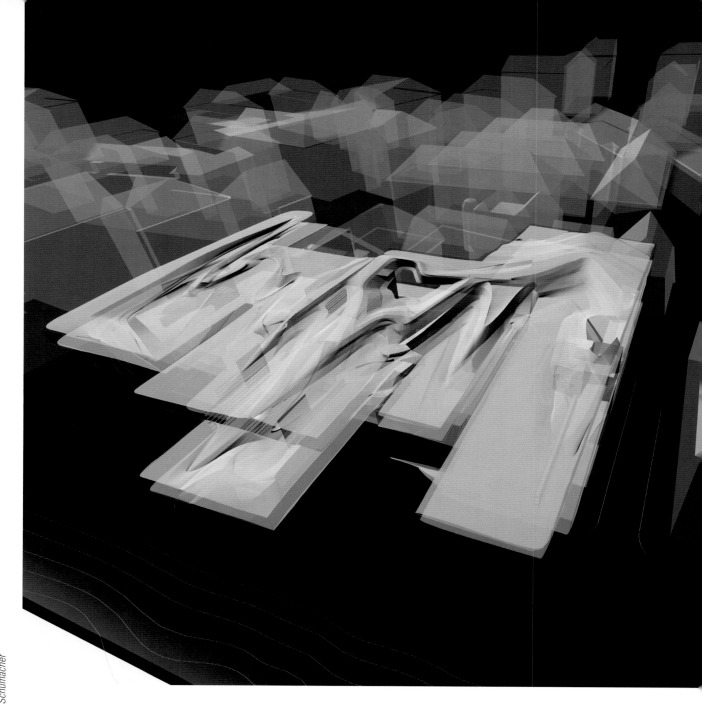

ART MUSEUM
Graz, Austria 2000
In collaboration with Patrik Schumacher

↑ The determining factor behind the design was the desire to project the museum over and across the Lendkai towards the riverbank. The cantilever needed to be high enough to let in sunlight, which led to the concept of a tall canopy, varying in height between three and six metres, which would cover a volume of flexible space and act as a large public room. The canopy's morphology is derived from the structural logic of the tapering mushroom columns – to be constructed from reinforced concrete. The art centre is located below the strongest cantilever, and the main vertical circulation through the building moves through the hollow stem of the largest mushroom. The effect of splaying the fans out at the top allows large hoop tensions at the upper levels of the form, which give way to hoop compression below. The space within the canopy is enclosed, designed to house elements that require intimacy, acoustic enclosure and darkness, such as lectures and performances.

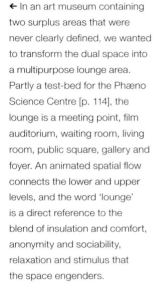

← In an art museum containing two surplus areas that were never clearly defined, we wanted to transform the dual space into a multipurpose lounge area. Partly a test-bed for the Phæno Science Centre [p. 114], the lounge is a meeting point, film auditorium, waiting room, living room, public square, gallery and foyer. An animated spatial flow connects the lower and upper levels, and the word 'lounge' is a direct reference to the blend of insulation and comfort, anonymity and sociability, relaxation and stimulus that the space engenders.

← ↙ Research in the form of preliminary diagrams for a set of dwellings considered the Kite Site as an extension of Glasgow Green. We proposed a footprint and structures for an urban site that would lead to a new interpretation of buildings. The orientation, height and location of the houses set up a dialectic to the masterplan model, with the aim of opening up unexpected views and axes across the site and onto the Green. Existing paths and lines across Glasgow Green are extended into and across the Kite Site towards London Road. Other line diagrams reshape and reorient the possible boundaries and locations of structures. Residents and visitors alike can cross the site on ramps, with paths to the buildings acting as landscape features, accentuated by hardscaping integrated into the buildings.

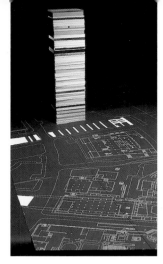

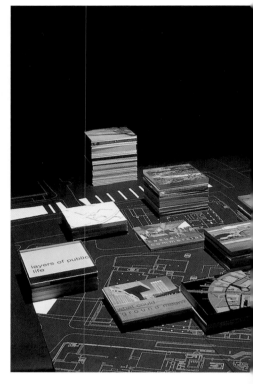

↗ → The overall masterplan for London's Hungerford and Jubilee Gardens site offered an excellent opportunity for a raised garden that would exploit the spatial repertoire of the artificial landscape. Because the River Thames is a vast open space that can be experienced from the South Bank, we envisioned a series of intimate spaces that would encourage strolling, reading, and other personal activities. Four formal languages would articulate the public landscape: slicing, warping and peeling of a continuous surface to mediate between inside and out, while maintaining continuity of movement; carving, burrowing and eroding to retain continuity in this new artificial landscape formation; layering, contouring and shifting of strata to produce terraces; and laminating and bending strips to guide parallel movements across the site.

→ The Singapore masterplan offered the first opportunity for us to explore an artificial landscape formation of an entire urban district. The advantages of such a bold move are striking: the possibility of an original urban skyline and identifiable panorama, along with the rich diversity of squares and alleys to create a strong sense of place. The concept of the dune-like megaform gives a sense of spatial coherence – achieved by allowing roof surfaces to join – that has become rare in the modern metropolis. At the same time, a huge variety of built volumes – tall, low, wide, small – is brought under the spell of a unifying force. The undulating pattern of lines that defines the streets and paths absorbs and harmonizes infinite varieties within a strong formal coherence, just one advantage of working with a 'natural', rather than Platonic, geometry.

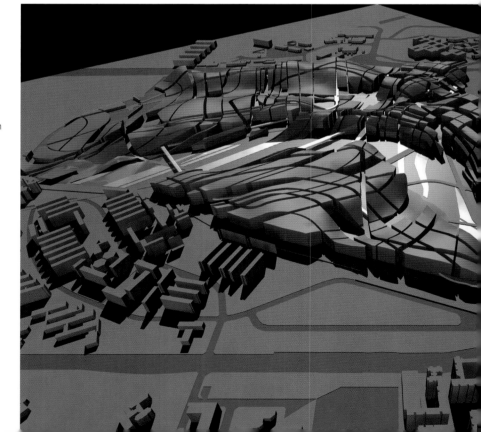

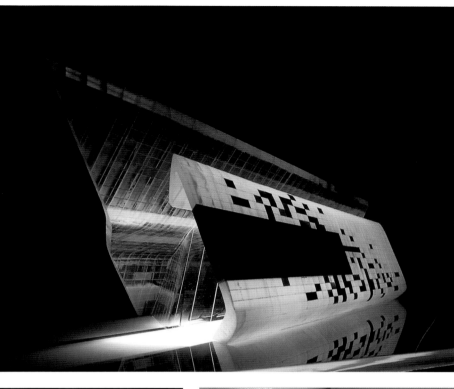

← A dynamic urban space built on synthetic land, Odaiba Island is the perfect location for cultural experimentation. The ten-year intervention of the temporary Guggenheim, therefore, will be an instant cultural hotspot. In line with the temporary nature of the structure, a lightweight envelope is used. Two folded planes, like sheets of paper, lean against each other and encapsulate a generous space, creating both a strong signature shape and a space that can constantly redefine itself. Although the spatial concept is extremely simple, the size, level of abstraction and dynamic profile of the folded planes – unified and animated by snakeskin-like pixellation – ensure an exhilarating spatial sensation.

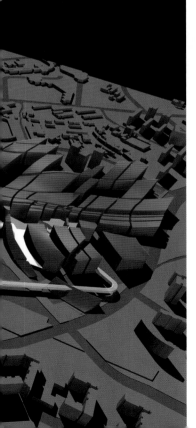

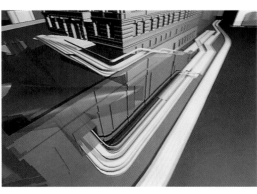

← ↙ The design for this museum addition works with graphic structures, weaving movement lines and visual connections around and through the existing museum plinth. Two different media were chosen to materialize these structures. The first is a linear web of steel and glass in a flowing movement, which is placed onto an extended sidewalk that swings up to the main entrance. The second is a composition of three diagonally attached projection cones that penetrate the massive volume of the Bastei (bastion or fortification) in the form of light and viewing tunnels. The idea of the projection line was inspired by the projective geometry of Albrecht Dürer and its application in architecture during the Baroque period.

ALBERTINA EXTENSION
Vienna, Austria 2001
In collaboration with Patrik Schumacher

BMW PLANT CENTRAL BUILDING
Leipzig, Germany *2001–05*
In collaboration with Patrik Schumacher

As the active nerve centre of the entire BMW factory complex, the point at which all threads of activity gather and branch out, the building needed to accommodate the cycles of production and the cycles of workers and visitors that traverse the space. This centrality is made manifest in the dynamic spatial system that encompasses the entire northern side of the factory, and articulates the central building as the point of confluence. This central area – or 'market place' – enhances communication by providing an area for staff and administrative services.

Structurally, the primary organizing strategy is a scissor-section that connects the ground and first floors in a continuous field. Two sequences of terraced plates, like giant staircases, step up from north to south and from south to north, capturing a long, connective void between them. At the bottom of this void is the auditing area, a central focus of everybody's attention; above the void, open to view, are half-finished cars that move along tracks between production units. The cascading floor plates are large enough to allow for flexible occupation patterns, thus opening more visual communication than with a single flat floor plate. This, in turn, is enhanced by the transparency of the internal organization. The mixing of functions avoid the traditional segregation of status groups; engineering and administrative offices, for example, are located within the trajectory of the manual workforce's daily movements.

We avoided the problems of a large car park in front of a building by turning it into a dynamic spectacle in its own right. The dynamism of vehicle movement within and seen through the building merges into the arrangement of parking spaces, which let the entire field to move, colour and sparkle with field lines that culminate inside the building.

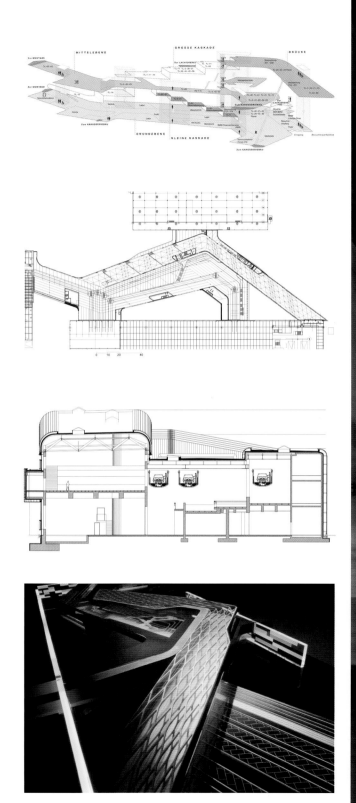

The growth of the Ordrupgaard Museum offered an opportunity to unite its different buildings and gardens into a single entity. At once a discrete feature in the landscape and an addition to the existing garden topography, this ensemble separates the flat terrain in front of the building from the sloping garden at the rear. Contours were studied and abstracted, then lifted and twisted to form a shell that becomes the museum enclosure. Visitors encounter art in the garden, as they approach the new extension, and works of different scales can be seen from various vantage points in the grounds. Transformed into a series of flowing, connected spaces, the interior landscapes of the galleries are a counterpoint to the exterior.

The new building is separated by a courtyard from the existing French Gallery. The galleries are aligned north–south behind the foyer and shop area, while a thick wall of lift, stairs and storage areas separates the foyer from the gallery spaces. A long, sloping ramp divides the temporary and permanent gallery spaces and leads to the multipurpose hall and café that face the garden. At the heart of the composition are the galleries for the Danish and French collections. A new gallery is physically connected to the existing Gauguin Gallery at the garden end, closing off a narrow courtyard. This new space is seen as the largest single area within the proposed building, and its views can be exploited to create visual connections to other galleries and out to the cloister-like spaces of the gardens beyond.

ORDRUPGAARD MUSEUM EXTENSION
Copenhagen, Denmark 2001–05

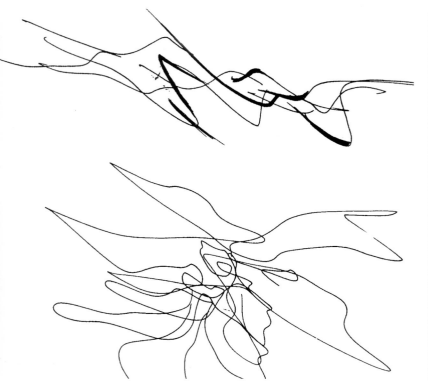

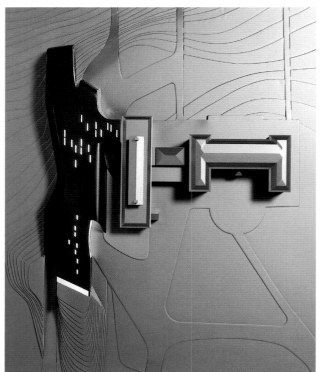

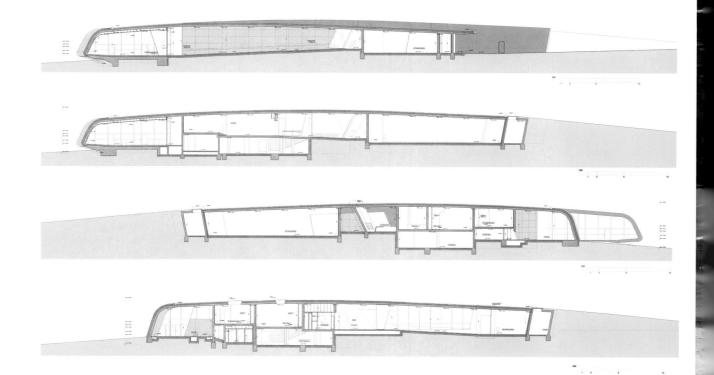

ORDRUPGAARD MUSEUM EXTENSION

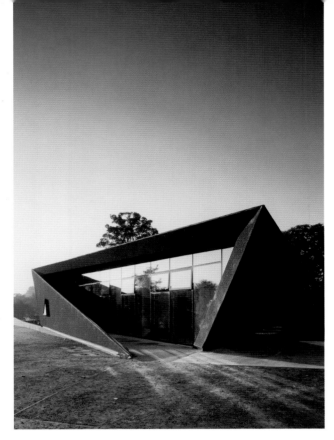

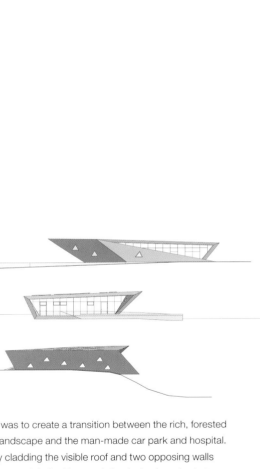

Elevations [above]

Our intention was to create a transition between the rich, forested surrounding landscape and the man-made car park and hospital. Articulated by cladding the visible roof and two opposing walls with the same material, Cor-Ten steel, the design is a play between a folding surface and a connecting ground slab. The roof's large overhangs extends the building down into the ground, while the concrete plinth connects the building outwards to the surrounding landscaped areas. Rooms inside are centred around an open-plan kitchen; offices are located on the north elevation with a direct view to the car park and the entrance. Rooms to the east are more private, and as such are seen externally as a semi-opaque façade. There is a direct view from the entrance at the northeast through the central kitchen space to the south-facing glass elevation.

MONOGRAPHIC EXHIBITION
Rome, Italy 2002
In collaboration with Patrik Schumacher

→ ↘ To celebrate the development of MAXXI [p. 156], the National Centre for Contemporary Arts held an exhibition on temporary premises in the Via Guido Reni. Taking MAXXI's flowing forms as a point of departure for the show's content, projects representing the whole of the practice's career are shown to overlap and intersect in a fluid interchange of ideas and design trajectories. The formal intervention of a curving wall, similar to some extent to the device used in the ICA exhibition, unifies the narrative arc of the works on display.

PRICE TOWER ARTS CENTER
Bartlesville, Oklahoma, USA 2002–
In collaboration with Patrik Schumacher

→ Our design for a new arts centre facility, located next to Frank Lloyd Wright's Price Tower, enters into a bold dialogue as dynamic forms are cantilevered, acute-angled and low-slung. Containing a new study centre and sitting next to a community centre designed by one of Wright's followers, the buildings form an architectural and cultural campus that will be the focal point of downtown Bartlesville. Through an exploration of urban and natural terrains, the city grid, and modes of movement through the city, the design superimposes the skewed axes of the tower's orientation and Wright's textile-block patterns. The end effect is a building that grows out of the site's patterns of living and landscape, thus remaining true to Wright's own philosophy.

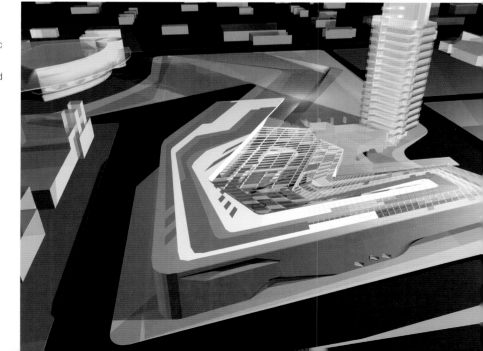

← The tragic destruction of New York's World Trade Center raised the question of what could replace it. Rather than calling for a symbolic response, our alternative question was to ask what kind of organizational structure would satisfy contemporary business life, and what kind of formal language would articulate it? What are the functionality and aesthetics of the contemporary metropolis? How – if at all – should its essence appear on the Manhattan skyline?

CITY OF TOWERS, VENICE BIENNALE

Venice, Italy 2002

In collaboration with Patrik Schumacher

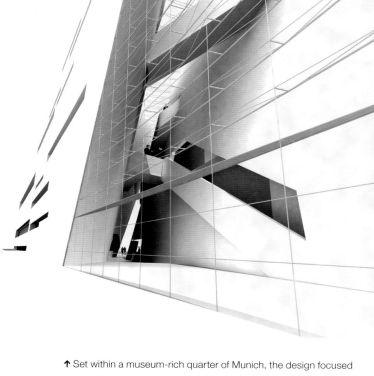

↑ Set within a museum-rich quarter of Munich, the design focused on a compact volume that would be tightly integrated into its urban context. A diagonal incision splits open the 'art box' like a canyon, creating a coherent full-height vertical circulation space within the volume and opening up a diagonal view and passage from the corner of Theresienstraße and Türkenstraße to the Pinakothek der Moderne museum. Within the building, this startling spatial experience contains the public lobby, reception and museum shop. Above and below, internal passages leading to gallery spaces spread along the two walls of the cleft, which serves as an interface between the varying heights of the galleries. The collection's complexity thus unfolds within this central volume, and allows for a diversity of gallery spaces.

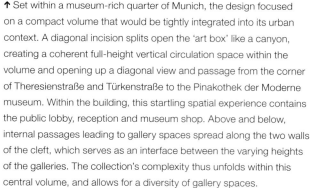

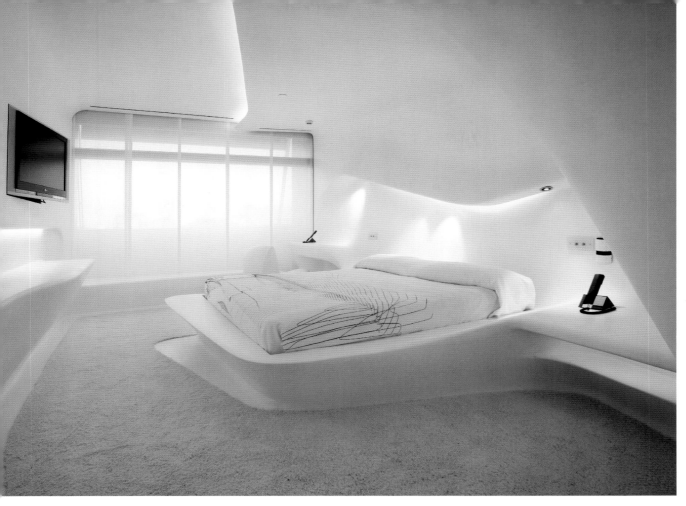

← ↖ ↑ Having been allowed full autonomy by the client, the brief was to design a hotel floor that comprised thirty rooms and all common parts. The objective was to ensure a dynamic and customized project, with the aim of ultimately allowing for a fluid space and seamless experience. We took the opportunity to create a new domestic language of architecture, driven by new developments in digital design and enhanced manufacturing capabilities. This new dialogue emphasizes the complex and continuous nature of the design and the merging of disparate forms and texture.

In the rooms, floor, walls and furniture are all one continuous surface or skin, making them pieces of art. Every single element – the walls, the bedroom doors with their LED signs, sliding doors to the bathroom, bathtubs and vanity units, beds, shelves, chairs and cantilevered benches by the window that double up as tables – is rounded in a single, curved sweep. A further unique element of this suite of bedrooms is the use of colour. Customers can opt for an alpine white or a black bedroom, or even choose a white bedroom with a black bathroom, a black bedroom and a white bathroom, or a black bedroom and an orange bathroom.

HOTEL PUERTA AMERICA – HOTELES SILKEN
Madrid, Spain 2003–05

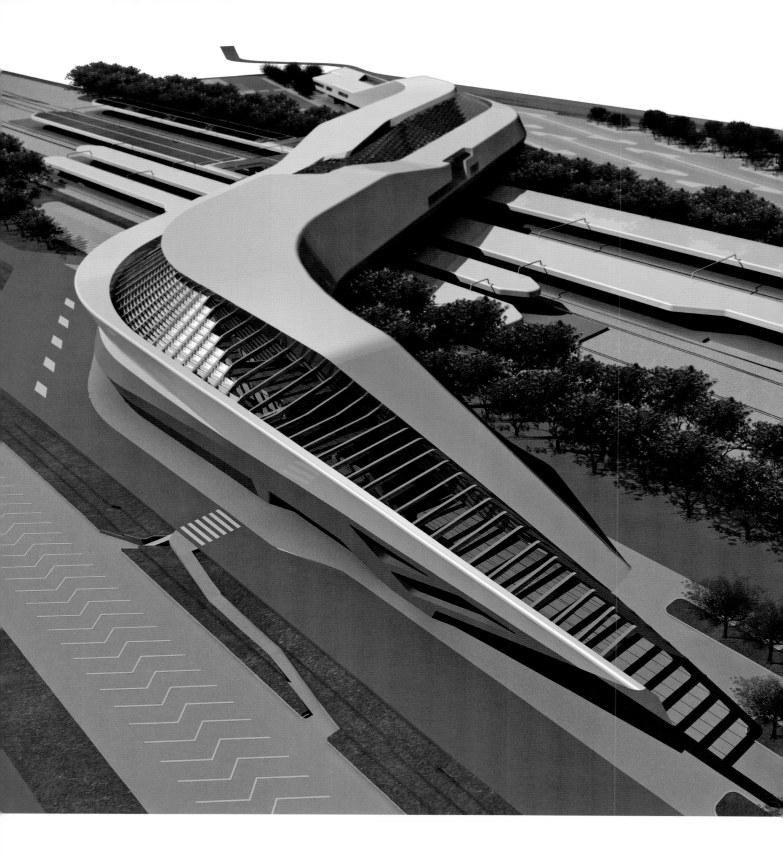

The new high-speed station Napoli Afragola is a bridge above the tracks. The key challenge of the architectural scheme was to create a well-organized transport interchange that can simultaneously serve as a new gateway to announce the approach to Naples. The form of the bridge emerges from the idea of enlarging the overhead concourse, which is required to access the various platforms, to such a degree that it can become the main passenger concourse itself.

Providing an urbanized public link across the tracks, the concourse bridge gives expression to a new kind of through-station that acts as the nucleus of a proposed business park linking the various surrounding towns. The bridge concept further allows two strips of extended park-land to move openly through the site alongside the tracks to open and connect the site to the surrounding landscape and business park. Geared towards the articulation of movement, the architectural language continues inside the building, where the trajectory and movements the travellers determines the geometry of the space.

HIGH-SPEED TRAIN STATION NAPOLI-AFRAGOLA

Naples, Italy 2004–14

In collaboration with Patrik Schumacher

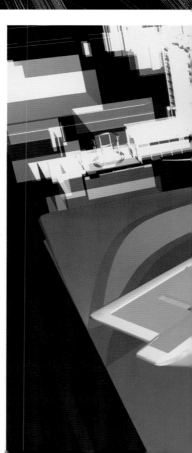

→ Our proposal for a new BBC music centre was to form the public centrepiece of a larger complex, with pedestrians guided onto the site under a high canopy. Studios are wrapped and surrounded by support facilities, while the acoustic aspects of separating circulation from performance space are differentiated by a 'belt' of rooms. A full-ring balcony for orchestra members, audience and technicians animates spaces for rehearsals and studio recordings.

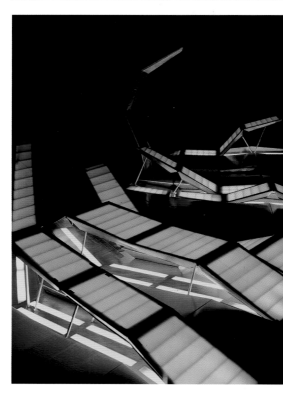

→ Commissioned by the Steirischer Herbst in Graz, 'Desire' is a contemporary opera by Beat Furrer, a present-day treatment of the myth of Orpheus that addresses the themes of psychological and emotional metamorphosis through the tragic love story of Orpheus and Eurydice. Our stage design was conceived as a landscape, a distorted grid that comprises a series of moving parts that change as the narrative journey and the music unfolds. Strong directional lines zig-zag across the set; the landscape splits open and is sliced in two. Boundaries between inside and outside, upper- and underworld, score and stage are blurred.

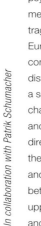

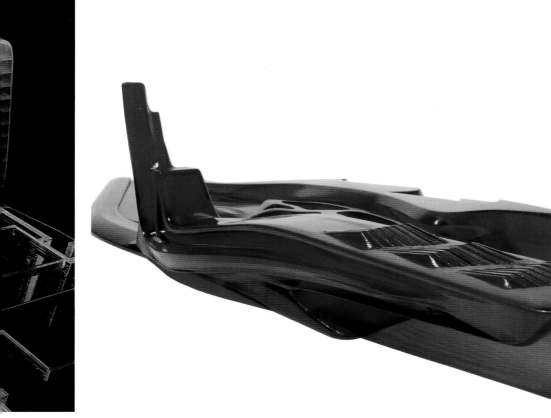

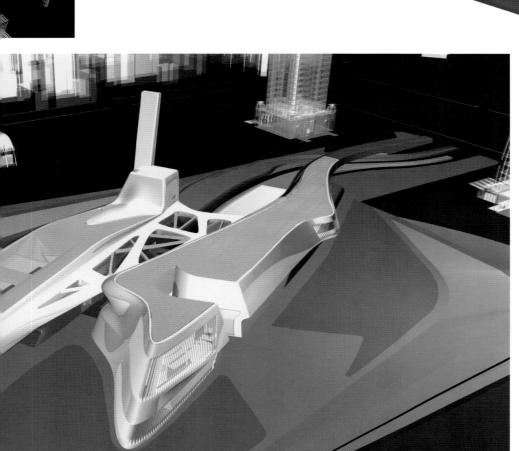

←↑ Our design concept is based on the museum as an ever-changing event space, with 'stage machinery' made up of large-scale kinetic elements that allow radical transformations of the gallery spaces. The transformations themselves can become a spectacle visible from the outside, a public sensation within the urban scenery. Public flow through the building and internal circulation through the exhibition spaces are expressed through swooping ramps, while movable levels, walls and platforms permit a multitude of interior spatial configurations.

GUGGENHEIM MUSEUM TAICHUNG
Taichung, Taiwan 2003

In collaboration with Patrik Schumacher

↗ Ice and snow are exciting natural elements, striking for their fluid shapes and coherent formations. Working with artist Cai Guo-Qiang, we created a landscape that both intensifies the conditions created by these elements and expresses the transformation from one state to the next. Two mirrored landscape formations emerge, one of snow, the other of ice. Floating spaces and canyons envelope visitors in a glowing glacier; walls curve into ceiling and into gravity-defying structures. Light informs the space, as 'veins' of illumination are interwoven into the structure. On this 'landscape', Cai Guo-Qiang created a surreal scene of flames that cascade down in blue streams, pools and terraces, thus reshaping the structure and transforming the piece into an (artificially) melted space. The remaining ice is left to nature.

→ Opening up Hunters Point to a rapidly changing future on the East River, our masterplan for the Olympic Village in New York's 2012 bid features a constellation of towers, whose minimal footprints offer an open and textured landscape that welcomes visitors with spectacular views towards Midtown and Lower Manhattan. The contoured ground and towers accentuate both the buildings' verticality and the horizontal plane, permitting maximum flexibility in the design process. Street and interior axes can be defined progressively through the layering and cutting of the ground, lighting strategies, and the integration of artworks.

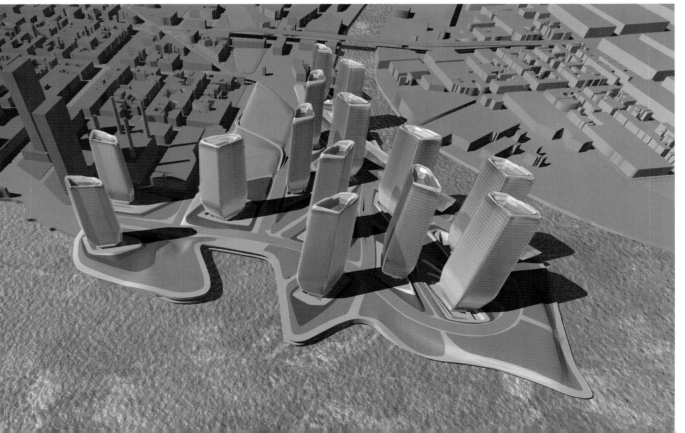

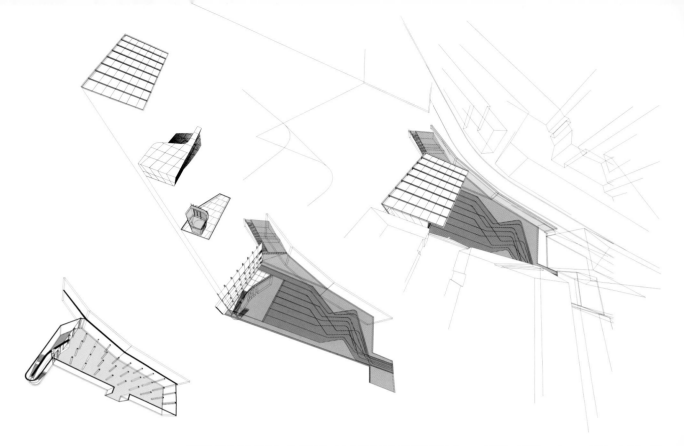

The client came to us with the intention of designing a *fin-de-siècle*-style pavilion that would contain an older pavilion originally commissioned by his great-grandfather in 1910. The old pavilion would become a jewel within the new container. Like a series of Russian dolls, the new pavilion would eventually be housed within the new extension at the bodegas – thus making the new pavilion another layer. Various studies led to a container developed in sectional cuts. The section distorts from a rectangle around the old pavilion to a distorted memory shape resembling a decanter. This was not an intentional end point, but once noticed it could not be ignored. We had designed a new bottle for an old wine.

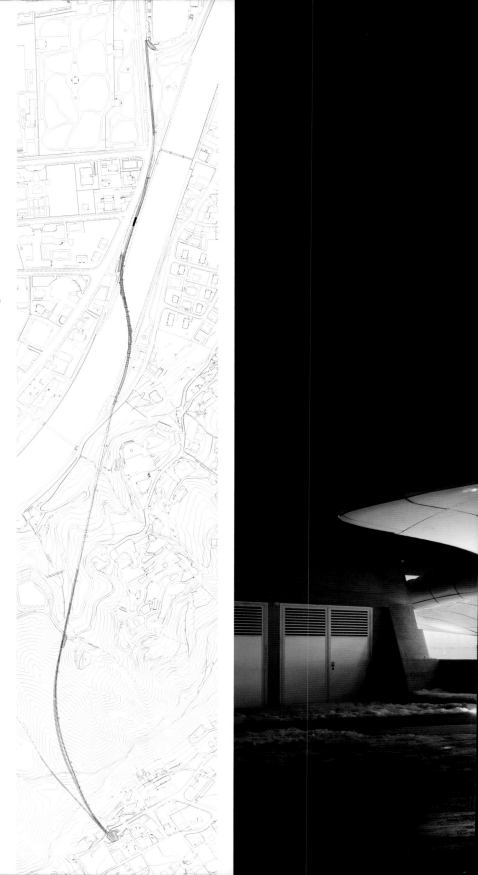

Site plan

This cable railway in the Tyrolean Alps, the result of a competition that we won with the contractor Strabag in 2005, comprises four new railway stations and a cable-stayed suspension bridge over the River Inn. It is our second project in the city of Innsbruck [see Bergisel Ski Jump; p. 112].

Each station has its own unique context, topography, altitude and circulation. Two contrasting elements, 'shell' and 'shadow', generate the stations' spatial qualities, with their lightweight organic roof structures of double-curvature glass 'floating' on top of concrete plinths to create artificial landscapes that describe the movement and circulation within. Because we wanted each station to use the fluid language of ice formations, like a frozen stream on the mountainside, we spent much of the development process studying such natural phenomena as glacial moraines and ice movements. A high degree of flexibility within this language enables the shell structures to adjust to these various parameters, while maintaining a coherent formal logic.

New production methods, including CNC milling, thermoforming and manufacturing technologies developed for the automotive industry, guaranteed a precise and automatic translation of the computer-generated design into the streamlined built structures.

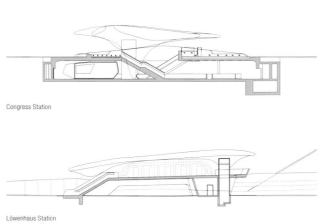

Congress Station

Löwenhaus Station

Alpenzoo Station

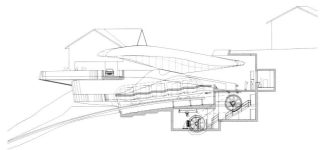

Hungerburg Station

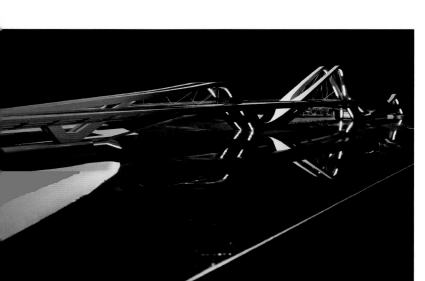

SHEIKH ZAYED BRIDGE
Abu Dhabi, UAE 1997–

154

↑ ↗ Today's highly mobile society requires a new route around the south shore of the Persian Gulf, connecting the Emirates together. In 1967, a steel arch bridge was built to connect the island of Abu Dhabi to the mainland, followed by a second bridge built in the 1970s, which connects downstream on the south side of the island. The location of the new (third) Gateway Crossing, close to the first bridge, is critical to the completion of the highway system. The bridge has the potential to become a destination in itself, a catalyst in the urban growth of Abu Dhabi. A collection of structural strands, gathered on one shore, are lifted and 'propelled' over the length of the channel. A sinusoidal waveform provides the structural silhouette. The mainland is the launch pad for the bridge structure as it emerges from the ground and approach road. The road decks are cantilevered on each side of the spine structure. Steel arches rise and spring asymmetrically from mass concrete piers between the road decks to mark the mainland and the central void position, diverging under the road decks to the outside of the roadways at the other end of the bridge. The main arch of the bridge rises to a height of 60 metres above water level, with the road cresting at a height of 20 metres above mean water level.

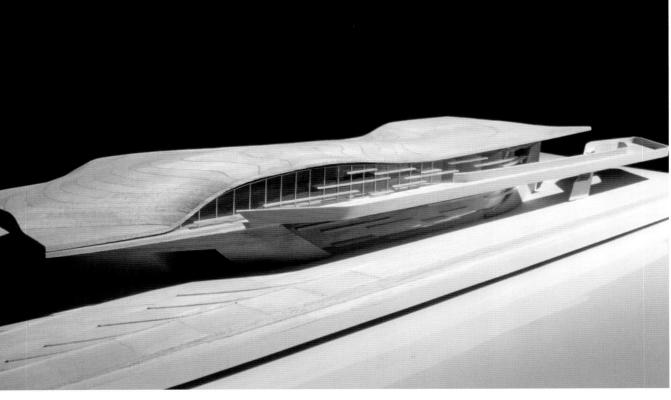

↑↓ The new ferry terminal forges an intimate, and innovative, relationship between the city and the waterfront. Like an oyster, the building has a hard shell enclosing soft, fluid elements, with a 'nerved' roof that acts as extended protection against the intense Mediterranean sun. The terminal is composed of three main interlocking elements: administrative offices, ferry terminal and cruise-ship terminal. As a whole, the building functions as a smooth transition between the land and sea, an artificial landform that constantly shifts from solid into liquid. Arriving passengers to the terminal drift into dynamic spaces organized around focal points, such as the restaurant and waiting room. Lighting, which will guide passengers through the length of the building, will glow on the outside, illuminated like a lighthouse to the port, a symbolic reference to the site's Norman and Saracen history.

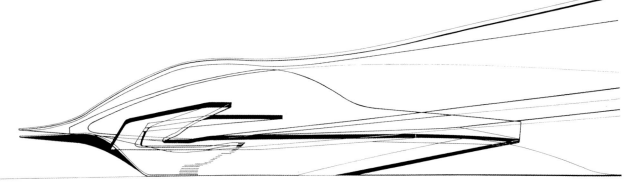

Externally, our design offers a quasi-urban field, a 'world' to dive into, rather than the building as an object. Internally, the move from object to field is critical to the relationship between the architecture and the art that it will house. Conventional object-focused paths are replaced by fields of multiple associations, so that the centre becomes a pliable and porous organism that promotes several forms of identification and activity at once. The conventional museum wall as the privileged and immutable vertical armature for displaying paintings here becomes a versatile system for the staging of exhibition effects. Movable elements enable 'sets' to be constructed, giving new curatorial freedom and redefining art spectatorship as a liberated dialogue with artefact and environment.

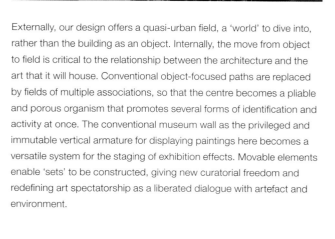

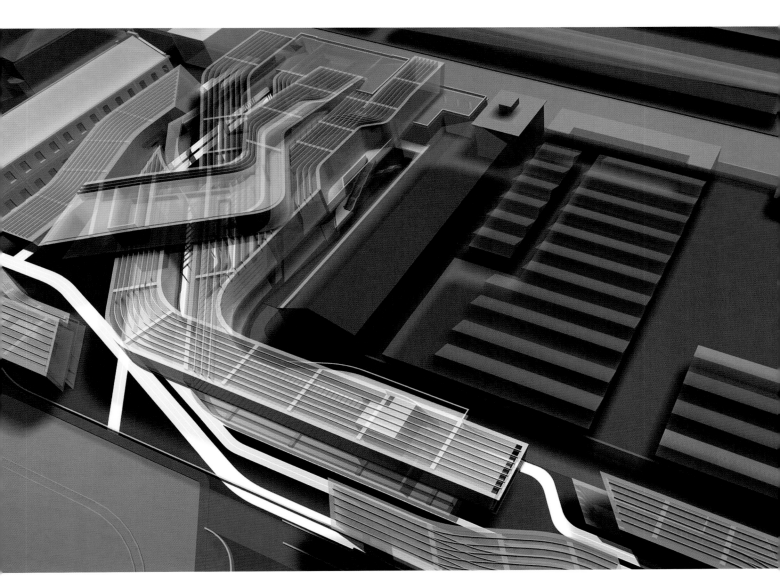

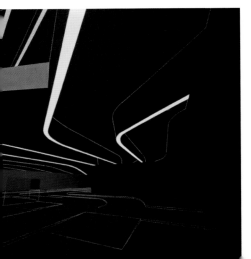

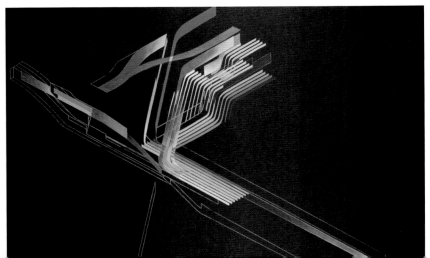

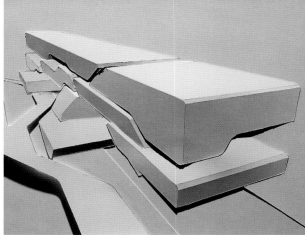

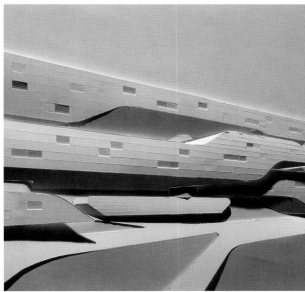

Although the design for a regional government complex containing an archive, library and sports department was developed rigorously along programmatic lines, the building's form recalls a large tree trunk, laid horizontally. The archive is located at the solid base of the trunk, followed by the slightly more porous library, with the sports department and well-lit offices at the end where the trunk bifurcates and becomes much lighter. The branches articulate points of access and entrances into the different institutions. At ground level, departments share various public spaces; above, each institution is distinct, with its own set of cores for internal vertical circulation.

PIERRES VIVES
Montpellier, France 2002–11

Occupying a site overlooking the Pearl River, the Guangzhou Opera House aims to sound the high notes of Chinese opera with its tantalizing contours. Featuring a unique 'twin boulder' design, the building will enhance urban function with open access to the riverside and dock areas, and establish a new dialogue with the emerging new town. When viewed from the park at the centre of Zhujiang Boulevard, the Opera House creates a visual prelude to the Haixinsha Tourist Park island beyond. An internal street is cut into the context's landscape from the direction of a proposed museum at the opposite side of the central boulevard. Café, bar, restaurant and retail facilities, embedded shell-like into these landforms, are located to one side of this promenade.

GLASGOW MUSEUM OF TRANSPORT RIVERSIDE PROJECT
Glasgow, Scotland 2004–10

↑ → ↘ The historical development of the River Clyde and the city of Glasgow offers a site where the building can flow from the city to the river, to be the transition from one to the other. A tunnel-like shed, a sectional extrusion open at opposite ends to the city and the Clyde, is porous to its context on either side. The cross-sectional outline is a responsive gesture to encapsulating a wave or a 'pleated' movement. Outer pleats are enclosed to accommodate support services and black-box exhibits, leaving the central space to be column-free and open. The end elevation is like the front elevation with an expansive glass façade and a large overhang to reduce solar exposure and allow views up and down the river. The landscape, made up of stone slabs in a shadow path around the building and an informal open courtyard space, is designed to direct the activities surrounding the building.

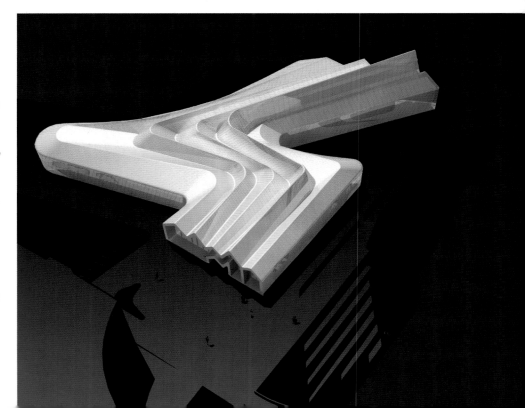

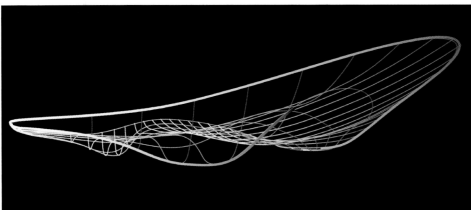

← ↑ Inspired by the fluid geometry of water in motion, our design aims to create spaces and a surrounding environment in sympathy with the river landscape of London's 2012 Olympic Park. An undulating roof sweeps up from the ground as a wave, enclosing the swimming and diving pools with a unifying gesture and describing their volume. Bridges connecting the building to the site are fluidly incorporated into the building.

The centre is planned on an orthogonal axis, along which the three pools are arranged. The training pool is located under a bridge; competition and diving pools within a larger hall. The overall strategy is to frame the base of the pool hall as a podium, by surrounding it and connecting it into the bridge. From the bridge level, the podium emerges from underneath the bridge to cascade around the hall to the lower level of the canalside area.

The pool hall is expressed by a large roof, grounded at three primary positions, that arches along the same axis as the pools. Double-curvature geometry is used to create a structure of parabolic arches that undulate to visually differentiate between the competition pool area and the diving pool. The roof projection over the bridge announces the entrance.

LONDON AQUATIC CENTRE
London, England 2003–12

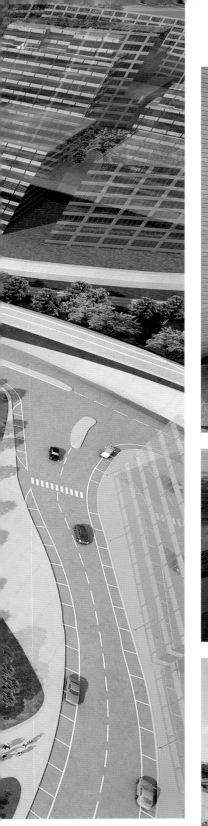

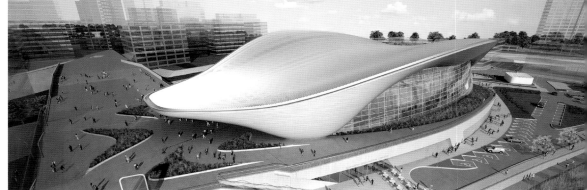

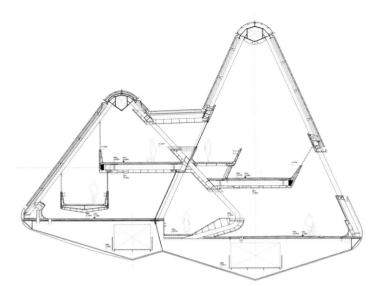

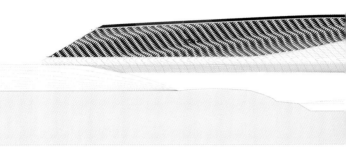

Our design for a bridge pavilion, which derives from an exploration of a diamond-shaped section that has been extruded along a curved path, is organized around four main truss elements, or 'pods', that perform as structural elements and spatial enclosures. The stacking and interlocking of these pods allow them to brace each other so that loads are distributed across all four, instead of a single element. The interlocking had unforeseen but felicitous effects on our design. Visitors move from pod to pod through small interstitial spaces, which act as filters or buffer zones, tuning down sound and visuals from one exhibition space to the next.

In designing the building's skin, shark scales provided fascinating paradigms, for both appearance and performance. Their pattern can easily wrap around complex curvatures with a simple system of rectilinear ridges that proves to be performative, visually appealing and economical. This skin was generated by a complex pattern of simple, overlapping shingles, some of which rotate around a pivot for opening or closing part of the façade. The quality of light can be modulated from rays through tiny, punctual apertures to wide, full-size openings.

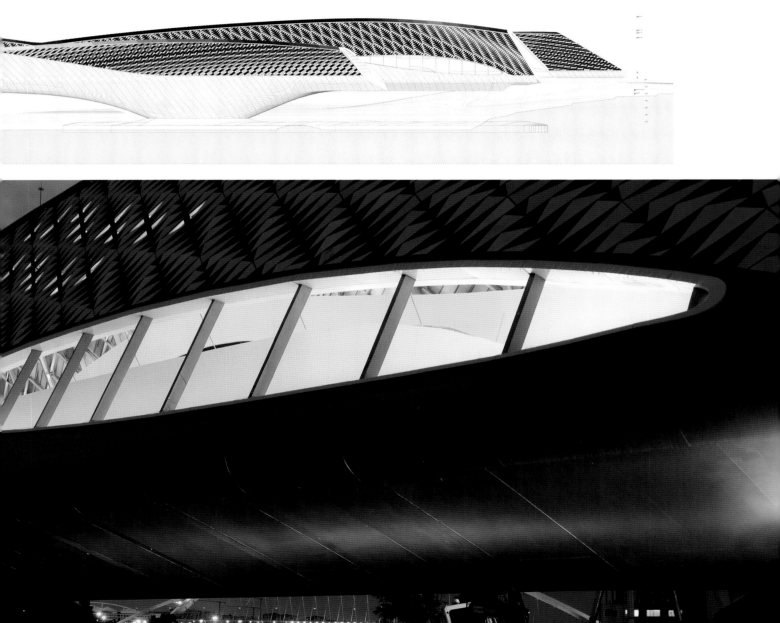

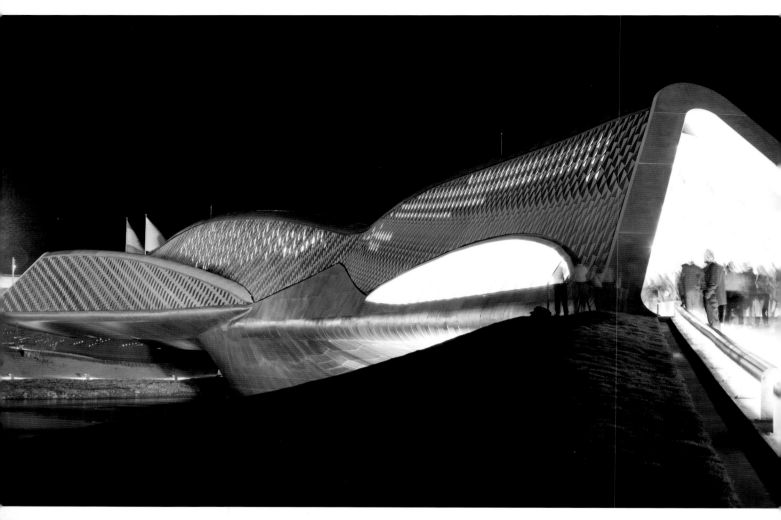

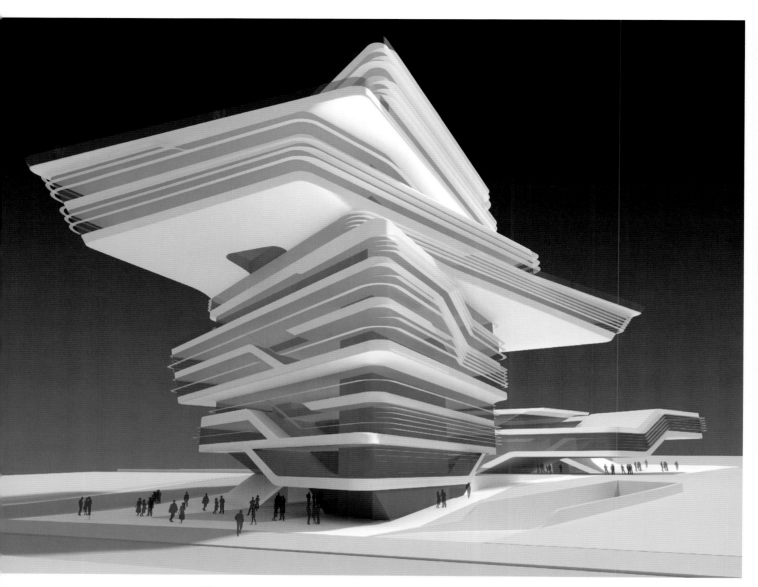

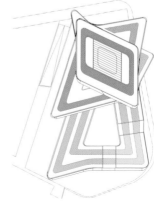

EDIFICI CAMPUS
Barcelona, Spain 2006–
In collaboration with Patrik Schumacher

← ↑ Responding to Barcelona's changing waterfront, we designed a spiralling tower that seamlessly stitches together the municipalities of Barcelona and Besòs. The Edifici Campus articulates the transition between the forum and the campus, between Barcelona's waterfront area and the requalification of the delta of the River Besòs, while anchoring itself on a functional mix of university and office spaces that promotes new opportunities of interaction through its diverse public spaces of the courtyard and the atrium.

The fluid character of the tower is generated through an intrinsically dynamic composition of volumes that dissolves the classic typology of the tower and the podium into an integrated whole. The building uses the site's inclined topography to redesign the landscape to maximize fluidity between the new campus and the forum. Through the use of cantilevers, the building lifts from street level, releasing the ground for public use. The continuous spiral movement weaves a series of public spaces, connecting the campus, through the courtyards and under the cantilevers, to the forum beyond.

← ↑ Marseille is France's second largest city, a historic Provençale port town with an ancient maritime past. The new tower offers an opportunity to create a vertical icon that will interact with the city's other significant landmarks. Seeking to diverge from the standard high-rise design protocol of a uniform floor plate that is replicated to minimize construction time and cost, our design focus shifted to the building envelope and a sculptural interior atrium/entrance, which is supported by the tower's programme: upper floors have conventional office spaces, while lower floors offer a continuous, horizontal arrangement. The CMA CGM tower rises from its Mirabeau site, adjacent to the quay and its waterways and characterized by medium- to low-rise post-war buildings, in a curving arc that gradually lifts from the ground into a vertical line. The tower's volumes are generated from a number of vectors that emerge from within the ground datum and trace the structural columns that define a double-façade system. At street level, a multi-modal transport exchange encourages pedestrian and mass-transit connectivity.

CMA CGM HEADQUARTERS TOWER

Marseille, France 2004–09

171

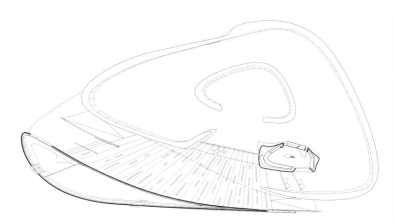

MOBILE ART PAVILION FOR CHANEL

Hong Kong, China *2007–08*
In collaboration with Patrik Schumacher

The form of the Mobile Art Pavilion is a celebration of the iconic work of Chanel, unmistakable for its smooth layering of exquisite details that together form an elegant, cohesive whole. The resulting building is very much tied to that original inspiration – chic, functional and versatile, both in its overall structure and detail. The pavilion's organic form evolved from the spiralling shapes found in nature, a system of organization and growth that is among the most frequent in nature. The pavilion follows the parametric distortion of a torus, which creates a constant variety of exhibition spaces around its circumference, with a 65-square-metre courtyard for visitors at its centre. This arrangement also allows visitors to see each other moving through the space, thus encouraging the viewing of art as a collective experience.

The shell was created with a succession of diminishing arched segments. Because the pavilion will travel across three continents, this segmentation allows the building to be easily transported in manageable elements no wider than 2.25 metres. The partitioning seams become a strong formal feature of the exterior façade and establish a spatial rhythm. Lines of energy converge within the pavilion, constantly redefining the quality of each exhibition space while guiding movement through the exhibition. Ultimately, the fascination of the Mobile Art Pavilion is the challenge of translating the intellectual and physical into the sensual – experimenting with completely unexpected and totally immersive environments for the global celebration of an iconic fashion label, a total artwork that continually reinvents itself as it moves from Asia to the USA and Europe.

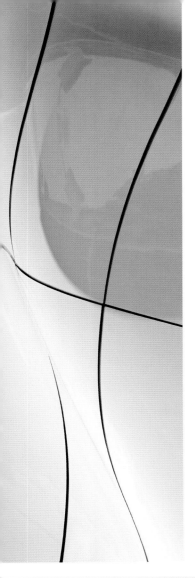
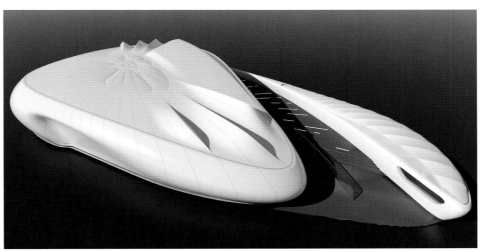

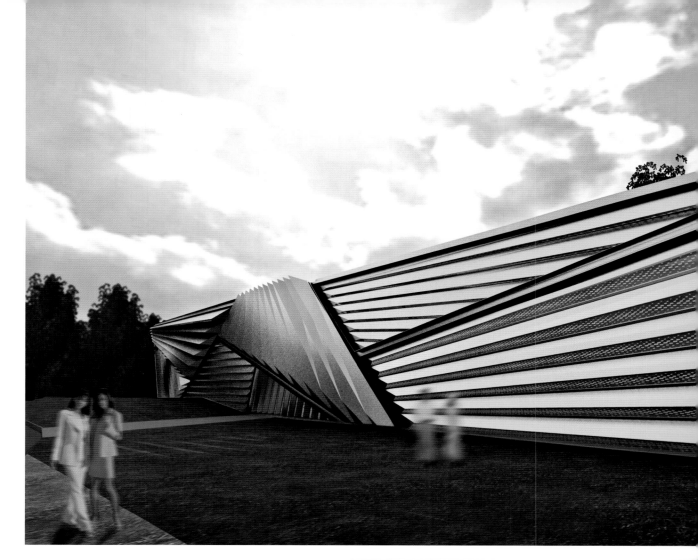

ELI & EDYTHE BROAD ART MUSEUM
Michigan State University, USA 2007–
In collaboration with Patrik Schumacher

↑ → The initial concept for a private art museum was generated by developing a 'landscape carpet' that would pick up the loose ends of the site's urban fabric, and interweave them with the different movement directions across and along the site. A pattern of linear movements is derived from the surrounding structures, forming the base for the carpet, which is folded up into the volume of the museum. Each patch of the façade picks up a different direction of the composition, creating the outer envelope as a sharp and directed body. The building leans to the west in a dramatic gesture, forming a raised head with a 12-metre-tall front face that looks towards the urban plaza, and continues in a linear shift to the east, facing the sculpture garden, where it blends into the landscape. The building's outer skin, a structure of glass and stainless steel with a gradual perforation, animates the building through its ever-changing appearance. The variation in glass and perforation is also used to filter and direct the daylight in each gallery.

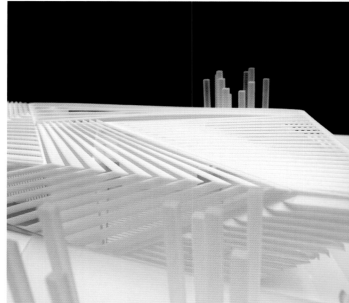

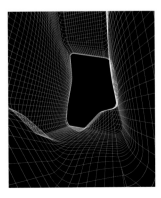

←↑ Located within the Business Bay masterplan, the site for the Omniyat flagship office/retail tower comprises two plots interlinked by a continuous low-level podium structure, which sits beneath two buildings that are conceived as a united mass: a cube hovering off the ground and carved by a free-form void. The cube is structured by a conventional system of vertically stacked slabs serviced by central cores, allowing the areas near the façade to be occupied on all eight sides. The eroded void, clad in tinted double-glazing, is treated as a volume in its own right, cutting through the cube's edges. Plateaus within the void will provide areas for recreation and rest. The ground floor is treated as an open field, to draw visitors into the interiors of the two separate lobbies. Reflective fritting patterns in the form of pixellated striations are applied to the glass façade to provide reflectivity and materiality, and to reduce solar gains. While the cube appears animated in daytime and the void empty, the night-time perception would be reversed: the cube appears dark and dematerialized, with the void activated by light, visible from a great distance.

'OPUS' OFFICE TOWER
Dubai, UAE 2007–10

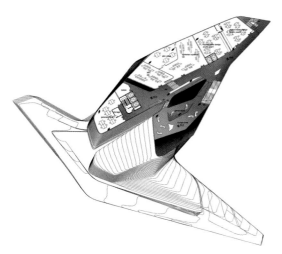

The new 'Innovation Tower', located at the northeast side of the Hong Kong Polytechnic University campus, will serve as a driving force in the development of the city as a design hub in Asia. Upon completion, the tower, our first permanent architectural design in Hong Kong, will provide some 12,000 square metres of floor area and will accommodate more than 1,500 students.

Hong Kong's diversity in its landscapes and history is reflected in an urbanism of layering and porosity. Our own explorations and research into an architecture of seamless fluidity follows this paradigm, so evident in the city. One of our seminal projects was designed for Hong Kong [p. 22], and the design for the Innovation Tower is a realization of this continued research. The design dissolves the classic typology of the tower and the podium into a seamless piece, and unashamedly aims to stimulate a vision of possibilities for the future, whilst reflecting the history of the institution.

The new tower will house the School of Design, as well as an advanced car design studio; fashion accessories materials labs; a sound studio for multimedia and entertainment design; a museum to showcase local and international design classics; and a public exhibition space.

INNOVATION TOWER
Hong Kong Polytechnic University, China 2007–11

In collaboration with Patrik Schumacher

MOSCOW EXPOCENTRE EXHIBITION HALLS
Moscow, Russia 2007–
In collaboration with Patrik Schumacher

↑ → The Moscow International Business Centre is one of the largest investment and construction projects in Europe, and the Expocentre will be the finishing keystone in this development, expanding the current usage as a business zone into a 24-hour living and events space. The project embraces the possibility of integrating vertical urban space with the site's existing horizontal urban fabric. The main function of the horizontal space is to house the large exposition and conference halls, which are lifted above ground to leave the ground floor free for offices, restaurants and bars. The residential tower, a large vertical volume divided into two smaller shapes, is designed as a continuation of the Moscow skyline. An elliptical form provides an elegant edge. The space between these volumes is structured with fluid passages, sky lobbies, apartments and a gym. The vertical urban space swoops to the ground to create a main lobby. The hotel rises to the 26th floor of the western tower; residences are located in the eastern tower and on the top floors of the western tower. The intersection of the horizontal and vertical volumes creates the main public plaza which serves as the project's focus.

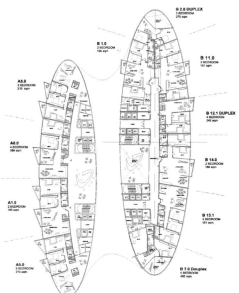

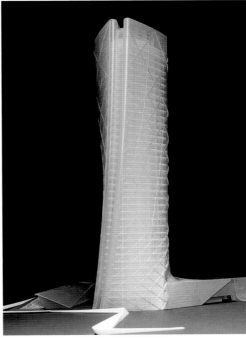

← ↑ This masterplan site encompasses a large park, three office towers, retail buildings, educational and social facilities, a museum, and four sites for residential development, each designed by a different architect. Our design includes a 190-metre-tall office tower of forty-three storeys, connected to a three-storey retail space and a housing complex of six buildings, ranging from three to fourteen storeys.

FIERA DI MILANO
Milan, Italy 2004–14

In collaboration with Patrik Schumacher

181

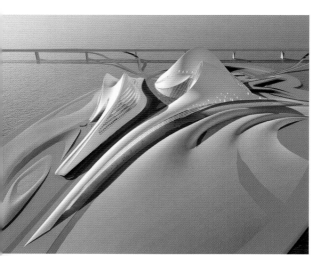
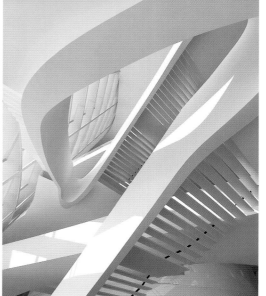

DUBAI OPERA HOUSE
Dubai, UAE 2006–
In collaboration with Patrik Schumacher

↑ ↗ This landmark development, located on an island in Dubai Creek, will include a 2,500-seat opera house, an 800-seat playhouse and a 5,000-square-metre arts gallery, as well as a performing arts school and six-star hotel. Our proposal houses all of these facilities in a single structure that evokes images of the nearby sand dunes. Two central peaks corresponding to the opera house and playhouse swoop down to earth, with entrances for the audience where the form has been scalloped away. The main foyer spaces create a gentle, multi-tiered landscape at one floor above ground level, serving the auditoria and arts gallery. Floating above are further foyers that afford surprising views across the space.

The auditoria are contained in flowing shapes that appear to emerge from the underside of the main shell. This inner shell does not quite touch the main shell, however. Instead, the two surfaces disappear into a light gap between them.

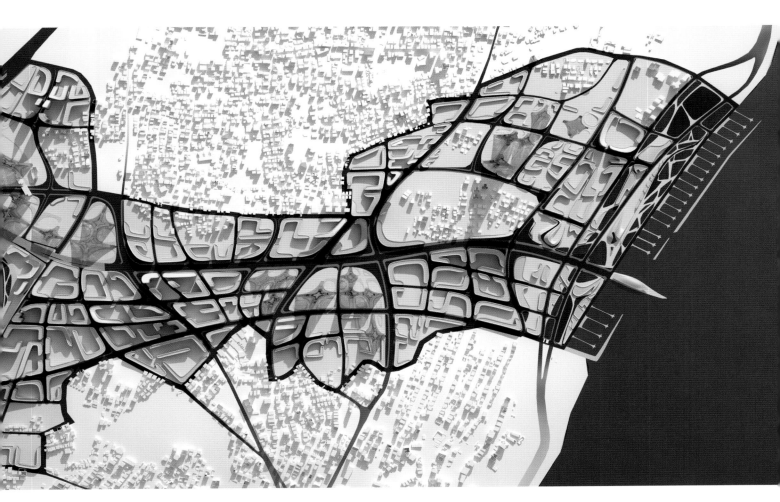

← ↑ Our vision of the Kartal-Pendik masterplan is to encourage the city of Istanbul to become polycentric as an antidote to the monocentric bias of its European side. This will generate an economic impetus, creating a ripple effect of wealth into the areas adjacent to the masterplan. Urban city quarters for 100,000 people to live and work will catalyze a vibrant area. To achieve this, we propose a gridded network of streets with three central clusters of density to allow for a dynamic skyline that takes advantage of the coastal disposition and sea views. A new main boulevard will be the primary artery – the 'spine' of the entire masterplan – providing connectivity between a new metro station in the north and the rail and motorway transport hub in the south. Two central business districts would be located in the north and south. The northern district, the quarry, will become an major recreational area, landscaped and centred around the lake, while the south, with its marina and seafront areas, will be developed with the cultural district.

KARTAL-PENDIK MASTERPLAN
Istanbul, Turkey 2006–
In collaboration with Patrik Schumacher

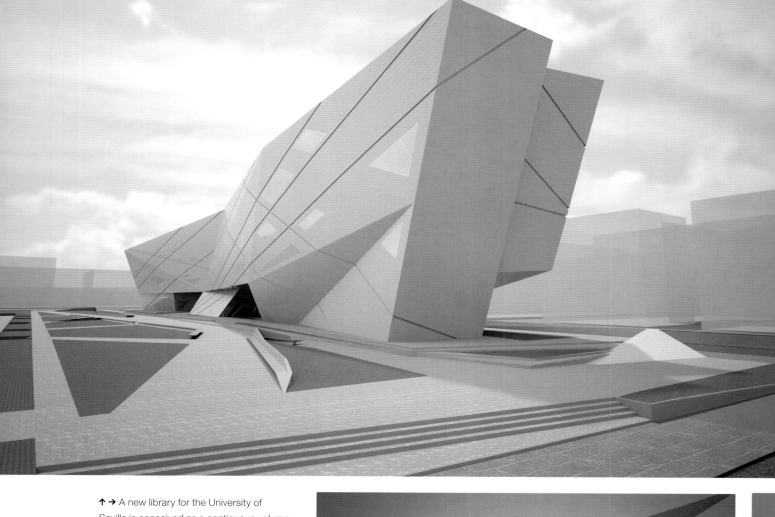

UNIVERSITY OF SEVILLE LIBRARY
Seville, Spain 2006–
In collaboration with Patrik Schumacher

↑ → A new library for the University of Seville is conceived as a continuous volume emerging from the extension of the Prado de San Sebastián park, progressively rising from a soft material into an elongated sculptural object. The 160-metre-long structure is lifted off the ground onto three structures that terminate in a shallow, half-basement-deep plinth to introduce the landscape at the entrance level through public terraces. This transitory area attracts visitors and promotes a variety of student activities. The monolithic structure above twists along its shape through a sequence of triangular planes, being more accentuated at the north end and straighter at the south. A striking kink at the centre defines the triple-height reception hall.

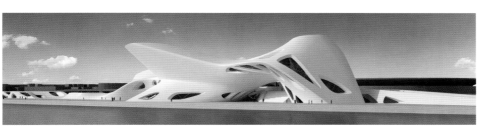

↙ ← ↑ Our design for a new museum resembles coral: empty inside, hard and porous outside. The erosion that forms the great cavity inside the building, intended to be a landmark announcing the arrival to the town from the sea, articulates the volume in a succession of open spaces for exhibitions and places of aggregation, spaces which accentuate the aesthetic dialogue between the contemporary and the Nuragic art. The inner cavity allows the creation of two continuous skins, one contained within the other. The museum programme is placed between the two skins, with the inner skin equipped with a flexible system of anchorage and electrification for multiple uses. The exhibition spaces and criss-crossing public paths create the building's fluid structure.

NURAGIC AND CONTEMPORARY ART MUSEUM

Cagliari, Italy 2006–

In collaboration with Patrik Schumacher

185

SZERVITA SQUARE
Budapest, Hungary 2006–10
In collaboration with Patrik Schumacher

↑ → Our design for a new building on Szervita Square will provide both a landmark structure and a new, enlarged public area, with the aim of moving away from closed forms and perimeter blocks, and making the public zones more porous and open. The building's fluid shape bends around the square and provides different views from all sides, at one point fading into the piazza and at another becoming a canopy that provides sun and noise protection. The square itself becomes a dish, offering distinct public spaces. The components of the building are layered, corresponding to one another structurally, aesthetically and formally: core, structure, skin *brise soleil*, which is echoed in the piazza, where it becomes urban furniture.

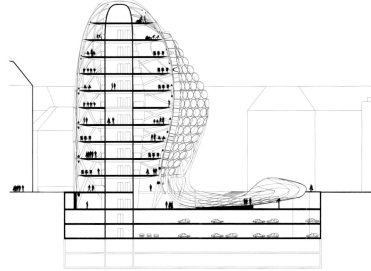

186

← ↑ Part of an ensemble of cultural institutions on Saadiyat Island, the centre's distinct formal language is derived from organizational systems found in the natural world. Growth-simulation processes were used to develop a set of basic geometries, and then superimposed with programmatic diagrams into a series of repeated cycles. The primary components of this biological analogy (branches, stems, fruits and leaves) were then transformed from these abstract diagrams into architectural design. The central axis of the cultural district is a pedestrian corridor that stretches from the Sheikh Zayed museum towards the sea. This axis interacts with the seafront promenade to generate a branching geometry in which islands are formed into distinct bodies to house the five main concert halls.

ABU DHABI PERFORMING ARTS CENTRE

Abu Dhabi, UAE 2008–

In collaboration with Patrik Schumacher

SIGNATURE TOWERS, MASTERPLAN AND PODIUM
Dubai, UAE 2006– and 2005–
In collaboration with Patrik Schumacher

↑ The programme for this development was addressed as a whole with the three Signature Towers corresponding to the three main functions: offices, hotel and residential. The towers share a common base, or podium, itself programmed with retail, restaurants and amenities to support the towers' population. The three towers are organized to share certain segments of the programme, allowing the development to be experienced throughout the day. Anchored in its residential population, it reaches the peak of activity during office hours and mutates through the diversity of the hotel's ever-changing residents.

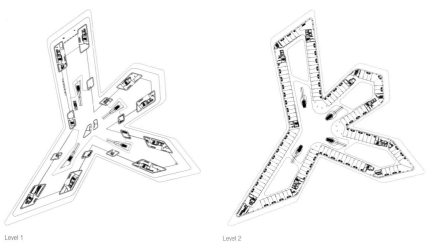

Level 1   Level 2

↑ Our aim here is to create a strong, sculptural element with a distinctive roof form that will be prominent when viewed from the waterfront or the nearby high-rise developments. The building is lifted above ground, with the heavier sculptural solid hovering above a light volume of glass. The challenge is to accommodate a large perimeter of stockbroker shopfronts around a single trading floor, while economizing on the overall area of the building and maintaining coherence of the central space. Our approach was to articulate the plan into a series of petals, allowing us to maximize the amount of frontage for any given area on the site. Each office has a glazed shopfront on the trading floor and an overlook from its mezzanine level. To bring light into this unbroken perimeter, a series of domed skylights draw light in from the roof.

DUBAI FINANCIAL MARKET
Dubai, UAE 2007–

In collaboration with Patrik Schumacher

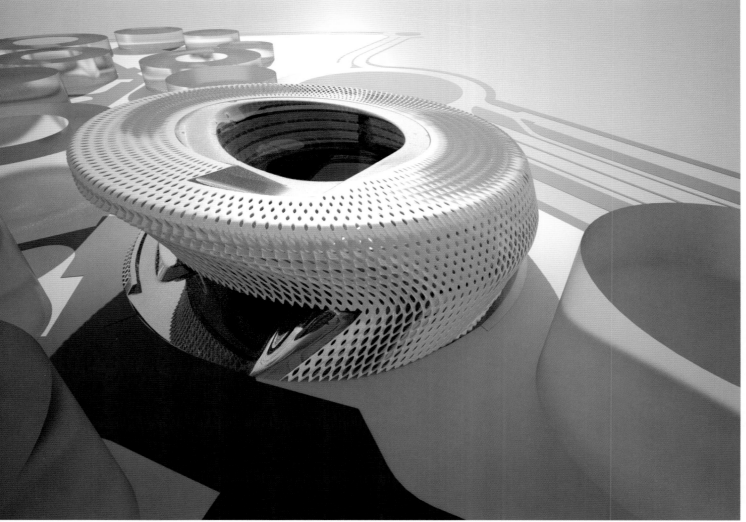

MADRID CIVIL COURTS OF JUSTICE
Madrid, Spain 2007–
In collaboration with Patrik Schumacher

↑ → Responding to the high demand for office space within the new masterplan for Madrid, our scheme for the Civil Courts of Justice inserts public space into its core to make it a pivot point for the entire complex. The design aims to break the static configuration of the surrounding buildings through the soft and dynamic tectonic and horizontal shifts in mass, which lend it elasticity that draws visitors into the interior. The envelope is composed of a double-ventilated façade composed of metallic panels that respond to environmental and programme conditions. Inside the building, a spiralling, semicircular atrium is developed around the courtyard, from which all public space evolves. This courtyard serves as an instant reference point for visitors when moving around the building, and extends to the lower ground floor, providing natural light to enter the courtrooms at that level.

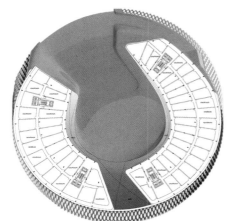

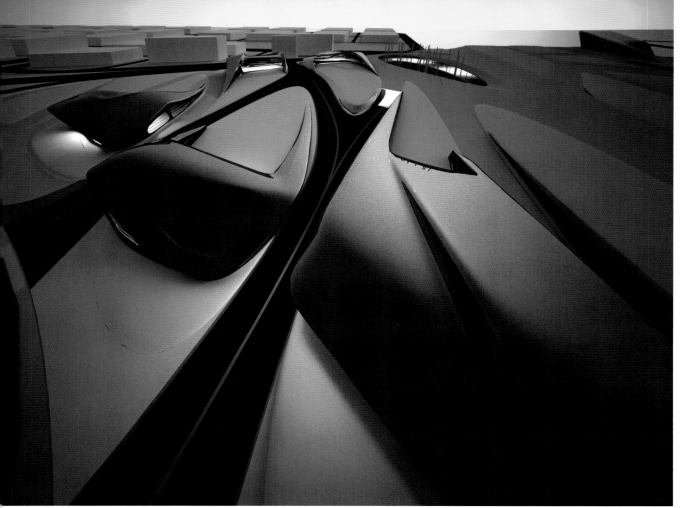

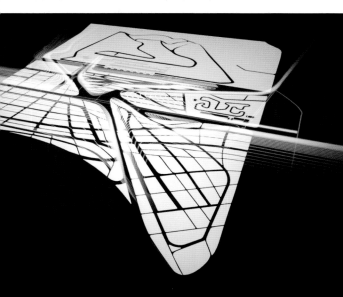

← ↑ The masterplan for the new Centre for Excellence and Car Experience at the Bahrain International Circuit combines a variety of programmes, from research and education to retail, hotel and clubhouse. Against the striking desert environment, high-tech machines speed around an immaculate surface of black tarmac, dramatically carved out of the yellow rock. With these initial conditions in mind, our design springs from several key design moves. A dynamic arrangement of zoned parcels creates visual drama on the site and gives the opportunity for an interchange of experience and ideas; movement through the site is choreographed by a system of streets that range from pragmatic flows to capricious drives through a man-made landscape. Cars dance through this landscape, interacting with the buildings, while parking, retail and storage areas form a podium structure that can be built efficiently using a rationalized construction grid. Within this solid podium, oases of green and landscaped areas allow these spaces to breathe. On top are showrooms or public buildings of high-end, customized architecture: jewels with a streamlined aesthetic that contrasts with the solid mass of the podium.

BAHRAIN INTERNATIONAL CIRCUIT
Sakhir, Bahrain 2007
In collaboration with Patrik Schumacher

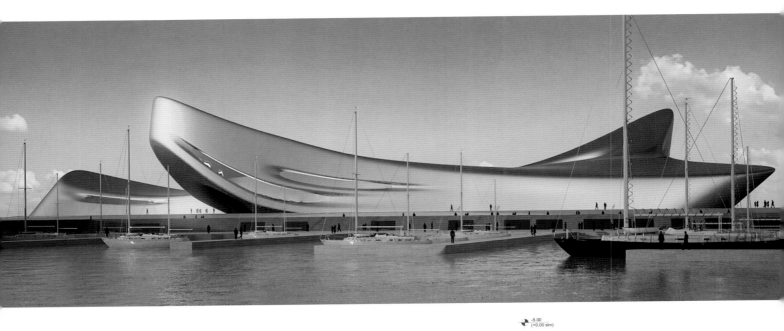

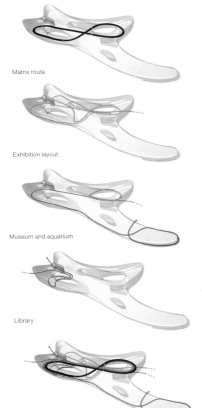

Matrix route

Exhibition layout

Museum and aquarium

Library

Public routes

REGIUM WATERFRONT
Reggio, Italy 2007–
In collaboration with Patrik Schumacher

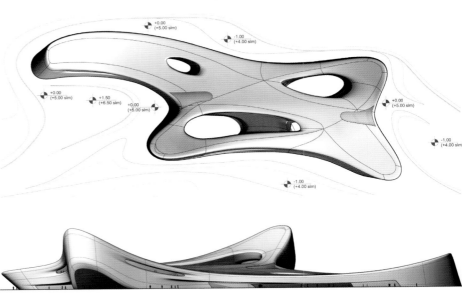

← ↑ The location for a museum of Mediterranean history and a multifunctional building is a narrow sea strait that separates Sicily from mainland Italy. Vaguely inspired by a starfish, the museum's shape is a continuation of our ongoing exploration of organic morphology. The radial symmetry of the shape clearly links the different sections and facilities, while movement and openness follow the fluid geometries of natural systems.

The museum will house exhibition spaces, restoration facilities, an archive, an aquarium and a library; the multifunctional building will comprise three structures that surround a partially covered 'piazza', which extends the seafront into the building.

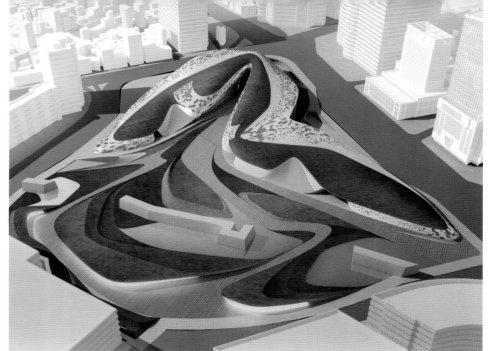

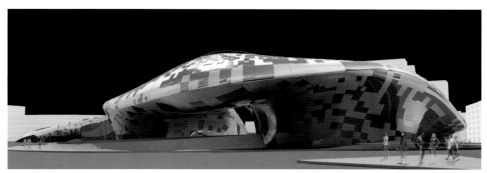

← This project is governed by the belief that architecture must enable people to 'think the unthinkable'. Taking the view that architecture should be enabling, liberating and life enhancing for the educational experience of designers and visitors, we propose to create a mobile learning resource and an 'anticipatory architecture', which is impermanent. Transparency, porosity and sustainability are key: double-skin façades curve up and over the structures, providing light and air movement to the interior; solar panels, rainwater recycling and heating/cooling systems are integrated into the design. The dynamic configuration of the complex continues into the park, a green oasis amid dense urban surroundings, which extends seamlessly onto the roof. Not unlike traditional Korean garden design, the proposed park expresses the natural flow and choreography of the unfolding scenery, with such typical elements as reflecting pools, lotus ponds, pebble beds and bamboo groves reinterpreted in a contemporary fashion. The park's ground plane is folded and mounded to create a sense of enclosure and spatial dynamics.

DONGDAEMUN WORLD DESIGN PARK AND PLAZA
Seoul, Korea 2007–
In collaboration with Patrik Schumacher

SURFERS PARADISE TRANSIT CENTRE SITE

Surfers Paradise, Queensland, Australia 2007

In collaboration with Patrik Schumacher

↑ → The entire site is considered as a single composition, rendered cohesive by the plinth's fluid extension into the public realm and by a podium roofscape with a generous outdoor terrace beneath the 101-storey tower. The tower itself is based on a simple circular plan, growing vertically from the base. The outward movement of the growing floor plates is accompanied by a carved concrete slot in the tower façade, which creates a source of natural light for circulation zones, and gently opens up towards the base, where it merges with the roof of the commercial part of the building. Glazing is interwoven with a modular shading device that alters its pattern according to the movements of the sun, adding a dynamic component to the striking altitude of the tower. A spectacular void below the tower is created by allowing the lowest 65 metres to remain open, raising the lobby and amenities for the residential units to level 16. At grade, the two footprints of the building are not joined, but leave a permeable, roofed gap that forms a pedestrian passage to a new public square.

← ↑ Rising to 240 metres, our proposed addition to the Warsaw skyline will be a progressive and prestigious building for the 21st century, with its distinctive profile set within an emerging cluster of tall structures. By avoiding sterile repetition, a clear identity is established through its dynamic, ever-changing appearance. The tower comprises a hotel, residential apartments, spa facilities, an underground retail area with an adjacent exterior mall, a restaurant and underground parking. The main access to the tower is at ground level, through a double-height lobby; all entrances are accessible via a bridge that crosses the mall area and connects the tower with the public realm.

LILIUM TOWER
Warsaw, Poland *2007–12*
In collaboration with Patrik Schumacher

195

BAHRAIN MUSEUM OF CONTEMPORARY ART
Al Muharraq, Bahrain 2007–12
In collaboration with Patrik Schumacher

↑ → On a narrow strip of land in the Gulf of Bahrain, our design begins as a gentle curve that rises from the ground to form a volume that bends slightly and reaches over the water towards Manama. Public fields flow around the sculptural mass of the museum, underlining its presence with contours that echo its volume. The fluidity of the elongated form encourages movement through and around the building, which lifts up towards the main entrance, forming a canopy and shaded public zone. The building's shape and organization follows a continuous path through daylit galleries and zones of diverse spatial qualities.

← ↑ At this family house overlooking the Pacific Ocean, a synthetic new topography is imposed over the site to shelter the new structure, while a perimeter fence contains the dynamic roof span where private and family spaces are clustered to emphasize the ocean view. The structural geometry responds to this internal dynamic by a polar distortion in plan and section, enabling the incorporation of all structural elements into one seamless skin with unimpeded views and clear access to the forecourt and the interior landscape. This single volume contracts with the neighbouring structures, critical of typological notions common in American suburbs.

LA JOLLA RESIDENCE
La Jolla, California, USA 2003–
In collaboration with Patrik Schumacher

197

EUSKOTREN CENTRAL HEADQUARTERS AND URBAN PLANNING

Durango, Spain 2004–
In collaboration with Patrik Schumacher

↑ ↗ → Key to the planning of this site are the degrees by which both public and private spaces are revealed, understood and encountered. Based on existing and proposed pedestrian flow diagrams, the site has been reorganized according to the civic importance and imagined popularity of potential circulation routes. By prioritizing some of these flows, new cross-town connections are made and structure and definition given to public spaces. At key circulation and service core positions, vertical access routes are generated. Topographic differentiations and ground-level changes are employed to create self-separation and to allow programmatic connections to the car park, buildings and adjacent streets.

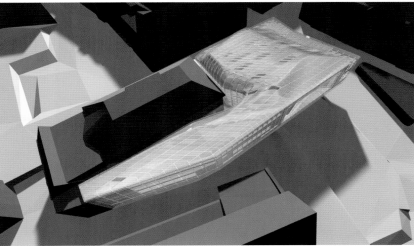

← ↑ The main design feature at this new concert hall in Basel is the idea of a homogeneous, plastic volume, expressed by the dramatic cantilever of the sculptural new building as it floats over the artificial topography of the square. Through the stylistic device of an inversion in the main façade, a strong connection between the interior and outside spaces is achieved. Underneath the new concert hall, a modulated entrance hall opens as a direct continuation of the square and connects the different levels by manipulating and terracing the ground. Two large cores grow out of this flowing surface and raise the floating volume.

NEUES STADT-CASINO
Basel, Switzerland 2004
In collaboration with Patrik Schumacher

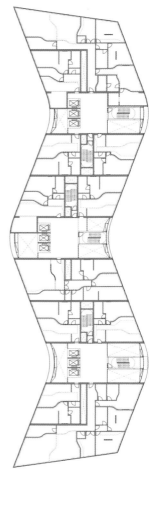

ZHIVOPISNAYA TOWER
Moscow, Russia 2004–
In collaboration with Patrik Schumacher

↑ → The proposed design is a development of the Modernist theme of the 'tower in the park', dissolving the podium into the tower's body and creating one single entity. The tower's mass is carved by sinuous lines in a choreographed movement, creating four blocks that are joined by a system of three cores. The building is generated through an elastic extrusion, incorporating diversity in its primary volume and enabling the creation of different apartment typologies within one overall modular frame.

← Our concept takes the form of an architectural intervention, part of a much larger urban planning gesture that aspires to organize and synthesize the whole of the Venetian wall, the moat and the fringes of the two parts of the city (inner and outer) into a unified whole. The moat becomes a 'green belt', surrounding and unifying the wall, which can be used for art exhibitions, sculpture installations and sports activities.

ELEFTHERIA SQUARE REDESIGN
Nicosia, Cyprus *2005–*
In collaboration with Patrik Schumacher

← The elegant design of the new Marina Villas allows the manipulation of ground and the articulation of structure as a new form of landscape, allowing some interior spaces to become external, and vice versa. Each villa consists of a main house and a guesthouse, which are connected by a landscape that works simultaneously as both cantilevered deck and terrace, with the latter merging into the front garden while offering spectacular views across the site to the ocean.

WEST BEACH VILLA DELLIS CAY
Turks and Caicos Islands *2005–*
In collaboration with Patrik Schumacher

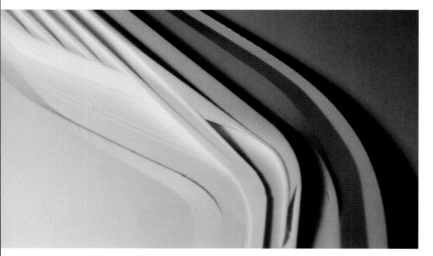

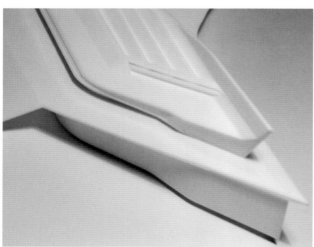

E.ON ENERGY RESEARCH DEPARTMENT
Aachen, Germany 2006–10

Our concept for a new building at RWTH University translates the direction and contours of the site as a primary form-generator, and connects the two arms of the campus into a larger spacial gesture. Structural and aerodynamic fins along the length of the roofscape allow for the modulation both of daylight and air flow, maximizing natural light and ventilation to all parts of the interior. A long, integrated landscaped path guides people to the main entrance. From here, a central corridor continues inside and divides the programme into two clear bands: an internal practical pocket with laboratories, and an enclosing academic band on two levels that includes a library and meeting rooms. At the northernmost corner of the building, the roof envelope rises, marking a turning point of the internal passage. Staircases at each end of the two-storey open gallery, together with a ramp, form a circulation loop, generating a constant fluency of movement between the practical and academic volumes.

Our plan for this former port and industrial area allows the dramatic topography and the broad curve of the River Nervion to subtly influence Bilbao's well-defined urban grid. The resulting building alignment generates a finely textured ground sweeping the length of the site, contracting to conform to the small scale of the existing fabric and expanding in response to more open spaces. In this way, the plan accommodates both historic buildings and new investment, while linking both to a generous public waterfront.

A sequence of bridges and an extended tram system establish a spine of activity that links downstream communities to the city centre, while an elegant system of building blocks, each over 1,000 square metres, gives the plan an overall unity. The platform level of the blocks both establishes the critical level of defence against floods and creates space for underground parking. By linking this level to the development of building clusters, the waterside promenade can dip closer to the river, allowing residents a closer engagement with the water's edge.

The rich pattern of public and private spaces can be achieved through the subtle differentiation of levels, promoting an easy balance between privacy and community life. The overall structure permits a densely built environment to accompany the fabric's strong feel of porosity, with future residents and workers all enjoying a rich tapestry of outdoor places.

ZORROZAURRE MASTERPLAN

Bilbao, Spain *2003–*
In collaboration with Patrik Schumacher

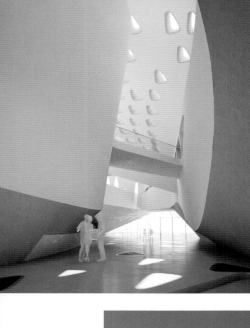

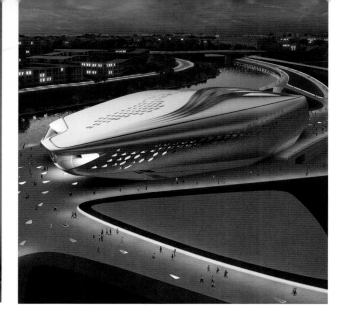

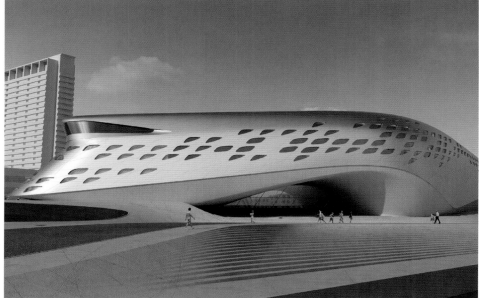

The sculptural volume of this new museum and cultural centre in Vilnius, the European 'capital of culture' for 2009, is designed along our characteristic conceptual terms of fluidity, velocity and lightness. The building appears like a mystical floating object that seems to defy gravity. Curvilinear lines echo the elongated contours of the building, offering an enigmatic presence that contrasts with the vertical skyline of the business district. It is a manifestation of the city's new cultural significance.

The museum's design points towards a future architectural language, and is part of an innovative research trajectory that embraces the latest digital design technology and fabrication methods. This enables a seamless transfer of our acceleration curves and sculpted surface modulations from drawing board to realization. Vilnius has a long history of art patronage, and as such will continue to develop as a cultural centre where the connection between culture and public life is critical. This museum will be a place of experimentation with the idea of galleries, spatial complexity and movement.

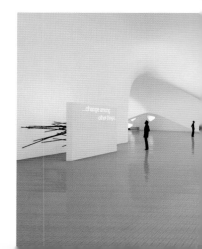

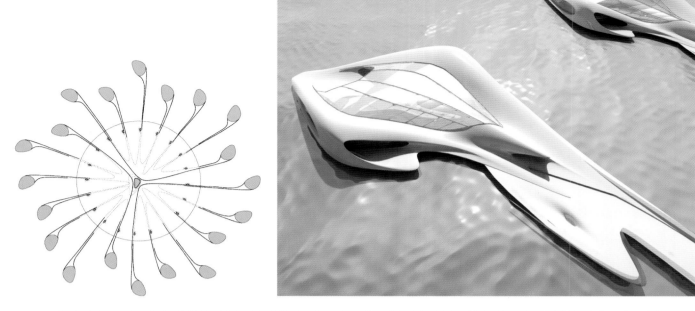

↑ ↗ This study for a high-end luxury resort is targeted at the pinnacle of the exclusive travel market. The resort's unique guest villas consist of both onshore and offshore components. The onshore units each contain private spa and sauna areas, and are connected via a pier to the 500-square-metre villas. The master bedroom and guest bedroom are housed in separate wings, centred around a multi-levelled living space, courtyard and pool area, all of which is contained beneath a retractable glass roof. A spectacular underwater living room is situated beneath the swimming pool. Minimum-footprint foundations on the sea bed increase to their maximum diameter at the surface to support each villa. The entire superstructure and all of each building's surfaces are finished in glass of different levels of opacity. This radical approach to surfaces, together with purist aesthetics and distinctive spatial features, create a unique experience for each guest.

← ↑ The site is located in a strategic position within the residential area of Singapore. The programme is organized into seven towers, which grow from sunken gardens within the landscape. The lower floors kink in to highlight the meeting point of buildings and ground, enabling a greater open area and the creation of private gardens. The towers are subdivided into petals, which are expressed three-dimensionally thanks to vertical cuts that give definition to the building's façades and allow for cross-ventilation. The buildings culminate at the top with a series of fingers stepped at different heights, blending the transition between the architectural fabric and the sky.

← ↖ The new building will allow for a less restrictive research environment and a better link between the college's academic and social functions. The intention is to create a suspended structure, where space is layered through contrasting use of built elements and materials, that allows for the more public aspects to infiltrate the building and spill into the college's curtiledge.

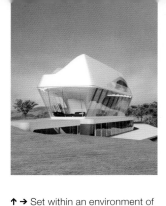

↑ → Set within an environment of lush green vegetation, this villa's conic systems afford flexible, open floor plans and panoramic visual connections with the landscape. Of the two main cones on the ground floor, one supports vertical circulation while the other is used for meditation and relaxation. On the top floor, three cuts form the outside terraces and balconies. Spanning largely without columns, the villa extends the ground floor into the natural surroundings.

→ The ancient city of Petra – and the principle of fluid erosion – is the inspiration behind this new performing arts centre. While the 'erosion' creates the public foyer spaces, the remaining mass represents the performance areas, which are then encapsulated by the support functions to create the exterior cubic volume. This volume is given tension by letting it gently swell, like the entasis of a column, in response to the public void in the centre of the building.

← ↑ The programme is divided into two main components: the first is strategically placed to merge with the sloped landscape, while a separate volume floats 22 metres above the ground. With its fluid geometries, the building emerges vertically from the landscape, yet remains partially embedded in the hillside. The horizontal form assimilates the existing land configuration, and occupies it by introducing artificial terraces. The external topography is pulled inside the building, articulated and released back into the natural surroundings. This two-way process dissolves the differentiation between interior and exterior, and creates the initial notion of flow which is then translated into the vertical and towards the second form.

CAPITAL HILL RESIDENCE
Moscow, Russia 2005–
In collaboration with Patrik Schumacher

→ The intervention designed for the exhibition hall is a carved-out solid, which allows visitors to walk through a series of carved voids. The spatial interrelation of the ellipsoids was developed according to the size and amount of the selected works. Along the visitors' route, the ellipsoids become ever more dynamic and turn into solids as they enter the atrium hall, where they become dramatic shell-like horizontal and vertical structures that rise up to the glass.

→ The aim of this installation was to explore the potential of concrete as a medium for repetitive and fluid form by combining traditional pre-cast techniques with CNC machine moulding. The individual elements of the piece create a fluidity that is at odds with the usual perception of concrete as an inert material. Areas of darkness and light visible in a nebula are evident here as hexagonal and triangular voids, produced by the positioning of each element of the installation.

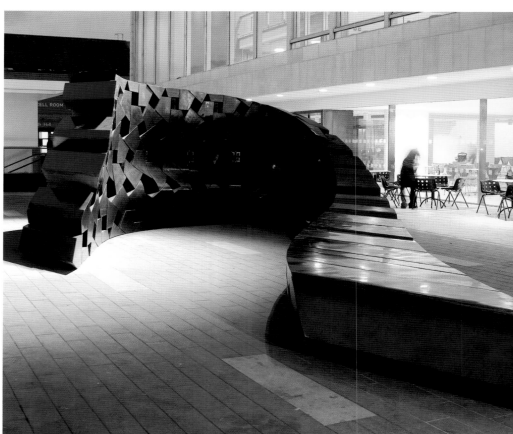

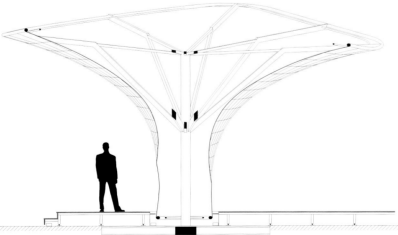

← ↑ This installation for the gallery's annual Summer Party is designed as an open-air space with three identical fabric 'parasols' arranged around a central point. Each parasol develops sculpturally from a small, articulated base to a large, cantilevered diamond shape. Taking inspiration from such complex natural geometries as flower petals, the parasols overlap, continually interweaving without touching. The pavilion, raised on a low platform in an open field, is free-standing and accessible from all sides. During the day, it provides shade, while at night the structure undergoes an energetic transformation into a source of illumination.

LILAS
*Serpentine Gallery, **London, England** 2007*
In collaboration with Patrik Schumacher

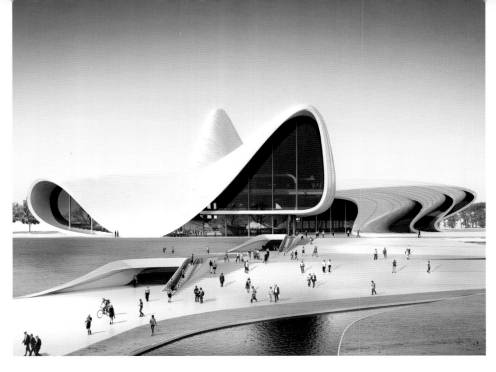

↑ ↗ This ambitious project will play an integral role in the intellectual life of the city. The proposal envisions a fluid form which emerges by the folding of the landscape's natural topography and by the wrapping of the centre's individual functions. All of these functions, together with the entrances, are represented by folds in a single, continuous surface. This fluid form allows the various spaces to be connected, while at the same time providing each element with its own identity and privacy. As it folds inside, the skin erodes away to become an element of the interior landscape.

↑ → The form of the museum harmonizes with the surrounding landscape, while the structural system of the conic walls give a distinct character to the interior, with the interstitial spaces of each wall creating a fluid circulation system between the two. The perforated patterns on the building's skin produce an ever-changing effect of natural light, allowing visitors inside to be able to sense the change of time, and extending the perception of interior to exterior and the natural world.

← ↑ The site is organized through a series of flow lines that define interweaving strips of intervention, favouring the longitudinal subdivision of the plot. This tapestry-like configuration is instrumental to phasing and expansion strategies, clearly outlining future capacity and growth vectors. A fluid grid is generated between the flow lines and the transport system, defining alignments and view lines that interplay between the terminal building and the airport city development, structuring the plot's occupation for the two stages of the terminal. The urban fabric is therefore organized in clusters, defining a close relationship between the blocks and generating nodes of activity through a common platform of services and facilities that bridge in between the buildings. Development by clusters is a flexible approach, creating a medium-density scheme with great connectivity features. The phasing of such a clustering system ensures development of critical mass and maximization of the shared facilities, such as plant and underground parking.

NEW PASSENGER TERMINAL AND MASTERPLAN

Zagreb, Croatia 2008

In collaboration with Patrik Schumacher

OBJECTS, FURNITURE AND INTERIORS

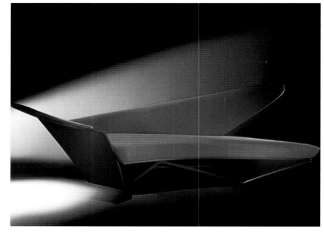

Red Sofa, 1988

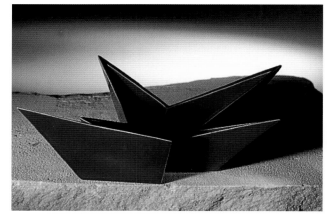

Waecthenberg Ceramics

Wave Sofa, 1988

Warped Plane Lamp, 1987

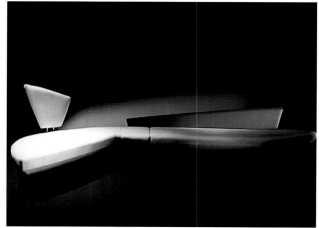

Whoosh Sofa, 1988

EARLY FURNITURE AND OBJECTS
Various makers 1987–90

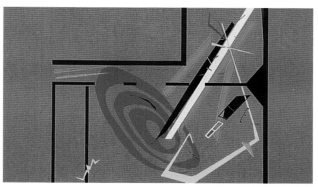

Vorwerk Wall-To-Wall Carpeting, 1990

Hommage à Verner Panton, 1990

TEA AND COFFEE SET
Sawaya & Moroni 1995–96

↑ → This table sculpture designed for Sawaya & Moroni splits into four distinct elements: teapot, coffee pot, milk jug and sugar bowl. Like a three-dimensional jigsaw puzzle, the pieces fit together to form a whole. When the set is not in use, the non-orthogonal volumes combine into a compact structure that can be carried as a single object. And when the set is in use, the object 'explodes' into shard-like volumes that reveal their function. As such, the service is a study of volumetric interaction that explores new possibilities of geometric interplay and dynamic sculpture on the scale of the domestic object, but which also holds lessons for larger-scale constructions.

← ↙ Like liquid metal, this tea and coffee set attempts to redefine the ritual use of everyday objects. By morphing objects that are normally distinct into a reconfigurable whole, the service can 'rest' as a sculptural object or 'function' as dynamic elements. The components sit within a tray that guides the user through the multiple configurations, the form changing according to whether or not the set is in use. Formally speaking, the sculpture exploits the idea of contrasting and combining extremely vertical with extremely horizontal objects: the teapot is a wide, flat organic shape, while the coffee pot rises from this landscape like a tower. In the 'functional' mode, objects can be flipped and turned, facilitated by the tray's template. Each shape has a cut or section that enables the piece to slide onto a different axis, exposing openings for pouring, and producing a completely different composition. 'Tea time' assumes a new significance: it becomes a sculptural riddle. The user manipulates the sliding, flipping and revolving parts, and finds the answers in the tea tray.

TEA AND COFFEE PIAZZA
Alessi 2003
In collaboration with Patrik Schumacher

↑ → The formal concept of this compact ensemble of lounge furniture is derived from dynamic landscape formations, with the different pieces acting as fragments of an overall mass. The eleven elements are shaped through typological, functional and ergonomic considerations, though predetermined use-patterns are rejected in favour of a degree of strangeness and indeterminacy. Melded together into a jigsaw puzzle, the pieces can be opened up and reconfigured. The lounging 'box', for example, chops off a piece from a flow of interwoven soft and hard space: the soft space emerges from the floor and is reshaped into comfortable seating elements; the hard space has vertical flat surfaces on top, giving rise to tables, desk and bar elements, and shelving.

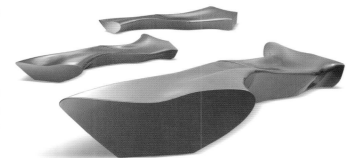

↑ A liquid form for a domestic setting, the Iceberg sofa/lounger allows sitters to assume a variety of orientations, positions and postures. Two icicle prongs appear to dart out in opposing directions, but they are in fact morphed together into a harmonious whole, a melting of formal inclination into a frozen state. The entity can be divided into two parts, one of which assumes a more vertical, throne-like orientation, the other suggesting a more horizontal, lounging posture. Constructed of steel and wood, with a shiny pearl-white car-paint finish, the structure is moulded to provide the most ergonomic contours.

ICEBERG
Sawaya & Moroni
In collaboration with Patrik Schumacher

223

ICE STORM
Österreichisches Museum für Angewandte Kunst *2003*
In collaboration with Patrik Schumacher

A built manifesto that suggested new kinds of living and lounging environments, this piece collected and fused previously designed furniture elements and installations: Z-Scape [p. 222], Iceberg [p. 223], Z-Play and Domestic Wave, including Ice-Flow. These diverse elements were drawn into a dynamic vortex, and integrated using two new hard sofas designed for the installation. The semi-abstract, moulded surface can be read as an apartment that has been carved from a single, continuous mass, with a complex interiorscape of folds, niches, recesses and protrusions. The design language emphasizes complex curvilinearity, seamlessness and smooth transition through the technique of 'morphing', through which the more conventional furniture pieces become integrated organs of a larger organism. Elements that are not contiguous with the overall figure (the Z-Play pieces) appear as loose fragments floating at the scene's periphery. Visitors are asked to inhabit the structure, and to explore an open aesthetic that invites us to rethink our accepted ideas of domestic lifestyle and behaviour.

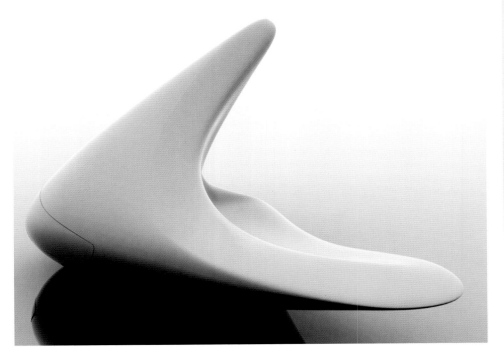

BELU BENCH
Kenny Schachter *2005*
In collaboration with Patrik Schumacher

→ ↘ Conceived as an autonomous single-celled body that allows for multifunctional use, this piece can be used as a table, counter, chair or container, or simply as a surface to lean on. With the dynamic complex geometry of a fluid volume, Belu is able to generate varying adjacency conditions in its direct relationship with the human body. It is not just an object for display, but a dynamic gesture that spatially defines its surroundings while serving a variety of functions. In a revisitation of the original concept, these unique geometries have been maintained yet scaled down in all three dimensions. This series affords further possibilities of direct intervention within the domestic environment.

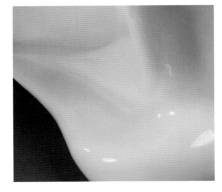 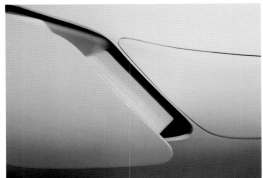

ZAHA HADID BOWLS 60, 70 AND METACRYLIC
Sawaya & Moroni *2007*
In collaboration with Patrik Schumacher

↘ A fluid form of curvilinear geometry, this silver bowl responds to the diffusion of energies that are generated at its perimeter, inviting an exploration of natural forces and affording a unique contextual relationship within any environment. While at first appearing unscripted and spontaneous, the total fluidity of the bowl's volume follows the overriding formal logic of our research into systems of continuous transformations and smooth transitions.

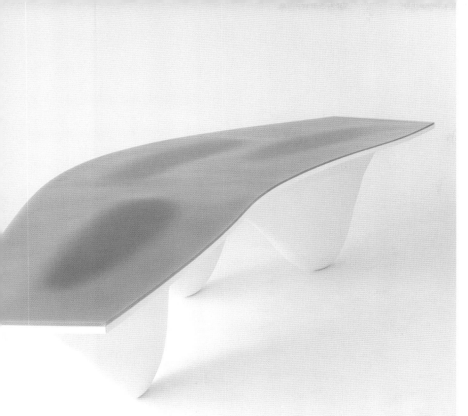

← ↑ The enigmatic, liquid form of the Aqua Table awakens one's curiosity. Blurring the relationship between horizontal top and vertical legs, the table implies motion by adopting the dynamic gestures of liquid to form a continuous surface. Through surface mutations at three points, the table's legs emerge to form an unbroken, tactile non-slip surface of translucent silicon gel. Gradual alterations in the tabletop's colour reflect these mutations, creating a surreal effect and accentuating the table's monolithic form. The lower structural body is made from polyester, which allows its geometry and enables weight reduction.

← ↑ An experiment in coupling advanced three-dimensional modelling techniques with the technology of rotational moulding, Flow defines a new typology in product design and sculpture, a sinuous object through which Cartesian geometries are blended in a continuous surface.

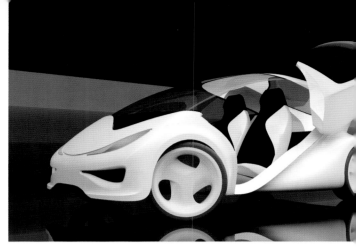
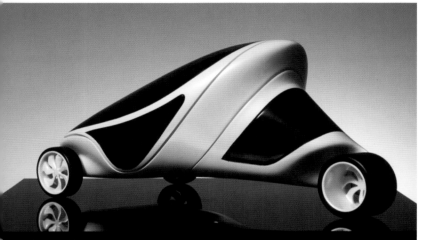
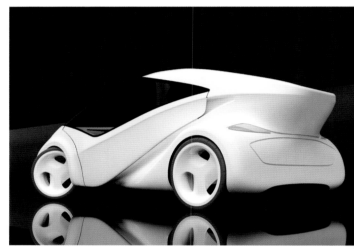

Z-CAR I AND II
Kenny Schachter *2005–08*
In collaboration with Patrik Schumacher

↑ → The Z-Car is a compact four-wheeled, four-seater city car that is based on its three-wheeled predecessor. It is an emission-free vehicle that is powered by rechargeable lithium-ion batteries. To save space and increase performance, the car is fitted with four electric in-wheel motors, which also make it very quiet. The large sliding passenger doors allow easy access, and the compact design takes advantage of a high degree of weight and space distribution for all the mechanical and electrical components.

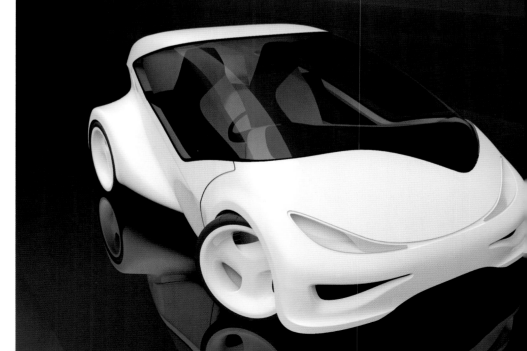

↑ From our observations of natural phenomena, such as the melting of ice or the flow of glaciers, we developed an island system that elaborates on this design language to create units that are continuous and blend in seamlessly with a kitchen's ergonomic needs. The composition contains a main island, a cantilevering shape that graduates from a horizontal cooking and eating surface into a vertical digital surface, and a secondary island containing sink, dishwasher and shelving unit, whose background is made up of wavy elements that can be rotated and assembled in various ways to create complex patterns. The cladding, fashioned from Corian Glacier White, was chosen for its thermoformable properties of translucency and endurance. The main island features electronics true to the 21st century: some 2,000 LED lights can be programmed to show a variety of information, while aromatic dispensers respond to the user's wishes and an invisible heating membrane keeps food warm.

Z-ISLAND
DuPont Corian 2005–06
In collaboration with Patrik Schumacher

↑ → This furniture collection for Established & Sons continues our exploration into a designed world of seamless fluidity, here at a domestic scale. Driven by the recent advancements in three-dimensional design software and in manufacturing capabilities, the collection's complex curvilinear geometries reflect detailed ergonomic research that allowed us to reconsider the balance between furniture and space. The pieces function and appear individually as stand-alone objects and collectively as a sensual universe in which soft meets sharp, convex encounters concave, as fragments that have been captured in a magnetic field. The rhythm of folds, niches, recesses and protrusions follows a coherent formal logic, previously seen in such pieces as Z-Scape [p. 222], Ice Storm [p. 224] and Aqua Table [p. 227], along with the interiors for the Hotel Puerta America [p. 141].

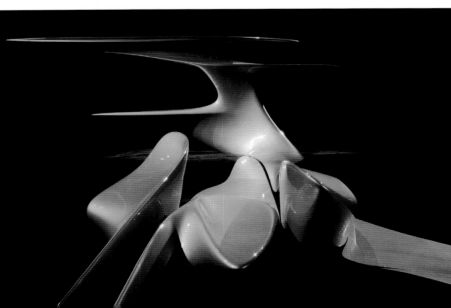

← ↑ This project for the Venice Biennale is an organic ensemble of furniture elements that range from shelving units, tables and benches to an artificial tree. Every part of the installation challenges Cartesian geometries by blending vertical and horizontal into sinuous resin surfaces that are finished with a bespoke golden orange colour. Following a common series of topological rules and differentiated by unique design features, the elements nest into each other while retaining their sculptural independence. Each piece suggests a multiplicity of possible uses, introducing a creative combination of surfaces, display areas and seating elements.

DUNE FORMATIONS
David Gill Galleries 2007

In collaboration with Patrik Schumacher

→ The essence of the table and the objects on its surface have been reduced to the purest of forms, an absolute expression of function that liberates our expectations and allows us to reconsider this relationship. Objects emerge from the Crater's surface that appear definite, yet when examined from an alternative perspective, these bowls or candle-holders have no independent solidity; they are simply integral elements of the table's continuous surface and are applied to three singularities beneath this same surface to form the table's signature. Three craters are moulded by seemingly invisible forces: two extend reassuringly to the floor; the third is suspended in space, and is clearly a bowl. To achieve the most dynamic and enigmatic surface, we have exploited the unique properties of aluminium to create the Crater's fluid forms.

↓ The Moon System is a unique new seating concept that combines the unrivalled manufacturing experience of a leading Italian furniture producer with our years of research into complex curvilinear geometries. Ergonomics and beauty are blended in a continuous shape. The collection redefines seating systems by making each element a module in its own right; the system reconfigures itself by rotating, interlocking and hiding its individual elements to allow an integration of formal disparate pieces within an overall ensemble, between solid and void, positive and negative, object and space. The conventional sofa form has been liquefied to accommodate a variety of users in a flexible and comfortable design.

← ↓ Drawing on our desire to create buildings that emerge from the city as sculpture yet knit together context, the Mesa Table evolved from an architectural experiment which was similarly to do with creating connections. Stripping the formal idea of a table to its constituent parts of ground, structure and surface, our design creates a world between two horizontal planes in which the voids express the form as much as the solids, appearing not merely as holes but defining the surface (not unlike water lilies, whose flat pads are supported by an unseen, complex and organic structure beneath). This unusual attenuation of surface from structure gives form to four organically shaped sections that define divisions on the surface, described as 'place mats'. As one end is attracted by an invisible gravitational force, it skews the symmetry, an attenuated prow dragging the other forms along with it while the structure below stretches to accommodate the distortions. The Mesa Table is thus a microcosm of some of the spatial ideas in our buildings. Form does not just follow function, it is drawn along by the plan's narrative and spatial flow, an evocation of a world shaped by unseen forces and dark matter.

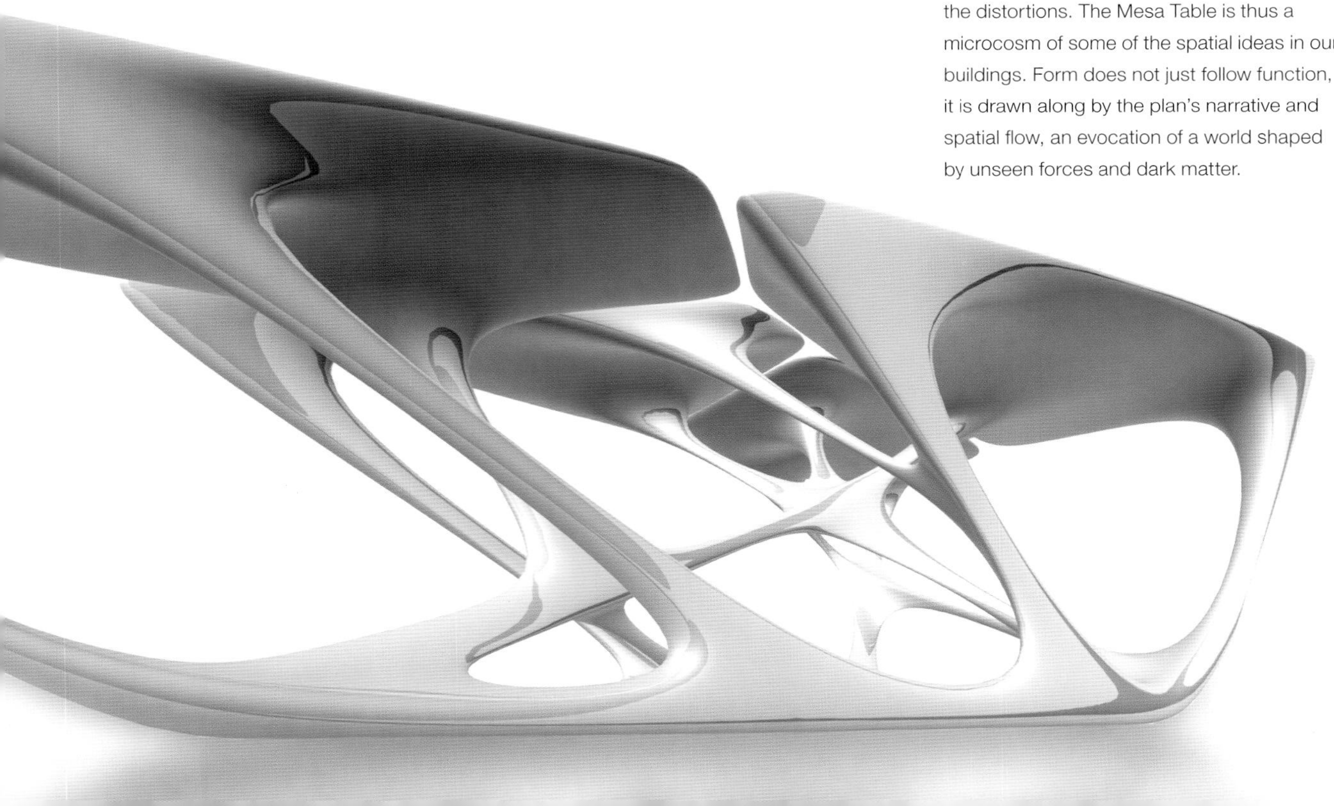

MESA TABLE
Vitra 2007
In collaboration with Patrik Schumacher

ZAHA HADID CHANDELIER
Swarovski Crystal Palace 2008
In collaboration with Patrik Schumacher

→ This design for a chandelier pushes the boundaries and preconceived notions of what a chandelier should be. The design draws inspiration from self-organizing systems and nanotechnology, redefining the chandelier from an object that is merely hung from the ceiling to one that engages the space more forcefully. Eighty-six cables, stretching from floor to ceiling at a 45° angle with over eight tons of tensile force, create a fluted cone that carries 2,700 internally lit crystals. Wrapping in a fluid vortex about the cone, the crystals inscribe an ethereality in a light-blue hue. More than 15 metres long and intended for a grand interior, the chandelier nonetheless maintains a high level of refinement.

SWARM CHANDELIER
Established & Sons 2006
In collaboration with Patrik Schumacher

→ Swarm, seen here at a 2007 exhibition at London's Design Museum, is a composition of black crystal volumes in forms that are dynamic rather than static, and that slash through space, creating movement through actual and perceived time. Its intricately layered formation does not presuppose any proportional system, nor does it privilege symmetry. Instead, integration is achieved via various modes and spatial relationships created from the dynamic forces of this controlled explosion. The chandelier's petals are brought together to form a larger organic whole. They do not remain pure and indifferent to each other, but are mutually adapting to the forces of the generating explosion.

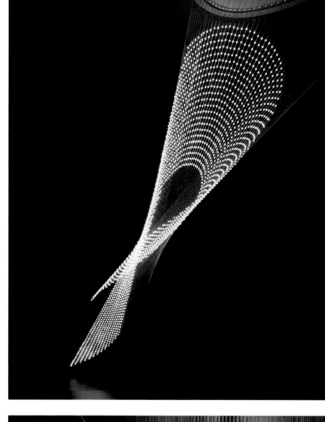

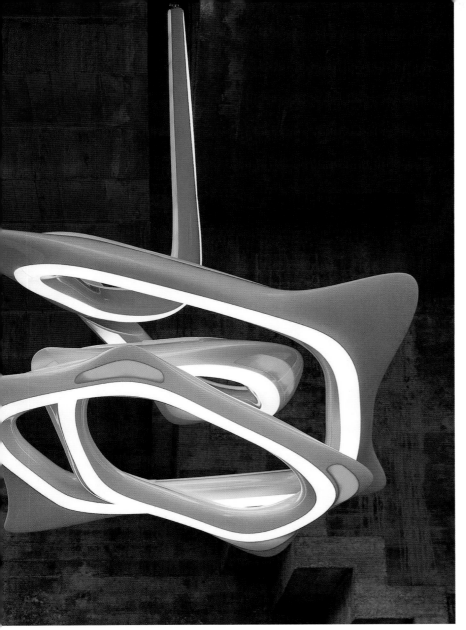

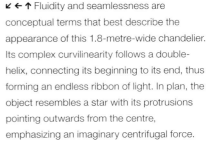

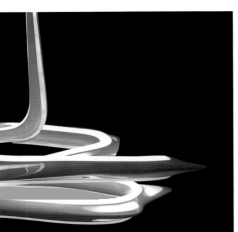

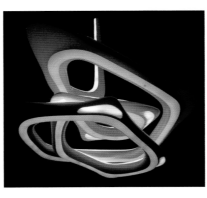

↙ ← ↑ Fluidity and seamlessness are conceptual terms that best describe the appearance of this 1.8-metre-wide chandelier. Its complex curvilinearity follows a double-helix, connecting its beginning to its end, thus forming an endless ribbon of light. In plan, the object resembles a star with its protrusions pointing outwards from the centre, emphasizing an imaginary centrifugal force.

Two transparent acrylic light spirals are inscribed in the otherwise opaque surface. A recessed LED light strip provides animated and programmable light sensations. Direct as well as indirect light can be emitted to the environment, and, consequently, different lighting atmospheres may be created by the user in order to match the specific space in which the chandelier is installed. This new interior design language is fuelled by advanced digital manufacturing methods; the user is invited to creatively explore the chandelier's interactive qualities and respond to its unfamiliar aesthetics.

VORTEXX CHANDELIER
Sawaya & Moroni 2005
In collaboration with Patrik Schumacher

↑ → The two vases are cut from a single block, and scored along two diagonal lines, thus creating a warped, inverted surface. They can be assembled together in alternative configurations, creating solid forms, or they can stand alone as distinct objects. The playful nature of the set means that the configurations can be altered to make a variety of different shapes, and the user can build a family of objects, like an endlessly mutating jigsaw puzzle.

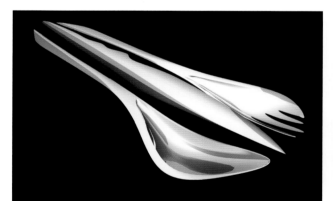

↑ → The tension between our formal architectural research and our exploration of industrial design resulted in this unique cutlery set. Each single piece has a formal expression of its own; combined, however, they complement one another as a unified single entity. The continuity of sculpted surfaces forms geometrically complex objects; accelerated curves normally used in car design give the pieces an extremely dynamic presence. The cutlery is forged from solid stainless steel that is polished to a mirror finish. The thickness of the material is extreme in some parts, allowing each item of the set to be ergonomically well balanced.

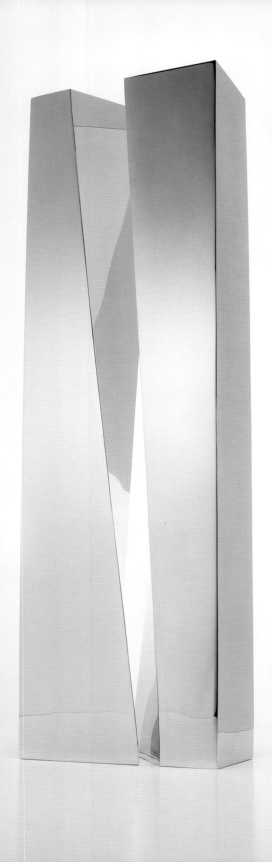

↑ These door handles were designed expressly for the communal spaces and the first-floor rooms of the Hotel Puerta America in Madrid [p. 141], and are characterized by a dynamic and strongly customized architecture. The coldness of the material fuses effortlessly with the sensual fluidity of the design, with the spatial formation defining both a beginning and an end. Pure lines merge organically into a harmonious link, creating a spatial journey of beauty and intricacy.

SERIES ZH DOOR HANDLES
Valli & Valli 2007

In collaboration with Woody K.T. Yao

↓ → The opportunities for reinterpretation afforded by Louis Vuitton's iconic Bucket bag led us to reflect on its condition as a generic container. The combination of a series of formal operations (extrusion, distortion, peeling and slicing), together with the materials selection, created a family of differentiated bags, hybrid crossings between traditional bag typologies – pochette, clutch, and the bucket. Blending these forms generated a series of possible relationships that allowed for the parts to be interchangeable within one coherent composition. The possibility of different combinations triggers a playful interaction with the user and a customization of the bucket's form and function to each occasion.

→ This collaboration into the field of fashion offered an exciting opportunity to express spatial ideas in a different scale and through different media. The design engages with the fluid, organic contours of the body, while the shoe's asymmetric quality conveys an inherent sense of movement, evoking continuous transformation. The concept addresses the perception of the shoe in motion, rather than the shoe as a static shop-window display. The shoes emerge from the ground and climb up the foot and leg with a soft, elegant movement; the plastic, organic quality of the choreography adheres to the skin. There is an implicit sense of lightness that blurs the boundary between body and object.

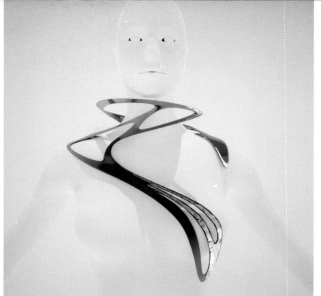

← ↑ Fluid movements leading to dynamic forms, the Celeste jewelry pieces reflect the seamless complexity of the vision we have explored and developed in architecture over the past three decades. The liquid, curvilinear shapes of the necklace and cuff follow the formal logic of continuous transformations observed in our morphological research.

The pieces are an obvious interpretation of the architectural language pursued by the practice: soft curves arise from the torso to create a dynamic form that wraps around the neck, coming to rest on the shoulder and eventually flowing down the arm to tentatively rest on the finger. The sculptural sensibility is strongly accentuated by the use of sterling silver, which brings to life the rhythm of folds and protrusions. Focusing on the dichotomy between the powerful solidity of silver and the organic fluidity of forms has resulted in exquisite, sensual and stunning pieces of jewelry.

CELESTE NECKLACE AND CUFF
Swarovski 2008
In collaboration with Patrik Schumacher

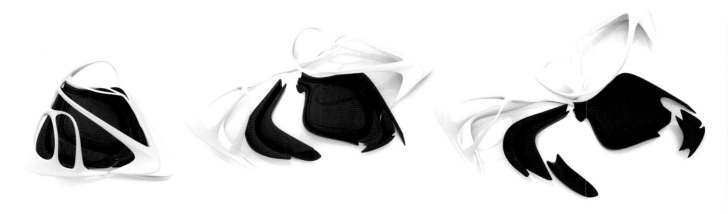

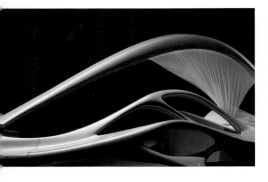

↑ → The room is conceived as a fragmented enclosure that can be compressed and expanded into areas for resting and sitting, or for storage. A multitude of folds structure these programmes both formally and functionally. The space of the room fluctuates between two extreme states: one that is condensed and exclusive of its surroundings, and the other being unfolded, dispersed and interlocked into its environment. Furniture and architecture become integrated and mobile as the various parts are released to reveal a desk with encased chair, bed, shelving, wardrobe rail and end table. Increased variety and possibilities for habitation are revealed as the Lotus seductively sheds and unveils its embedded counterparts.

LOTUS
Venice Biennale *2008*
In collaboration with Patrik Schumacher

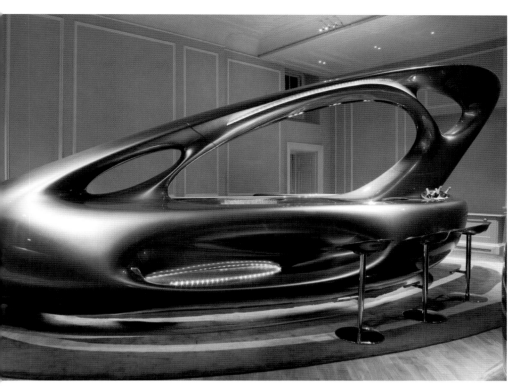

← Our first London interior for two decades explodes against the Georgian backdrop of the Home House members' club. The furniture installations, in saturated period colours, flow through the bar and reception rooms to create an interior landscape of sculptural islands. While further informed by the ergonomic considerations of a social environment, each piece is conceived through the morphological language that remains its primary formal determination. The installations demonstrate a new type of living environment that continues our investigations into dynamic space-making, creating a new open aesthetic that plays with the user's interaction.

HOME BAR
Home House 2008
In collaboration with Patrik Schumacher

← To mark the 500th anniversary of Palladio's birth, we decided to explore the logic and relational system of a single room in Venice's Villa Foscari (known as La Malcontenta), designed by Palladio in 1555 and conceived and built as a manifesto to demonstrate his architectural theories. The building's natural equilibrium has been shaken by the dynamic component we have introduced, abandoning the Euclidian mathematics that generated Palladio's proportional theories to explore the potential of advanced digital techniques. Aura is thus generated as a spatial morphology that reflects the structure of this void, the skeleton of this ethereal space.

AURA
Fondazione La Malcontenta 2008
In collaboration with Patrik Schumacher

CIRRUS

Lois & Richard Rosenthal Center for Contemporary Art *2008*

In collaboration with Patrik Schumacher

↓ → This installation for the Lois & Richard Rosenthal Center for Contemporary Art in Cincinnati [p. 104] offers a 'carpet' of interiority as its striated and weaved articulations unravel from wall to ground. An encompassed series of voids structure the sculpture, providing areas for sitting, leaning and reclining. These dynamic sculptural qualities follow an architectural language of fluidity and porosity, with each unique striation an essential element in the woven topology of the piece.

SEOUL DESK AND TABLE

NY Projects *2008*

In collaboration with Patrik Schumacher

→ This desk and table explore the moment of transition between horizontal and vertical by blending their structural elements into one streamlined formation. Taking advantage of advanced automotive design and manufacturing techniques, the desk and table are built through a complex process using carbon fibre, giving these pieces an extraordinary lightness and strength, as well as a characteristic textured finishing.

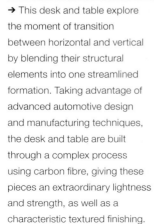

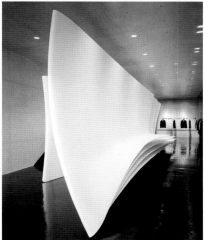

← ↑ Our concept for this flagship store in Tokyo is based on the brand's minimal design and uses the same design parameters of fixed points, folding, pleating and cut-outs. Furniture is staged in key points and creates the spatial concept of a narrow enclosure changing to an open condition. In two formal elements the design shifts between architecture and sculpture, where a compact mass of surface layers unravel and fold to form the shelving display and seating. The use of the latest 3D modelling and CNC programming solutions guarantees a precise and automatic translation of the design into the built structure.

NEIL BARRETT FLAGSHIP STORE
Neil Barrett 2008
In collaboration with Patrik Schumacher

Citadel Capital Office Buildings [15]
Cairo, Egypt, 2008–
Client Citadel Capital
Design Zaha Hadid with Patrik Schumacher
Project Architect Joris Pauwels
Design Team Paulo E. Flores, Sandra Riess, Sofia Danillidou, Alexander Janowsky, Feng Xu, Lulu Aldihani

Nassim Villas [16]
Singapore, 2007–12
Client Satinder Garcha
Design Zaha Hadid with Patrik Schumacher
Project Designers Ting Ting Zhang, William Tan
Structural Engineer Web Structures Pte Ltd
M&E Engineer Ace-Tech Design Pte Ltd
Local Architect Aedas (Singapore) Pte Ltd
Cost Consultant TJ Chiam Surveyors Pte Ltd

Malevich's Tektonik [18]
London, England, 1976–77
Fourth-year Student Project

Dutch Parliament Extension [19]
The Hague, Netherlands, 1978–79
Design Team Office for Metropolitan Architecture (OMA): Zaha Hadid, Rem Koolhaas, Elia Zenghelis, with Richard Perlmutter, Ron Steiner, E. Veneris

Museum of the Nineteenth Century [19]
London, England, 1977–78
Fifth-year Student Design Thesis

Irish Prime Minister's Residence [20]
Dublin, Ireland, 1979–80
Design Team Zaha Hadid with K. Ahari, Jonathan Dunn

Parc de la Villette [21]
Paris, France, 1982–83
Science Park Masterplan
Design Team Zaha Hadid with Jonathan Dunn, Marianne van der Waals, Michael Wolfson

59 Eaton Place [21]
London, England, 1981–82
Residential Conversion
Design Team Zaha Hadid with Jonathan Dunn, K. Knapkiewicz, Bijan Ganjei, Wendy Galway

The Peak [22]
Hong Kong, 1982–83
Leisure Club, International Competition: First Prize
Design Team Zaha Hadid with Michael Wolfson, Jonathan Dunn, Marianne van der Waals, N. Ayoubi
Presentation Michael Wolfson, Alistair Standing, Nan Lee, Wendy Galway
Structural Engineer Ove Arup & Partners: David Thomlinson

The World (89 Degrees) [24]
1983
Painting

Melbury Court [24]
London, England, 1985
Residential Conversion
Design Team Zaha Hadid with Brian Ma Siy, Michael Wolfson

Grand Buildings, Trafalgar Square [25]
London, England, 1985
Mixed-use Development
Design Team Zaha Hadid with (in the early stages) Brian Ma Siy
Competition Team Michael Wolfson, Brian Ma Siy, Marianne Palme, Kar Hwa Ho, Piers Smerin

Halkin Place [28]
London, England, 1985
Residential Conversion
Design Team Zaha Hadid with Brian Ma Siy, Piers Smerin

Kyoto Installations [28]
Kyoto, Japan, 1985
Installations

Tents and Curtains, Milan Triennale [29]
Milan, Italy, 1985
Design Team Zaha Hadid with Piers Smerin, Michael Wolfson

24 Cathcart Road [29]
London, England, 1985–86
Residential Interior and Furniture
Client Bitar
Design Team Zaha Hadid with Michael Wolfson, Brett Steele, Nan Lee, Brenda MacKneson

Hamburg Docklands [30]
Hamburg, Germany, 1986
Masterplanning Workshops

New York, Manhattan: A New Calligraphy of Plan [31]
1986
Painting

Kurfürstendamm 70 [32]
Berlin, Germany, 1986
Office Building
Client EUWO Holding AG
Design Team Zaha Hadid with Michael Wolfson, Brett Steele, Piers Smerin, Charles Crawford, Nicola Cousins, David Gomersall
Client Feasibility Berlin Senate
Co-architect Stefan Schroth
Structural Engineer Ove Arup & Partners: Peter Rice, John Thornton
Glazing Consultant RFR Engineers: Hugh Dutton
Quantity Surveyor Büro am Lützowplatz: Wilfraed Kralt
Total Area 820 m² (7 floors)

IBA-Block 2 [33]
Berlin, Germany, 1986–93
Client Degewo AG
Design Team Zaha Hadid with Michael Wolfson, David Gomersall, Piers Smerin, David Winslow, Päivi Jääskeläinen
Co-architect Stefan Schroth
Total Area 2,500 m² (long block: 3 floors; tower: 8 floors)

Azabu-Jyuban [34]
Tokyo, Japan, 1986
Commercial Development
Client K-One Corporation
Design Team Zaha Hadid with Michael Wolfson, Brenda MacKneson, Alistair Standing, Signy Svalastoga, Paul Brislin, Nicola Cousins, David Gomersall, Edgar González, Erik Hemingway, Simon Koumjian, Päivi Jääskeläinen
Models Daniel Chadwick, Tim Price
Project Architect (Japan) Satoshi Ohashi
Co-architect Hisashi Kobayashi & Associates
Structural Engineer Ove Arup & Partners: Peter Rice, Yasuo Tamura
Total Area 340 m² (6 floors)

Tomigaya [35]
Tokyo, Japan, 1986
Office Building
Client K-One Corporation
Design Team Zaha Hadid with Michael Wolfson, Brenda MacKneson, Alistair Standing, Signy Svalastoga, Paul Brislin, Nicola Cousins, David Gomersall, Edgar González, Erik Hemingway, Simon Koumjian, Päivi Jääskeläinen, Patrik Schumacher
Models Daniel Chadwick, Tim Price
Project Architect (Japan) Satoshi Ohashi
Co-architect Hisashi Kobayashi & Associates
Structural Engineer Ove Arup & Partners: Peter Rice, Yasuo Tamura
Total Area 238 m² (2 floors)

West Hollywood Civic Center [36]
Los Angeles, California, USA, 1987

Al Wahda Sports Centre [37]
Abu Dhabi, UAE, 1988
Client Sheikh Tahnoon bin Saeed Al Nahyan
Design Team Zaha Hadid with Michael Wolfson, Satoshi Ohashi
Structural Engineer Ove Arup & Partners: Peter Rice

Metropolis [38]
1988
Painting

Berlin 2000 [39]
1988
Painting

Victoria City Areal [40]
Berlin, Germany, 1988
Mixed-use Development
Client City of Berlin (Building Authority)
Design Team Zaha Hadid with Michael Wolfson, Nicholas Boyarsky, Patrik Schumacher, Edgar González, Paul Brislin, Nicola Cousins, Signy Svalastoga, C.J. Lim, Kim Lee Chai, Israel Numes, Mathew Wells, Simon Koumjian
Model Daniel Chadwick
Structural Engineer Ove Arup & Partners: Peter Rice, Mathew Wells
Total Area c. 75,000 m² (15 floors)

A New Barcelona [42]
Barcelona, Spain, 1989
Urban Masterplan
Design Team Zaha Hadid with Patrik Schumacher, Simon Koumjian, Edgar González

Tokyo Forum [43]
Tokyo, Japan, 1989
Cultural Centre
Client Tokyo Metropolitan Government
Design Team Zaha Hadid with Brian Ma Siy, Patrik Schumacher, Vincent Marol, Philippa Makin, Bryan Langlands, David Gomersall, Jonathan Nsubuga
Model Daniel Chadwick
Total Area 135,000 m² (8 floors)

Hafenstraße Development [44]
Hamburg, Germany, 1989
Mixed-use Development
Client Free and Hanseatic City of Hamburg (Building Authority)
Design Team Zaha Hadid with Patrik Schumacher, Signy Svalastoga, Edgar González, Bryan Langlands, Philippa Makin, Nicola Cousins, Mario Gooden, Ursula Gonsior, Claudia Busch, Vincent Marol
Model Daniel Chadwick
Co-architect Mirjane Markovic
Structural Engineer Ove Arup & Partners: Peter Rice
Total Area Corner building: 871 m² (8 floors); middle site building: c. 2,800 m² (10 floors)

Moonsoon [46]
Sapporo, Japan, 1989–90
Restaurant
Client JASMAC Corporation
Design Team Zaha Hadid with Bill Goodwin, Shin Egashira, Kar Hwa Ho, Edgar González, Bryan Langlands, Ed Gaskin, Yuko Moriyama, Urit Luden, Craig Kiner, Dianne Hunter-Gorman, Patrik Schumacher
Consultants Michael Wolfson, Satoshi Ohashi, David Gomersall
Model Daniel Chadwick
Producer Axe Co Ltd
Total Area 435 m² (2 floors)

Osaka Folly, Expo 90 [48]
Osaka, Japan, 1989–90
International Garden Festival
Client and Sponsor Fukuoka Jisho Co Ltd
Organizer Workshop for Architecture & Urbanism
Design Team Zaha Hadid with Edgar González, Urit Luden, Satoshi Ohashi, Kar Hwa Ho, Patrik Schumacher, Voon Yee-Wong, Simon Koumjian, Dianne Hunter-Gorman, Nicola Cousins, David Gomersall
Model Daniel Chadwick
General Producer Arata Isozaki
Contractor Zenitaka Corporation
Total Area 435 m²

Leicester Square [49]
London, England, 1990
Client *Blueprint Magazine*
Design Team Zaha Hadid with Graham Modlen, Vincent Marol, Simon Koumjian, Patrik Schumacher, Craig Kiner, Cristina Verissimo, David Gomersall, Philippa Makin, Dianne Hunter-Gorman, Maria Rossi, Mya Manakides

Vitra Fire Station [50]
Weil am Rhein, Germany, 1990–94
Client Vitra International AG: Rolf Fehlbaum
Design Zaha Hadid
Project Architect Patrik Schumacher
Consultant Architect Roland Mayer
Detail Design Patrik Schumacher, Signy Svalastoga
Design Team Simon Koumjian, Edgar González, Kar Wha Ho, Voon Yee-Wong, Craig Kiner, Cristina Verissimo, Maria Rossi, Daniel R. Oakley, Nicola Cousins, David Gomersall, Olaf Weishaupt
Models Daniel Chadwick, Tim Price
Project Manager, Construction Drawings and Building Supervision GPF & Assoziierte: Roland Mayer, Jürgen Roth, Shahrir Eetezadi, Eva Weber, Wolfgang Mehnert

Zollhof 3 Media Park [54]
Düsseldorf, Germany, 1989–93
Client Kunst- und Medienzentrum Rheinhafen GmbH
Design Zaha Hadid
Project Architects Brett Steele, Brian Ma Siy
Project Team Paul Brislin, Cathleen Chua, John Comparelli, Elden Croy, Craig Kiner, Graeme Little, Yousif Albustani, Daniel R. Oakley, Patrik Schumacher, Alistair Standing, Tuta Barbosa, David Gomersall, C.J. Lim
Models Ademir Volic, Daniel Chadwick
Feasibility and Competition Michael Wolfson, Anthony Owen, Signy Svalastoga, Edgar González, Craig Kiner, Patrik Schumacher, Ursula Gonsior, Bryan Langlands, Ed Gaskin, Yuko Moriyama, Graeme Little, Cristina Verissimo, Maria Rossi, Yousif Albustani
Consultant Architect Roland Mayer
Project Manager Vebau GmbH
Project Co-ordinator Weidleplan Consulting GmbH
Structural Engineers Boll und Partner; Ove Arup & Partners
Services Engineers Jaeger, Mornhinweg und Partner; Ove Arup & Partners; Ingenieurbüro Werner Schwarz GmbH
Façade Consultant Institut für Fassadentechnik
Fire Specialist Wilfred Teschke
Building Physicist Dr. Schäcke & Bayer GmbH
Traffic Consultant Waning Consult GmbH
Cost Consultant Tillyard GmbH

Music-Video Pavilion [56]
Groningen, Netherlands, 1990
Client City Planning Department Groningen
Design Team Zaha Hadid with Graham Modlen, Urit Luden, Edgar González, Vincent Marol, Maria Rossi, Dianne Hunter-Gorman, Cristina Verissimo, Yousif Albustani, Craig Moffatt, Craig Kiner
Model Daniel Chadwick
Co-architect Karelse Van der Meer
Total Area 24.5 m² (4 levels: ground floor, 2 balconies and video room)

Hotel and Residential Complex [58]
Abu Dhabi, UAE, 1990
Client Sheikh Tahnoon bin Saeed Al Nahyan
Design Team Zaha Hadid with Vincent Marol, Craig Kiner, Yousif Albustani, Satoshi Ohashi, Patrik Schumacher, Daniel R. Oakley, Philippa Makin, Dianne Hunter-Gorman
Model Daniel Chadwick
Structural Engineer Ove Arup & Partners
Total Area 47,000 m² (2 retail floors, 1 office floor, 28 hotel floors)

Interzum 91 [59]
Gluzendorf, Germany, 1990
Exhibition Stand Design

London 2066 [60]
1991
Painting
Client British *Vogue*
Design Team Zaha Hadid with Daniel R. Oakley, Voon Yee-Wong, Graham Modlen, Craig Kiner, Cristina Verissimo, Yousif Albustani, Patrik Schumacher, Mascha Veech-Kosmatschof, Graeme Little
Computer Modelling Daniel R. Oakley

The Hague Villas [62]
Hague Housing Festival, The Hague, Netherlands, 1991
Residential Development
Design Team Zaha Hadid with Craig Kiner, Patrik Schumacher, Yousif Albustani, James Braam, Daniel R. Oakley, John Stuart, Cristina Verissimo, David Gomersall
Model Craig Kiner
Structural Engineer Ove Arup & Partners

The Great Utopia [63]
Solomon R. Guggenheim Museum, New York, New York, USA, 1992
Exhibition Design
Design Team Zaha Hadid with Patrik Schumacher, Yousif Albustani, Daniel R. Oakley, David Gomersall, Simon Koumjian
Models Tim Price, Ademir Volic

Vision for Madrid [64]
Madrid, Spain, 1992
Urban Masterplan
Design Team Zaha Hadid with Patrik Schumacher, Daniel R. Oakley, Simon Koumjian, Yousif Albustani, Craig Kiner, Paco Mejias

Arthotel Billie Strauss [65]
Nabern, Germany, 1992
Design Team Zaha Hadid with Patrik Schumacher, Yousif Albustani, Daniel R. Oakley, David Gomersall

Concert Hall [65]
Copenhagen, Denmark, 1992–93
Design Zaha Hadid with Patrik Schumacher
Design Team Paul Brislin, Brian Ma Siy, John Comparelli, Nicola Cousins, Edgar González, Douglas Grieco, C.J. Lim, Mya Manakides, Guido Schwark
Structural Engineer Ove Arup & Partners
Acoustics Consultant Arup Acoustics: Malcolm Wright
Theatre Consultant Theatre Projects Consultants

Rheinauhafen Redevelopment [66]
Cologne, Germany, 1992
Urban Masterplan
Design Zaha Hadid
Design Team Patrik Schumacher, Daniel R. Oakley, Craig Kiner, Yousif Albustani, Cathleen Chua, David Gomersall, John Stuart, Simon Koumjian
Model Tim Price

Carnuntum [68]
Vienna, Austria, 1993
Archaeological Museum with Belvedere, Amphitheatre, Folly, Pavilion
Design Team Zaha Hadid with Patrik Schumacher, Douglas Grieco, Wendy Ing, Brian Ma Siy, Paola Sanguinetti, Edgar González, David Gomersall
Model Daniel Chadwick

Spittelau Viaducts [70]
Vienna, Austria, 1994–2005
Mixed-use Development
Client SEG Developers
Design Zaha Hadid with Edgar González, Douglas Grieco, Paul Brislin, Patrik Schumacher, Woody K.T. Yao
Project Architects Woody K.T. Yao, Markus Dochantschi
Detail Design Zaha Hadid with Woody K.T. Yao, Markus Dochantschi, Wassim Halabi, Garin O'Aivazian, James Geiger
Design Team Clarissa Mathews, Paola Sanguinetti, Peter Ho, Anne Save de Beaurecueil, David Gomersall
Structural Engineer Friedreich & Partner
Total Area 2,600 m²

Spittalmarkt [74]
Berlin, Germany, 1995
Corporate Headquarters for German Building Society
Design Zaha Hadid with Patrik Schumacher
Competition Team Patrik Schumacher, Woody K.T. Yao, Wassim Halabi, David Gomersall, Graham Modlen
Design Development Patrik Schumacher, James Geiger

Lycée Français Charles de Gaulle [75]
London, England, 1995
Schoolhouse Extension
Design Team Zaha Hadid with Douglas Grieco, Edgar González, Paul Brislin, Brian Ma Siy, Paola Sanguinetti, Woody K.T. Yao, David Gomersall

Pancras Lane [75]
London, England, 1996
Office Building over Public Space
Design Team Zaha Hadid with Brian Ma Siy, Paul Brislin, Edgar González, Patrik Schumacher, Douglas Grieco, Woody K.T. Yao, Paola Sanguinetti

Blueprint Pavilion, Interbuild 95 [76]
Birmingham, England, 1995
Exhibition Stand
Clients *Blueprint Magazine*; Montgomery Exhibitions Ltd
Design Zaha Hadid with Paul Brislin and Woody K.T. Yao
Design Team Tomás Amat Guarinos, Oliviero Godi, Maha Kutay, Clarissa Mathews, Graham Modlen, Anne Save de Beaurecueil, Leena Ibrahim
Computer Imagery Flexagon Studio: Thomas Quihano, Wassim Halabi
Structural Engineer Ove Arup & Partners: Rob Devey, Shiguru Hikone, Colin Jackson, Darren Sri-Tharan, Jane Wernick
Quantity Surveyor Tillyard: Brett Butler
Total Area 120 m²

42nd Street Hotel [77]
New York, New York, USA, 1995
Hotel and Commercial Complex
Clients Weiler Arnow Management Co; Milstein Properties
Design Team Zaha Hadid with Douglas Grieco, Peter Ho, Clarissa Mathews, Anne Save de Beaurecueil, Voon Yee-Wong, Woody K.T. Yao, Paul Brislin, Graham Modlen, Patrik Schumacher, David Gomersall, Bijan Ganjei
Model Richard Armiger
Images for Model Dick Stracker
Computer Imagery Rolando Kraeher
Structural Engineer Ove Arup & Partners
Total Area 180,000 m²

Prado Museum Extension [78]
Madrid, Spain, 1996
Design Team Zaha Hadid with Tomás Amat Guarinos, Patrik Schumacher, Joaquin López, Ivan Pajares Sanchez, Anne Save de Beaurecueil, Markus Dochantschi, David Gomersall, Wassim Halabi, Paul Karakusevic, Simon Koumjian, Maha Kutay, Graham Modlen, Woody K.T. Yao, Simon Yu
Design Team (Spain) Jesús Bermejo, Luis A. Gutiérrez, Juan Carlos Rico

Cardiff Bay Opera House [80]
Cardiff, Wales, 1994–96
Client Cardiff Bay Opera House Trust: The Rt Hon Lord Crickhowell, Chairman
Design Zaha Hadid
Project Architect Brian Ma Siy
Design Team Patrik Schumacher, Ljiljana Blagojevic, Graham Modlen, Paul Brislin, Edgar González, Paul Karakusevic, David Gomersall, Tomás Amat Guarinos, Wendy Ing, Paola Sanguinetti, Nunu Luan, Douglas Grieco, Woody K.T. Yao, Voon Yee-Wong, Anne Save de Beaurecueil, Simon Koumjian, Bijan Ganjei, Nicola Cousins
Models Ademir Volic, Michael Kennedy, James Wink
Percy Thomas Partnership Ian Pepperell, Richard Roberts, Russell Baker, Richard Puckrin
Project Manager Stanhope Properties: Peter Rogers
Structural Engineer Ove Arup & Partners: Jane Wernick, David Glover, John Lovell
Services Consultant Ove Arup & Partners: Simon Hancock
Acoustics Consultant Arup Acoustics: Richard Cowell, Nigel Cogger
Theatre Consultant Theatre Projects Consultants: David Staples, Alan Russell, Anne Minors
Quantity Surveyor Gardiner & Theobald; Tillyard: Brett Butler, Peter Coxall
Arts Consultant AEA Consulting: Adrian Ellis, Jan Billington
Brief Consultant Inter Consult Culture: Charlotte Nassim
Construction Manager Lehrer McGovern Bovis: Alan Lansdell
Total Area 25,000 m²

Boilerhouse Extension [84]
Victoria & Albert Museum, London, England, 1996
Client Victoria & Albert Museum
Design Team Zaha Hadid with Patrik Schumacher, Brian Ma Siy, Graham Modlen, Ljiljana Blagojevic, Paul Karakusevic, David Gomersall, Woody K.T. Yao, Markus Dochantschi, Wassim Halabi, Ivan Pajares Sanchez, Maha Kutay, Simon Yu, Tomás Amat Guarinos, James Geiger, Tilman Schall, Alan Houston
Structural Engineer Ove Arup & Partners: Jane Wernick
Building Services Ove Arup & Partners: Simon Hancock
Construction Manager Ove Arup & Partners (PMS): Peter Platt-Higgins
Cost Consultant Davis Langdon & Everest: Rob Smith
Total Area 10,000 m²

Wish Machine: World Invention [85]
Kunsthalle, Vienna, Austria, 1996
Exhibition Design
Client Kunsthalle Wien: Herbert Lachmeyer, Curator, Brigitte Felderer
Design Team Zaha Hadid with Patrik Schumacher, Simon Yu, Wassim Halabi, Markus Dochantschi, David Gomersall, Woody K.T. Yao, Paul Karakusevic
Total Area 900 m²

Master's Section, Venice Biennale [86]
Palazzo Grassi, Venice, Italy, 1996
Exhibition
Design Team Zaha Hadid with Patrik Schumacher, Markus Dochantschi, Woody K.T. Yao, Wassim Halabi, Garin O'Aivazian, David Gomersall, Simon Yu, Yousif Albustani, Giuseppe Anzalone Gherardi

Habitable Bridge [86]
London, England, 1996
Mixed-use Development
Client The Rt Hon John Gummer, Secretary of State for the Environment; Royal Academy
Sponsor Thames Water
Design Team Zaha Hadid with Patrik Schumacher, Ljiljana Blagojevic, Paul Karakusevic, Graham Modlen, Woody K.T. Yao, Markus Dochantschi, Tilman Schall, Colin Harris, Thilo Fuchs, Shumon Basar, Katrin Kalden, Anne-Marie Foster
Models Ian Houston, Michael Howe
Computer Design Wassim Halabi, Simon Yu, Garin O'Aivazian
Structural Engineer Ove Arup & Partners: Jane Wernick, Sophie Le Bourva
Services Consultant Ove Arup & Partners: Simon Hancock, Dorte Rich Jorgensen
Transportation Consultant Ove Arup & Partners: John Shaw
Construction Manager Ove Arup & Partners: Harry Saradjian
Cost Consultant Davis Langdon & Everest: Rob Smith, Sam Mackenzie
Total Area 40,000 m²

La Fenice [88]
1996
Painting
Design Team Zaha Hadid with Graham Modlen, Maha Kutay, Simon Yu
Computer Design Wassim Halabi

Philharmonic Hall [89]
Luxembourg, 1997
Client Ministry of Public Buildings
Design Zaha Hadid with Patrik Schumacher
Design Team Garin O'Aivazian, Markus Dochantschi, Woody K.T. Yao, Wassim Halabi, Jan Hübener, Anna Klingmann, Tilman Schall, Filipe Pereira, Shumon Basar, Mark Hemel, Yousif Albustani, Graham Modlen, Anuschka Kutz, David Gomersall
Total Area 7,100 m²

Landesgartenschau 1999 [90]
Weil am Rhein, Germany, 1996–99
Exhibition Space, Café, Centre of Enviromental Research
Client Landesgartenschau Weil am Rhein GmbH
Design Zaha Hadid with Patrik Schumacher and Mayer Bährle
Project Architect Markus Dochantschi
Project Team Oliver Domeisen, Wassim Halabi, Garin O'Aivazian, Barbara Pfenningstorff, James Lim
Models June Tamura, Jim Heverin, Jon Richards, Ademir Volic
Co-architect Mayer Bährle Freie Architekten BDA
Total Area 800 m²

Museum of Islamic Arts [94]
Doha, Qatar, 1997
Client State of Qatar
Design Zaha Hadid with Patrik Schumacher and Woody K.T. Yao
Design Team Shumon Basar, Graham Modlen, Markus Dochantschi, Anuschka Kutz, Garin O'Aivazian, Filipe Pereira, Ivan Pajares Sanchez, Wassim Halabi, Ali Mangera, Edgardo Torres, Julie Fisher, Andrew Schachman, Oliver Domeisen, Julie Richards, Irene Huttenrauch, Tia Lindgren
Total Area 28,000 m²

Hackney Empire [96]
London, England, 1997
Design Team Zaha Hadid with Markus Dochantschi, Graham Modlen, Anuschka Kutz, Oliver Domeisen, Irene Huttenrauch, Woody K.T. Yao, Patrik Schumacher, David Gomersall, Tia Lindgren

Campus Center, Illinois Institute of Technology [97]
Chicago, Illinois, USA, 1998
Design Zaha Hadid with Patrik Schumacher
Design Team Yousif Albustani, Anuschka Kutz, Oliver Domeisen, Shumon Basar, Inken Witt, Jee-Eun Lee, Wassim Halabi, Ivan Pajares Sanchez, David Gomersall, Stéphane Hof, Woody K.T. Yao, Markus Dochantschi, Marco Guarnieri, Ali Mangera, Jim Heverin, Jon Richards, Terence Koh, Simon Yu, James Lim, Tilman Schall
Structural and Civil Engineer Ove Arup & Partners: Jane Wernick
Building Services Ove Arup & Partners: Simon Hancock
Acoustics Consultant Arup Acoustics: Andrew Nicol
Construction Manager Ove Arup & Partners: Peter Platt-Higgins
Quantity Surveyor Davis Langdon & Everest: Sam Mackenzie, Brian Irving
Fire and Means of Escape Ove Arup & Partners: Chris Barber
Information Technology Ove Arup & Partners: Volker Buscher
Urban Context Report Space Syntax Laboratory: Bill Hillier, Mark David Major

The Mind Zone [98]
Millennium Dome, London, England, 1998–2000
Client New Millennium Experience Company
Design Zaha Hadid
Project Architect Jim Heverin
Project Team Barbara Kuit, Jon Richards, Paul Butler, Ana Sotrel, Christos Passas, Graham Modlen, Oliver Domeisen
Competition Team Graham Modlen, Patrik Schumacher, Oliver Domeisen, Garin O'Aivazian, Simon Yu, Wassim Halabi, Jim Heverin, Jon Richards
Models Jon Richards, Jim Heverin, Eddie Can, Helmut Kinzler; A Models
Artist Liaison Doris Lockhart-Saatchi
Artists/Exhibit Collaborators Research Studios: Neville Brody; Richard Brown, Nancy Burson, Brian Butterworth, Helen Chadwick, Hussein Chalayan, Richard Deacon, Escape, Ryoji Ikeda, Herbert Lachmayer (with Matthias Fuchs and Sylvia Eckermann), Langlands & Bell, Ron Mueck, New Renaissance, Urs B. Roth, Gavin Turk
Structural Engineer Ove Arup & Partners
Building Services Ove Arup & Partners
Cladding Design Consultant DCAb
Construction Manager McAlpine/Laing Joint Venture
Principal Contractor Hypsos Expo
Steel Contractor Watson Steel Structures Ltd
GRP Contractor SP Offshore
Quantity Surveyor Davis Langdon & Everest
Lighting Consultant Hollands Licht

Future TV Media Centre [99]
Beirut, Lebanon, 1998
Design Zaha Hadid
Project Architect Wassim Halabi
Design Team Garin O'Aivazian, Ali Mangera, Sara Klomps, Oliver Domeisen

UNL/Holloway Road Bridge [99]
London, England, 1998
Design Team Zaha Hadid with Christos Passas, Ali Mangera, Patrik Schumacher, Woody K.T. Yao, Sonia Villaseca, Eddie Can, Jorge Ortega, Helmut Kinzler
Structural Engineer Jane Wernick Associates
Building Services Ove Arup & Partners: Simon Hancock
Transport and Flow Capacity Ove Arup & Partners: Fiona Green
Construction Programme Ove Arup & Partners: Harry Saradjain
Quantity Surveyor Davis Langdon & Everest: James Woodrough

Car Park and Terminus Hoenheim-Nord [100]
Strasbourg, France, 1998–2001
Client Compagnie des Transports Strasbourgeois
Design Zaha Hadid
Project Architect Stéphane Hof
Sketch Design Team Stéphane Hof, Sara Klomps, Woody K.T. Yao, Sonia Villaseca
Project Team Silvia Forlati, Patrik Schumacher, Markus Dochantschi, David Salazar, Caroline Voet, Eddie Can, Stanley Lau, David Gerber, Chris Dopheide, Edgar Gonzáles
Project Consultant Mayer Bährle Freie Architekten BDA: Roland Mayer
Local Architect Albert Grandadam
General Engineer Getas/Serue
Structural Engineer Luigi Martino
Total Area 25,000 m²; tram station: 3,000 m²

Lois & Richard Rosenthal Center for Contemporary Art [104]
Cincinnati, Ohio, USA, 1997–2003
Design Zaha Hadid
Project Architect Markus Dochantschi
Assistant Project Architect Ed Gaskin
Project Team Ana Sotrel, Jan Hübener, David Gerber, Christos Passas, Sonia Villaseca, James Lim, Jee-Eun Lee, Oliver Domeisen, Helmut Kinzler, Patrik Schumacher, Michael Wolfson, David Gomersall
Competition Team Shumon Basar, Oliver Domeisen, Jee-Eun Lee, Terence Koh, Marco Guarinieri, Stéphane Hof, Woody K.T. Yao, Ivan Pajares Sanchez, Wassim Halabi, Nan Atichapong, Graham Modlen
Study Models Chris Dopheide, Thomas Knüvener, Sara Klomps, Bergendy Cooke, Florian Migsch, Sandra Oppermann, Ademir Volic
Presentation Model Ademir Volic
Local Architect KZF Design: Donald L. Cornett, Mark Stedtefeld, Dale Beeler, Amy Hauck-Hamilton, Deb Lanius
Construction Manager Turner Construction Company: Craig Preston, Bill Huber, Bob Keppler
Structural Engineer THP Limited Inc: Shayne O. Manning, Murray Monroe, Andreas Greuel, Jason Jones
Acoustics Consultant Arup Acoustics: Neill Woodger, Andrew Nicol, Richard Cowell
Services Consultant Heapy Engineering: Ron Chapman, Gary Eodice, Kirby Morgan, Fred Grable
Security Consultant Steven R. Keller & Associates: Steven Keller, Pete Rondo
Theatre Consultant Charles Cosler Theatre Design
Lighting Consultant Office for Visual Interaction: Enrique Peiniger, Jean M. Sundin

Pet Shop Boys World Tour [108]
1999
Design Zaha Hadid
Project Architect Oliver Domeisen
Design Team Bergendy Cooke, Jee-Eun Lee, Christos Passas, Caroline Voet, Susann Schweizer, Thomas Knüvener
Lighting Design Marc Brickman

L.A. Eyeworks Store [108]
Los Angeles, California, USA, 1999
Design Zaha Hadid
Project Architect Oliver Domeisen
Design Team Jee-Eun Lee, Bergendy Cooke, Sonia Villaseca
Models Zahira Nazer, Chris Dopheide
CAD Model Caroline Voet

Reina Sofía Museum Extension [109]
Madrid, Spain, 1999
Design Zaha Hadid with Patrik Schumacher
Design Team Sonia Villaseca, Jorge Ortega, Eddie Can, Paola Cattarin, Christos Passas, Chris Dopheide, Bergendy Cooke, Jee-Eun Lee, Caroline Voet, Oliver Domeisen, David Gomersall, Electra Mikelides
Structural Engineer Ove Arup & Partners: David Glover, Ed Clark
Services Engineer Ove Arup & Partners: Simon Hancock
Cost Consultant Davis Langdon & Everest: Eloi Ruart
Museum Design Consultant Bruce McAllister

Rothschild Bank Insurance Hall and Furniture [109]
London, England, 1999
Client N.M. Rothschild & Sons
Design Zaha Hadid
Design Team Graham Modlen, Barbara Kuit, Zahira Nazer, Oliver Domeisen
Models Florian Migsch, Bergendy Cooke, Thomas Knüvener, Jee-Eun Lee

Museum for the Royal Collection [110]
Madrid, Spain, 1999
Design Zaha Hadid with Patrik Schumacher
Design Team Sonia Villaseca, Caroline Voet, Jorge Ortega, Eddie Can, Paola Cattarin, Jee-Eun Lee, David Gomersall, Chris Dopheide, Silvia Forlati, J.R. Kim
Structural Engineer Ove Arup & Partners: David Glover, Ed Clark
Services Engineer Ove Arup & Partners: Simon Hancock
Cost Consultant Davis Langdon & Everest: Eloi Ruart
Museum Design Consultant Bruce McAllister

Royal Palace Hotel and Casino [111]
Lugano, Switzerland, 1999
Design Zaha Hadid
Design Team Ali Mangera, Barbara Kuit, Thomas Knüvener, Paola Cattarin, Woody K.T. Yao, Patrik Schumacher, Jorge Ortega, Eddie Can, Silvia Forlati, Oliver Domeisen, Jee-Eun Lee, Bergendy Cooke
Collaborators Zahira Nazer, Jan Hübener, Yoash Oster
Structural Engineer Ove Arup & Partners: David Glover, Colin Jackson, Ed Clark
Environmental Engineer Ove Arup & Partners: Simon Hancock
Casino Consultant Edward Lyon Design

Metapolis, Charleroi/Danses [111]
Charleroi, Belgium, 1999
Design Zaha Hadid
Design Team Caroline Voet, Woody K.T. Yao, Stéphane Hof, Shumon Basar, Paola Cattarin, Bergendy Cooke, Chris Dopheide
Technical Consultant DCAb
Costume Consultant Susan Schweizer
Fabrics Consultant Marie O'Mahony
Couturier Thomas Zaepf

Bergisel Ski Jump [112]
Innsbruck, Austria, 1999–2002
Design Zaha Hadid
Project Manager Markus Dochantschti
Project Architect Jan Hübener
Project Team Matthias Frei, Cedric Libert, Silvia Forlati, Jim Heverin, Garin O'Aivazian, Sara Noel Costa de Araujo
Competition Team Ed Gaskin, Eddie Can, Yoash Oster, Stanley Lau, Janne Westermann
Structural Engineer Christian Aste
Project Management Georg Malojer
Services Engineers Technisches Büro Ing. Heinz Pürcher; Technisches Büro Matthias Schrempf; Peter Fiby
Ski Jump Technology Bauplanungsbüro Franz Fuchslueger
Lighting Consultant Office for Visual Interaction: Enrique Peiniger, Jean M. Sundin

Phæno Science Centre [114]
Wolfsburg, Germany, 1999–2005
Client City of Wolfsburg, Ministry of Culture and Sport
Design Zaha Hadid with Christos Passas
Project Architect Christos Passas
Assistant Project Architect Sara Klomps
Special Contributor Patrik Schumacher
Project Team David Salazar, Helmut Kinzler, Günter Barczik, Gernot Finselbach, Silvia Forlati, Ken Bostock, Enrico Kleinke, Liam Young, Lida Charsouli, Barbara Kuit, Patrik Schumacher, Markus Dochantschi, Edgar Gonzáles
Competition Team Christos Passas, Janne Westermann, Chris Dopheide, Stanley Lau, Eddie Can, Yoash Oster, Jan Hübener, Caroline Voet
Co-architect Mayer Bährle Freie Architekten BDA: Rene Keuter, Tim Oldenburg
Project Team (Mayer Bährle) Sylvia Chiarappa, Stefan Hoppe, Andreas Gaiser, Roman Bockemühl, Annette Finke, Stefanie Lippardt, Marcus Liermann, Jens Hecht, Christoph Volckmar
Structural Engineers Adams Kara Taylor; Ingenieurgruppe Tokarz Frerichs Leipold
Services Engineers NEK Consults Ltd; Büro Happold
Lighting Consultants Fahlke & Dettmer; Office for Visual Interaction
Cost Consultant Hanscomb GmbH
Total Area 12,000 m²; underground car park: 15,000 m²

Meshworks [120]
Villa Medici, Rome, Italy, 2000
Design Zaha Hadid
Design Team Simon Koumjian, Patrik Schumacher, Caroline Voet
Installation Team Justin Porcano, Alfredo Greco, Michael Osmen, Daniel Arbelaez, Peter Kohn

Serpentine Gallery Pavilion [121]
London, England, 2000
Client The Serpentine Gallery
Design Zaha Hadid
Project Architect Jim Heverin
Project Manager Eric Gabriel
Structural Engineer CETEC Consultants
Quantity Surveyor Howard Associates
Lighting Consultant Maurice Brill Lighting Design
Contractor Gap Sails + Structures

British Pavilion, Venice Biennale [121]
Venice, Italy, 2000
Design Zaha Hadid
Project Architect Woody K.T. Yao
Design Team Eddie Can, Jan Hübener, Gianluca Racana
Installation Team Chris Dopheide, Alessandra Calglia, Justin Porcano, Michael Osmen, Daniel Arbelaez

Pescara Urban Plan [122]
Pescara, Italy, 2000
Design Zaha Hadid with Patrik Schumacher
Competition Team Gianluca Racana, Paola Cattarin, David Gerber, Silvia Forlati, Chris Dopheide

National Library of Quebec [122]
Montreal, Quebec, Canada, 2000
Design Zaha Hadid with Patrik Schumacher
Design Team Sonia Villaseca, Stéphane Hof, Chris Dopheide, Djordje Stojanovic, Dillon Lin, Lida Charsouli, Garin O'Aivazian, David Gerber, Andreas Durkin, Liam Young, Christos Passas, Sara Klomps
Competition Model Ademir Volic
Local Architect Albert Grandadam
Structural Engineer Adams Kara Taylor: Hanif Kara
Cost Consultants Davis Langdon & Everest: Guy Rezeau; Hanscomb Consultants
Environmental Engineer Max Fordham Partnership: Henry Luker, Sam Archer
Acoustics Consultants Arup Acoustics; Peutz & Associes France
Lighting Consultant Office for Visual Interaction: Enrique Peiniger, Jean M. Sundin

La Grande Mosquée de Strasbourg [123]
Strasbourg, France, 2000
Design Zaha Hadid with Patrik Schumacher
Design Team Ali Mangera, David Gerber, David Salazar, Jorge Ortega, Caroline Voet, Eddie Can, Patrik Schumacher, Woody K.T. Yao, Stéphane Hof, Hon Kong Chee, Steve Power, Edgar González, Garin O'Aivazian
Local Architect Albert Grandadam
Structural Engineer Adams Kara Taylor: Hanif Kara
Environmental Engineer Max Fordham Partnership: Henry Luker, Sam Archer
Acoustics Consultants Arup Acoustics; Peutz & Associes France
Lighting Consultant Office for Visual Interaction: Enrique Peiniger, Jean M. Sundin
Cost Consultant Davis Langdon & Everest: Guy Rezeau

Centro JVC Hotel [123]
Guadalajara, Mexico, 2000
Client Omnitrition de México
Design Zaha Hadid
Project Architect Jim Heverin
Project Team Helmut Kinzler, Edgar Gonzáles, Eddie Can, Jorge Ortega, Zulima Nieto, Jose Rojo
Structural Engineer Adams Kara Taylor
Building Services Büro Happold
Fire Consultant Arup Fire

Art Museum [124]
Graz, Austria, 2000
Design Zaha Hadid with Patrik Schumacher
Design Team Sonia Villaseca, Stanley Lau, Paola Cattarin, David Gerber, Eddie Can, Gianluca Racana, Yoash Oster, Janne Westermann
Structural Engineer Adams Kara Taylor: Hanif Kara
Façade Consultant Adams Kara Taylor: Hanif Kara
Cost Consultant Davis Langdon & Everest: Sam Mackenzie

Zaha Hadid Lounge [125]
Kunstmuseum, Wolfsburg, Germany, 2001
Design Zaha Hadid
Project Architects Woody K.T. Yao, Djordje Stojanovic

Homes for the Future 2, Kite Site [125]
Glasgow, Scotland, 2001
Residential Development
Clients MacTaggart & Mickel; Logan Construction Management Ltd
Design Zaha Hadid
Project Architect Graham Modlen
Design Team Ken Bostock, Amin Taha, Sandra Oppermann
Local Architect Wren Rutherford ASL
Structural Engineer Adams Kara Taylor
Services Consultant Max Fordham Partnership
Landscape Consultant Turnbull Jeffrey Partnership
Cost Consultant Robinson Low Francis

Hungerford and Jubilee Gardens [126]
South Bank Centre, London, England, 1999
Design Zaha Hadid
Project Architect Jim Heverin
Design Team Patrik Schumacher, Ken Bostock, David Salazar, Helmut Kinzler, Edgar González, Eddie Can, Tiago Correia

one-north Masterplan [126]
Singapore, 2002
Design Zaha Hadid with Patrik Schumacher
Project Director Markus Dochantschi
Project Architects (Masterplan Phase) David Gerber, Dillon Lin, Silvia Forlati
Project Team (Masterplan Phase) David Mah, Gunther Koppelhuber, Rodrigo O'Malley, Kim Thornton, Markus Dochantschi
Project Architects (Rochester Detail Planning Phase) Gunther Koppelhuber
Project Team (Rochester Detail Planning Phase) Kim Thornton, Hon Kong Chee, Yael Brosilovski, Fernando Pérez Vera
Competition Team David Gerber, Edgar González, Chris Dopheide, David Salazar, Tiago Correia, Ken Bostock, Patrik Schumacher, Paola Cattarin, Dillon Lin, Barbara Kuit, Woody K.T. Yao
Models Riann Steenkamp, Chris Dopheide, Ellen Haywood, Helena Feldman
Presentation Models Delicatessen Design Ltd: Ademir Volic
Urban Strategy Lawrence Barth, Architectural Association
Infrastructural Engineer Ove Arup & Partners: Simon Hancock, Ian Carradice, David Johnston
Infrastructural Audits JTC Consultants Pte Ltd
Transport Engineer MVA: Paul Williams, Tim Booth
Landscape Architect Cicada Pte Ltd
Lighting Consultant Lighting Planners Associates: Kaoru Mende
Planning Tool Consultant B Consultants: Tom Barker, Graeme Jennings

Temporary Museum, Guggenheim Tokyo [127]
Tokyo, Japan, 2001
Client Guggenheim Foundation
Design Zaha Hadid
Project Architect Patrik Schumacher
Design Team Gianluca Racana, Ken Bostock, Vivek Shankar
Total Area 7,000 m²

Albertina Extension [127]
Vienna, Austria, 2001
Design Zaha Hadid with Patrik Schumacher
Project Architect Lars Teichmann
Design Team Ken Bostock, Dillon Lin, Tiago Correia, Sandra Oppermann, Raza Zahid

BMW Plant Central Building [128]
Leipzig, Germany 2001–05
Design Zaha Hadid with Patrik Schumacher
Project Architects Jim Heverin, Lars Teichmann
Project Team Matthias Frei, Jan Hübener, Annette Bresinsky, Manuela Gatto, Fabian Hecker, Cornelius Schlotthauer, Wolfgang Sunder, Anneka Wegener, Markus Planteu, Robert Neumayr, Christina Beaumont, Achim Gergen, Caroline Anderson
Competition Team Lars Teichmann, Eva Pfannes, Ken Bostock, Stéphane Hof, Djordje Stojanovic, Leyre Villoria, Liam Young, Christiane Fashek, Manuela Gatto, Tina Gregoric, Cesare Griffa, Yasha Jacob Grobman, Filippo Innocenti, Zetta Kotsioni, Debora Laub, Sarah Manning, Maurizio Meossi, Robert Sedlak, Niki Neerpasch, Eric Tong, Tiago Correia
Partner Architects IFB Dr Braschel AG; Anthony Hunt Associates
Structural Engineers IFB Dr Braschel AG; WPW Ingenieure GmbH
M&E Engineer IFB Dr Braschel AG
Cost Consultant IFB Dr Braschel AG
Lighting Design Equation Lighting Design
Landscape Architect Gross.Max

Ordrupgaard Museum Extension [132]
Copenhagen, Denmark, 2001–05
Design Zaha Hadid
Project Architect Ken Bostock
Design Team Caroline Krogh Andersen
Competition Team Patrik Schumacher, Ken Bostock, Adriano De Gioannis, Sara Noel Costa de Araujo, Lars Teichmann, Vivek Shankar, Cedric Libert, Tiago Correia
Model Riann Steenkamp
Associate Architect PLH Arkitekter
Structural Engineers Jane Wernick Associates; Birch & Krogboe
M&E Design Ove Arup & Partners; Birch & Krogboe
Lighting Consultant Arup Lighting
Acoustics Consultant Birch & Krogboe

Maggie's Centre Fife, Victoria Hospital [136]
Kirkcaldy, Scotland, 2001–06
Drop-in Cancer Care Centre
Client Maggie's Centre
Design Zaha Hadid
Project Architects Jim Heverin, Tiago Correia
Project Team Zaha Hadid, Jim Heverin, Tiago Correia
Structural Engineer Jane Wernick Associates
Services Engineer K.J. Tait Engineers
Underground Drainage SKM Anthony Hunts
Quantity Surveyor CBA Chartered Quantity Surveyors
Planning Supervisor Reiach & Hall Architects
Landscape Architect Gross.Max
Building Surveyor GLM Ltd
Total Area 250 m²

Monographic Exhibition [138]
Rome, Italy, 2002
Design Zaha Hadid with Patrik Schumacher
Project Architects Gianluca Racana, Woody K.T. Yao
Design Team Tiago Correia, Adriano De Gioannis, Barbara Pfenningstorff, Ana M. Cajiao, Maurizio Meossi, Manuela Gatto, Thomas Vietzke, Natalie Rosenberg, Ken Bostock, Barbara Kuit, Christos Passas, Sara Klomps
Local Architect ABT s.r.l.

Price Tower Arts Center [138]
Bartlesville, Oklahoma, USA, 2002–
Design Zaha Hadid with Patrik Schumacher
Project Architect Markus Dochantschi
Project Team Matias Musacchio, Ana M. Caijao, Jorge Seperizza, Mirco Becker, Tamar Jacobs, Viggo Haremst, Christian Ludwig, Ed Gaskin

City of Towers, Venice Biennale [139]
Venice, Italy, 2002
Client Alessi
Design Zaha Hadid with Patrik Schumacher
Design Team Thomas Vietzke, Natalie Rosenberg, Woody K.T. Yao

Museum Brandhorst [140]
Munich, Germany, 2002
Design Zaha Hadid with Patrik Schumacher
Project Architect Barbara Pfenningstorff
Design Team Adriano De Gioannis, Cornelius Schlotthauer, Maurizio Meossi, Filippo Innocenti, Rocio Paz, Eric Tong, Ana M. Cajiao, Flavio La Gioia, Viggo Haremst, Manuela Gatto, Tamar Jacobs, Thomas Vietzke, Natalie Rosenberg, Christos Passas
Structural Engineer ASTE: Andreas Glatzl, Christian Aste
NME and General Lighting Max Fordham Partnership: Henry Luker
Exterior Lighting Office for Visual Interaction: Enrique Peiniger, Jean M. Sundin
Glass Façade RFR Ingénieurs: Jean-François Blassel

248

Hotel Puerta America – Hoteles Silken [141]
Madrid, Spain, 2003–05
Interior for a Hotel Floor
Client Grupo Urvasco
Design Zaha Hadid
Project Architect Woody K.T. Yao
Project Design Thomas Vietzke, Yael Brosilovski, Patrik
Schumacher
Design Team Ken Bostock, Mirco Becker
Total Area 1,200 m²

High-Speed Train Station Napoli-Afragola [142]
Naples, Italy, 2004–14
Client TAV s.p.a.
Design Zaha Hadid with Patrik Schumacher
Project Architect Filippo Innocenti
Project Managers Paola Cattarin, Filippo Innocenti
Design Team Cesare Griffa, Federico Bistolfi, Mario Mattia, Paolo
Zilli, Tobias Hegemann, Michele Salvi, Chiara Beccarini, Alessandra
Belia, Serena Pietrantonj, Roberto Cavallaro, Karim Muallem
Competition Team Fernando Pérez Vera, Ergian Alberg, Hon Kong
Chee, Cesare Griffa, Karim Muallem, Steven Hatzellis, Thomas
Vietzke, Jens Borstelmann, Robert Neumayr, Elena Perez, Adriano De
Gioannis, Simon Kim, Selim Mimita
Structural and Geotechnical Engineers Adams Kara Taylor: Hanif
Kara, Paul Scott; Interprogetti: Giampiero Martuscelli
Environmental Engineers Max Fordham Partnership: Henry Luker,
Neil Smith; Studio Reale: Francesco Reale, Vittorio Criscuolo Gaito
Building Regulation, Coordination Local Team Interplan
Seconda: Alessandro Gubitosi
Fire Safety Macchiaroli & Partners: Roberto Macchiaroli
Transport Engineer JMP: Max Matteis
Acoustics Consultant Paul Gillieron Acoustic
Landscape Architect Gross.Max: Eelco Hooftman
Cost Consultant Building Consulting: Pasquale Miele
Total Area 20,000 m²

BBC Music Centre [144]
London, England, 2003
Client BBC
Design Zaha Hadid with Patrik Schumacher
Project Architects Steven Hatzellis, Graham Modlen, Ergian Alberg
Project Team Karim Muallem, Ram Ahronov, Adriano De Gioannis,
Simon Kim, Yansong Ma, Rafael Schmidt, Markus Planteu
Structural Engineer Ove Arup & Partners: Bob Lang
Services Consultant Ove Arup & Partners: Nigel Tonks
Acoustics Consultant Arup Acoustics: Richard Cowell
Theatre Consultant Anne Minors Performance Consultants
Cost Consultant Davis Langdon & Everest: Sam Mackenzie

Desire [144]
Graz, Austria, 2003
Stage Set for a Contemporary Opera
Design Zaha Hadid with Patrik Schumacher
Project Architect Rocio Paz
Design Team Filippo Innocenti, Zetta Kotsioni, Alexander de Looz
Structural Engineer B Consultants

Guggenheim Museum Taichung [145]
Taichung, Taiwan, 2003
Design Zaha Hadid with Patrik Schumacher
Project Architect Dillon Lin
Design Team Jens Borstelmann, Thomas Vietzke, Yosuke Hayano
Production Team Adriano De Gioannis, Selim Mimita, Juan Ignacio
Aranguren, Ken Bostock, Elena Perez, Ergian Alberg, Rocio Paz,
Markus Planteu, Simon Kim
Structural Engineer Adams Kara Taylor: Hanif Kara, Andrew
Murray, Sebastian Khourain, Reuben Brambleby, Stefano Strazzullo
Services Consultant IDOM Bilbao
Cost Consultant IDOM UK Ltd; IDOM Bilbao
Model Photography David Grandorge

The Snow Show [146]
Lapland, Finland, 2003–04
Collaboration with Cai Guo-Qiang
Design Zaha Hadid with Patrik Schumacher
Project Architects Rocio Paz, Woody K.T. Yao
Design Team Yael Brosilovski, Thomas Vietzke, Helmut Kinzler
Structural Engineer Adams Kara Taylor
Lighting Design Zumtobel Illuminazione s.r.l., with HFG-Karlsruhe
Scenography class, Prof. M. Simon

NYC 2012 Olympic Village [146]
New York, New York, USA, 2004
Design Zaha Hadid with Patrik Schumacher
Project Manager StudioMDA: Markus Dochantschi
Project Architect Tiago Correia
Design Team Ana M. Cajiao, Daniel Baerlecken, Judith Reitz, Simon
Kim, Dillon Lin, Yosuke Hayano, Ergian Alberg, Yael Brosilovski,
Daniel Li, Yang Jingwen, Li Zou, Laura Aquili, Jens Borstelmann,
Juan Ignacio Aranguren
Urban Strategy Lawrence Barth
Structural Engineer Ove Arup & Partners: Bob Lang
Infrastructural Engineer Ove Arup & Partners: Ian Carradice
Transport Engineer Ove Arup & Partners: David Johnston
Building Services Ove Arup & Partners: Andrew Sedgwick
Lift Consultant Ove Arup & Partners: Mike Summers, Warrick
Gorrie
Mechanical Engineer Ove Arup & Partners: Emmanuelle Danisi
Fire Consultant Ove Arup & Partners: Barbara Lane, Tony Lovell
Security Consultant Arup Security Consulting: John Haddon,
Simon Brimble
Façade Consultant Ove Arup & Partners: Edith Mueller
Materials Ove Arup & Partners: Clare Perkins
Lighting Design L'Observatoire International: Hervé Descottes
Landscape Architect Gross.Max: Eelco Hooftmann
Cost Consultant Davis Langdon Adamson: Nick Butcher, Ethan
T. Burrows
Video Animation and 3D Visuals Neutral
Photography David Grandorge

López de Heredia Pavilion [148]
Haro la Rioja, Spain, 2001–06
Client López de Heredia
Design Zaha Hadid
Project Architect Jim Heverin
Project Team Tiago Correia, Matthias Frei, Ana M. Cajiao
Partner Architect IOA Arquitectura: Joan Ramon Rius, Nuria Ayala,
Xavier Medina, Candi Casadevall
Structural Engineer Jane Wernick Associates
M&E Engineer Ove Arup & Partners: Ann Dalzell

Nordpark Cable Railway [150]
Innsbruck, Austria, 2004–07
Client INKB (Innsbrucker Nordkettenbahnen GmbH)
Design Zaha Hadid with Patrik Schumacher
Project Architect Thomas Vietzke
Design Team Jens Borstelmann, Markus Planteu
Production Team Caroline Krogh Andersen, Makakrai Suthadarat,
Marcela Spadaro, Anneka Wegener, Adriano De Gioannis, Peter
Pichler, Susann Berggren
Local Partner Office/Building Management Malojer
Baumanagement
Structural Engineer Bollinger Grohmann Schneider Ziviltechniker
Façade Planning Pagitz Metalltechnik GmbH
Contractor Strabag AG
Engines and Cables Contractor Leitner GmbH
Planning Advisors ILF Beratende Ingenieure ZT GmbH; Malojer
Baumanagement
Concrete Base Baumann + Obholzer ZT
Bridge Engineer ILF Beratende Ingenieure ZT GmbH
Lighting Zumtobel Illuminazione s.r.l.

Sheikh Zayed Bridge [154]
Abu Dhabi, UAE, 1997–
Client Sheikh Sultan Bin Zayid Al Nahyan
Design Zaha Hadid
Project Architect Graham Modlen
Project Team Garin O'Aivazian, Zahira Nazer, Christos Passas, Sara
Klomps, Steve Power
Project Engineer Mike King
Structural Consultant Rendel Palmer & Tritton
Lighting Consultant Hollands Licht
Size 800m (length) × 64m (height) × 61m (width)

Maritime Terminal Salerno [155]
Salerno, Italy, 2000–12
Client Comune di Salerno
Design Zaha Hadid
Project Architect Paola Cattarin
Design Team Andrea Parenti, Giovanna Sylos Labini, Cedric Libert,
Filippo Innocenti, Paolo Zilli, Eric Tong
Competition Team Paola Cattarin, Sonia Villaseca, Chris Dopheide
Local Architect Interplan Seconda
Structural Engineer Ingeco
Structural Engineer (Preliminary Design) Ove Arup & Partners
M&E Engineer Macchiaroli & Partners
M&E Engineer (Preliminary Design) Ove Arup & Partners
Maritime/Transport Engineer Ove Arup & Partners
Lighting Consultant Equation Lighting Design
Cost Consultants Interplan Seconda; Studio Miele
Total Area 4,500 m²

MAXXI: National Museum of XXI Century Arts [156]
Rome, Italy, 1998–2009
Client Italian Ministry of Culture
Design Zaha Hadid with Patrik Schumacher
Project Architect Gianluca Racana
Site Supervision Team Paolo Matteuzzi, Anja Simons, Mario Mattia
Project Team Anja Simons, Paolo Matteuzzi, Fabio Ceci, Mario
Mattia, Maurizio Meossi, Paolo Zilli, Luca Peralta, Maria Velceva,
Matteo Grimaldi, Ana M. Cajiao, Barbara Pfenningstorff, Dillon Lin,
Ken Bostock, Raza Zahid, Lars Teichmann, Adriano De Gioannis,
Amin Taha, Caroline Voet, Gianluca Ruggeri, Luca Segarelli
Local Architect ABT s.r.l.
Structural Engineers Anthony Hunt Associates; OK Design Group
M&E Consultants Max Fordham Partnership; OK Design Group
Lighting Consultant Equation Lighting Design
Acoustics Consultant Paul Gillieron Acoustic
Total Area 30,000 m²

Pierres Vives [158]

Montpellier, France, 2002–11
Library, Archive, Office
Client Département de l'Hérault
Design Zaha Hadid
Project Architect Stéphane Hof
Project Team Joris Pauwels, Philipp Vogt, Rafael Portillo, Melissa Fukumoto, Jens Borstelmann, Jaime Serra Avila, Kane Yanegawa, Loreto Flores, Edgar Payan, Lisamarie Villegas Ambia, Stella Nikolakaki, Karouko Ogawa, Hon Kong Chee, Caroline Krogh Andersen, Judith Reitz, Olivier Ottevaere, Achim Gergen, Daniel Baerlecken, Yosuke Hayano, Martin Henn, Rafael Schmidt, Daniel Gospodinov, Kia Larsdotter, Jasmina Malanovic, Ahmad Sukkar, Ghita Skalli, Elena Perez, Andrea Balducci Castè, Lisa Cholmondeley, Douglas Chew, Larissa Henke, Steven Hatzellis, Jesse Chima, Adriano De Gioannis, Simon Kim, Stéphane Carnuccini, Samer Chamoun, Ram Ahronov, Ross Langdon, Ivan Valdez, Yacira Blanco, Marta Rodriguez, Leonardo Garcia, Sevil Yazici
Competition Team Thomas Vietzke, Achim Gergen, Martin Henn, Christina Beaumont, Yael Brosilovski, Lorenzo Grifantini, Carlos Fernando Pérez, Helmut Kinzler, Viggo Haremst, Christian Ludwig, Selim Mimita, Flavio La Gioia, Nina Safainia
Structural Engineer Ove Arup & Partners: Paul Nuttall, Sophie Le Bourva, Mits Kanada, David Rutter
Services Consultant (Concept Design) Ove Arup & Partners: Emmanuelle Danisi, Michael Stych; GEC Ingénierie: Francis Petit, Philippe Vivier, Rene Andrian, Gregory Makarawiez
Infrastructure GEC Ingénierie: Jean Paul Sulima
Acoustics Consultant Rouch Acoustique: Nicolas Albaric
Cost Consultant GEC-LR: Ivica Knenovic

Guangzhou Opera House [160]

Guangzhou, China, 2003–09
Client Guangzhou Municipal Government
Design Zaha Hadid
Project Directors Woody K.T. Yao, Patrik Schumacher
Project Architect Simon Yu
Project Team Jason Guo, Yang Jingwen, Long Jiang, Ta-Kang Hsu, Yi-Ching Liu, Zhi Wang, Christine Chow, Cyril Shing, Filippo Innocenti, Lourdes Sánchez, Hinki Kwong
Competition Team (1st Stage) Filippo Innocenti, Matias Musacchio, Jenny Huang, Hon Kong Chee, Markus Planteu, Paola Cattarin, Tamar Jacobs, Yael Brosilovski, Viggo Haremst, Christian Ludwig, Christina Beaumont, Lorenzo Grifantini, Flavio La Gioia, Nina Safainia, Fernando Pérez Vera, Martin Henn, Achim Gergen, Graham Modlen, Imran Mahmood
Competition Team (2nd Stage) Cyril Shing, Yansong Ma, Yosuke Hayano, Adriano De Gioannis, Barbara Pfenningstorff
Structure, Services and Acoustics (Competition Stage) Ove Arup & Partners
Cost Consultant (Competition Stage) Davis Langdon & Everest
Local Consultant Ove Arup & Partners Hong Kong Ltd
Local Design Institute Guangzhou Pearl River Foreign Investment Architectural Designing Institute
Structural Engineer Shanghai Tongking Science & Technology Development Co Ltd; Guangzhou Pearl River Foreign Investment Architectural Designing Institute
Façade Engineer King Glass Engineering Group
Building Services Guangzhou Pearl River Foreign Investment Architectural Designing Institute
Acoustics Consultant Marshall Day Acoustics
Theatre Consultant ENFI
Lighting Consultant Beijing Light & View
Project Manager Guangzhou Municipal Construction Group Co Ltd
Construction Manager Guangzhou Construction Engineering Supervision Co Ltd
Cost Consultant Guangzhou Jiancheng Engineering Costing Consultant Office Ltd
Principal Contractor China Construction 3rd Engineering Bureau Co Ltd
Total Area 70,000 m²

Glasgow Museum of Transport Riverside Project [162]

Glasgow, Scotland, 2004–10
Client Glasgow City Council
Design Zaha Hadid
Project Director Jim Heverin
Project Architect Johannes Hoffman
Project Team Matthias Frei, Agnes Koltay, Malca Mizrahi, Tyen Masten, Gemma Douglas, Johannes Hoffmann, Daniel Baerlecken, Achim Gergen, Christina Beaumont, Markus Planteu, Claudia Wulf, Alasdair Graham, Rebecca Haines-Gadd, Brandon Buck, Naomi Fritz, Liat Muller, Elke Presser, Hinki Kwong, Michael Mader, Mike Chong, Mikel Bennett, Jee-Eun Lee, Chun Chiu, Aris Giorgiadis, Lole Mate, Thomas Hale, Andreas Helgesson, Andrew Summers, Des Fagan
Competition Team Malca MizManagrahi, Michele Pasca di Magliano, Viviana R. Muscettola, Mariana Ibanez, Larissa Henke
Services Consultant Büro Happold
Acoustics Consultant Büro Happold
Fire Safety Büro Happold Fire Engineering Design and Risk Assessment Group (FEDRA)
Project Manager Capita Symonds
Cost Consultant Capita Symonds
Total Area 10,000 m²; exhibition: 7,000 m²

London Aquatic Centre [163]

London, England, 2003–12
Facility for the 2012 London Olympics
Client Olympic Delivery Authority
Design Zaha Hadid
Project Director Jim Heverin
Project Architect Glenn Moorley, Sara Klomps
Project Team Alex Marcoulides, Carlos Carijo, Clay Shorthall, Ertu Erbay, Giorgia Cannici, Hannes Schafelner, Hee Seung Lee, Kasia Townend, Nannette Jackowski, Nicholas Gdalewitch, Seth Handley, Thomas Soo, Tom Locke, Torsten Broeder, Tristran Job, Yamac Korfali, Yeena Yon
Competition Team Agnes Koltay, Feng Chen, Gemma Douglas, Makakrai Suthadarat, Karim Muallem, Marco Vanucci, Mariana Ibanez, Saffet Kaya Bekiroglu, Sujit Nair
Sports Architect S&P Architects
Structural Engineer Ove Arup & Partners
Services Consultant Ove Arup & Partners
Fire Safety Arup Fire
Acoustics Consultant Arup Acoustics
Façade Engineer Robert-Jan Van Santen Associates
Lighting Design Arup Lighting
Kitchen Design Winton Nightingale
Maintenance Access Reef
Temporary Construction Consultant Edwin Shirley Staging
Security Consultant Arup Security Consulting
AV and IT Consultant Mark Johnson Consultants
Disability Consultant Access = Design
CDM Co-coordinator Total CDM Solutions Ltd
BREEAM Consultant Ove Arup & Partners
Total Area 20,000 m²

Zaragoza Bridge Pavilion [166]

Zaragoza, Spain, 2005–08
Interactive Exhibition for Expo 2008
Client Expoagua Zaragoza 2008
Design Zaha Hadid with Patrik Schumacher
Project Architect Manuela Gatto
Project Team Fabian Hecker, Matthias Baer, Soohyun Chang, Feng Chen, Atrey Chhaya, Ignacio Choliz, Federico Dunkelberg, Dipal Kothari, Maria José Mendoza, José M. Monfa, Marta Rodriguez, Diego Rosales, Guillermo Ruiz, Lucio Santos, Hala Sheikh, Marcela Spadaro, Anat Stern, Jay Suthadarat
Competition Team Feng Chen, Atrey Chhaya, Dipal Kothari
Engineering Consultant Ove Arup & Partners
Cost Consultant Ove Arup & Partners; IDOM
Size 270m (length); 185m from island to right bank, plus 85m from island to Expo riverbank

Edifici Campus [170]

Barcelona, Spain, 2006–
Mixed-use Development
Client El Consorcio de la Zona Franca de Barcelona; España Consorci del Campus Interuniversitari del Besòs
Design Zaha Hadid with Patrik Schumacher
Project Architect Tiago Correia
Design Team Alejandro Díaz, Aurora Santana
Project Team Fabiano Continanza, Mónica Bartolomé, Raquel Gallego, Oihane Santiuste, Rafael González, Esther Rivas, Jessica Knobloch, Hooman Talebi, Maria Araya, Ebru Simsek
Technical Architect J/T Ardèvol i Associats SL
Local Architect Ferran Pelegrina Associats SL
Structural Engineer Adams Kara Taylor; Brufau, Obiol, Moya & Associats SL
M/E/P Engineer Max Fordham Partnership; Grupo JG
Façade Engineer Ferrés Arquitectos y Consultores
Lighting Design Architectural Lighting Solutions
Total Area 27,650 m²; offices: 12,150 m²; university: 8,500 m²; parking: 7,000 m²

CMA CGM Headquarters Tower [171]

Marseille, France, 2004–09
Head Offices and Parking
Client CMA CGM Marseille
Design Zaha Hadid
Project Director Jim Heverin
Project Architect Stéphane Vallotton
Project Team Karim Muallem, Simone Contasta, Leonie Heinrich, Alvin Triestanto, Muriel Boselli, Eugene Leung, Bhushan Mantri, Jerome Michel, Nerea Feliz, Prashanth Sridharan, Birgit Eistert, Evelyn Gono, Marian Ripoll
Competition Team Jim Heverin, Simon Kim, Michele Pasca di Magliano, Viviana R. Muscettola
Partner Architect SRA – RTA
Structural Engineer Ove Arup & Partners
Services Consultant Ove Arup & Partners
Façade Engineers Ove Arup & Partners; Robert-Jan Van Santen Associates
Cost Consultant R2M
Total Area 64,000 m² (33 floors)

Mobile Art Pavilion for Chanel [172]

Hong Kong, China, 2007–08
Travelling Exhibition Pavilion
Client Chanel
Design Zaha Hadid with Patrik Schumacher
Project Architects Thomas Vietzke, Jens Borstelmann
Project Team Helen Lee, Claudia Wulf, Erhan Patat, Tetsuya Yamazaki, Daniel Fiser
Structural Engineer Ove Arup & Partners
Cost Consultant Davis Langdon & Everest
Main Contractor/Tour Operator ESS Staging
FRP Manufacturing Stage One Creative Services Ltd
Materials Façade cladding: fibre-reinforced plastic; roof: PVC; ETFE roof lights; secondary structure: aluminium extrusions; primary structure: 74 tons of steel (pavilion: 69 tons; ticket office: 5 tons); 1,752 different steel connections
Total Area 700 m²

Eli & Edythe Broad Art Museum [176]

Michigan State University, USA, 2007–
Client Michigan State University
Design Zaha Hadid with Patrik Schumacher
Project Director Craig Kiner
Project Architect Alberto Barba
Project Team Ruven Aybar, Michael Hargens, Edgar Payan Pacheco, Sophia Razzaque, Arturo Revilla, Charles Walker
Project Director (Competition) Nils-Peter Fischer
Project Architects (Competition) Britta Knobel, Fulvio Wirz
Competition Team Daniel Widrig, Melike Altinisik, Mariagrazia Lanza, Rojia Forouhar
Structural Consultant Adams Kara Taylor: Hanif Kara
Environmental/M&E Consultant Max Fordham Partnership: Henry Luker

'Opus' Office Tower [177]
Dubai, UAE, 2007–10
Client Omniyat Properties
Design Zaha Hadid
Project Director Christos Passas
Project Architect Vincent Nowak
Project Team Dimitris Akritopoulos, Chiara Ferrari, Thomas Frings, Jesus Garate, Sylvia Georgiadou, Javier Ernesto Lebie, Wen-Yuan Peng, Paul Peyrer-Heimstaett, Phivos Skroumbelos, Marilena Sophocleous
Competition Team Daniel Baerlecken, Gemma Douglas, Alvin Huang, Paul Peyrer-Heimstaett, Saleem Abdel-Jalil
Project Management Gleeds
Local Architect Arex Consultants
Structural Engineer Ramboll Whitbybird Ltd; BG&E Engineers
M&E Engineer Ramboll Whitbybird Ltd
Fire Engineer SAFE Consulting
Lift Consultant Roger Preston Dynamics
Traffic Consultant Cansult Limited
Main Contractor Multiplex Construction
Façade Contractor Permasteelisa/Gartner
Total Area 85,641 m²; 100m (width) × 67m (depth) × 93m (height)

Innovation Tower [178]
Hong Kong Polytechnic University, China, 2007–11
Client Hong Kong Polytechnic University
Design Zaha Hadid with Patrik Schumacher
Project Director Woody K.T. Yao
Project Leader Simon Yu
Competition Team Hinki Kwong, Melodie Leung, Long Jiang, Zhenjiang Guo, Yang Jingwen, Miron Mutyaba, Pavlos Xanthopoulus, Margarita Yordanova Valova
Local Architects AGC Design Ltd; AD+RG
Structural and Geotechnical Engineer Ove Arup & Partners
Building Services Ove Arup & Partners
Landscape Architect Team 73 HK Ltd
Acoustics Consultant Westwood Hong & Associates Ltd
Total Area 15,000 m²; 76m (height)

Moscow Expocentre Exhibition Halls [180]
Moscow, Russia, 2007–
Office and Retail
Client BCI Construction Limited
Design Zaha Hadid with Patrik Schumacher
Design Leader Inanc Eray
Design Team Yevgeniy Beylkin, Melike Altinisik, Erhan Patat
Visualizations Stack! Studios
Presentation Models A-Models; ARRK Product Development Group

Fiera di Milano [181]
Milan, Italy, 2004–14
Office Tower and Residential Development
Design Zaha Hadid with Patrik Schumacher
Project Director Gianluca Racana
Tower Project Architect Paolo Zilli
Tower Design Team Giuseppe Morando, Andrea Balducci Castè, Annarita Papeschi, Matteo Pierotti, Mario Mattia
Residential Project Architect Maurizio Meossi
Residential Design Team Vincenzo Barilari, Cristina Capanna, Giacomo Sanna, Arianna Francioni, Massimiliano Piccinini, Samuele Sordi, Mario Mattia, Alessandra Belia
Competition Team Simon Kim, Yael Brosilovski, Adriano De Gioannis, Graham Modlen, Karim Muallem, Daniel Li, Yang Jingwen, Tiago Correia, Ana M. Cajiao, Daniel Baerlecken, Judith Reitz
Structural Engineer Adams Kara Taylor
M&E Consultants Max Fordham Partnership; MilanoProgetti
Lift Consultant Roger Preston Dynamics
Fire Safety Silvestre Mistretta
Transport Systematica

Dubai Opera House [182]
Dubai, UAE, 2006–
Design Zaha Hadid with Patrik Schumacher
Project Director Charles Walker
Project Architect Nils-Peter Fischer
Project Team Melike Altinisik, Alexia Anastasopoulou, Dylan Baker-Rice, Domen Bergoc, Shajay Bhooshan, Monika Bilska, Alex Bilton, Elizabeth Bishop, Torsten Broeder, Cristiano Ceccato, Alessio Constantino, Mario Coppola, Brian Dale, Ana Valeria Emiliano, Elif Erdine, Camilla Galli, Brandon Gehrke, Aris Giorgiadis, Pia Habekost, Michael Hill, Shao-Wei Huang, Chikara Inamura, Alexander Janowsky, DaeWha Kang, Tariq Khayyat, Maren Klasing, Britta Knobel, Martin Krcha, Effie Kuan, Mariagrazia Lanza, Tyen Masten, Jwalant Mahadevwala, Rashiq Muhamadali, Mónica Noguero, Diogo Brito Pereira, Rafael Portillo, Michael Powers, Rolando Rodriguez-Leal, Federico Rossi, Mireia Sala Font, Elke Scheier, Rooshad Shroff, William Tan, Michal Treder, Daniel Widrig, Fulvio Wirz, Susu Xu, Ting Ting Zhang
Project Director (Competition) Graham Modlen
Project Architect (Competition) Dillon Lin
Competition Team Christine Chow, Daniel Dendra, Yi-Ching Liu, Simone Fuchs, Larissa Henke, Tyen Masten, Lourdes Sánchez, Johannes Schafelner, Swati Sharma, Hooman Talebi, Komal Talreja, Claudia Wulf, Simon Yu
Engineering Consultant Ove Arup & Partners: Steve Roberts
Acoustics Consultant Arup Acoustics: Neill Woodger
Theatre Consultant Anne Minors Performance Consultants
Lighting Consultant Office for Visual Interaction

Kartal-Pendik Masterplan [183]
Istanbul, Turkey, 2006–
Proposal for a New City Centre
Client Greater Istanbul Municipality and Kartal Urban Regeneration Association
Design Zaha Hadid with Patrik Schumacher
Overall Project Architect Bozana Komljenovic
Stage 2 Project Team Amit Gupta, Marie-Perrine Placais, Susanne Lettau, Elif Erdine, Jimena Araiza
Stage 1 Project Leaders Bozana Komljenovic, DaeWha Kang
Stage 1 Project Team Sevil Yazici, Vigneswaran Ramaraju, Brian Dale, Jordan Darnell, Oznur Erboga
Competition Leaders DaeWha Kang, Saffet Kaya Bekiroglu
Competition Team Sevil Yazici, Daniel Widrig, Elif Erdine, Melike Altinisik, Ceyhun Baskin, Inanc Eray, Fulvio Wirz, Gonzalo Carbajo
Total Area 5.5 million m² (555 hectares)

University of Seville Library [184]
Seville, Spain, 2006–
Client University of Seville
Design Zaha Hadid with Patrik Schumacher
Project Architects Sophie Le Bienvenu, Sara Klomps
Project Architects (Execution) Sophie Le Bienvenu, Alberto Barba
Project Team Loreto Flores, Edgar Payan, Keji Majekodunmi, Lourdes Sánchez, Tarek Shamma, Susann Berggren, Ben Holland
Competition Team Sophie Le Bienvenu, Federico Dunkelberg, Tarek Shamma, Ebru Simsek, Fulvio Wirz, Mariagrazia Lanza, Miya Ushida
Local Architect IDOM Sevilla
Structural Consultant IDOM Bilbao
Façade and Coordination Consultant IDOM UK Ltd
Cost, Services, Sustainability Consultant IDOM Sevilla
Total Area 10,500 m²

Nuragic and Contemporary Art Museum [185]
Cagliari, Italy, 2006–
Client Regione Autonoma della Sardegna
Design Zaha Hadid with Patrik Schumacher
Project Architect Paola Cattarin
Team Leader Paolo Matteuzzi
Design Team Federico Bistolfi, Michele Salvi, Serena Pietrantonj, Alessandra Belia, Cristina Capanna
Competition Team Paola Cattarin, Paolo Matteuzzi, Federico Bistolfi, Michele Salvi, Serena Pietrantonj, Vincenzo Barilari, Samuele Sordi
Structural Consultant Adams Kara Taylor: Albert Taylor
Environmental Sustainability Max Fordham Partnership: Neil Smith
Mechanical and Electrical System Max Fordham Partnership: Neil Smith
Cost Consultant Building Consulting: Pasquale Miele
Environmental Prefeasibility Silvia Serreli
Health and Safety Luca Peralta
Total Area 12,000 m²

Szervita Square [186]
Budapest, Hungary, 2006–10
Office and Retail
Client Orco Property Group
Design Zaha Hadid with Patrik Schumacher
Project Architect Ebru Simsek
Project Team Federico Rossi, Alexander Janowsky, William Tan, Ting Ting Zhang
Local Architects Laszlo Vancza, Zoltan Szecsi
Structural Consultant Adams Kara Taylor: Hanif Kara, Reuben Brambleby, Valentina Galmozzi, Marco Vanucci
Climate Engineer Transsolar Energietechnik GmbH: Volkmar Bleicher, Kai Babetzki
Renderings Stack! Studios
Additional Renderings for City Silhouette Study DPI: Tamas Pinter
Total Area *c.* 32,000 m² (11 storeys)

Abu Dhabi Performing Arts Centre [187]
Abu Dhabi, UAE, 2008–
Client Tourism Development & Investment Company of Abu Dhabi
Design Zaha Hadid with Patrik Schumacher
Project Director Nils-Peter Fischer
Project Architects Britta Knobel, Daniel Widrig
Project Team Jeandonne Schijlen, Melike Altinisik, Arnoldo Rabago, Zhi Wang, Rojia Forouhar, Jaime Serra Avila, Diego Rosales, Erhan Patat, Samer Chamoun, Philipp Vogt, Rafael Portillo
Structural, Fire, Traffic and Building Services Consultants WSP Group, with WSP (Middle East): Bill Price, Ron Slade
Acoustics Consultant Sound Space Design: Bob Essert
Façade Sample Construction King Glass Engineering Group
Theatre Consultant Anne Minors Performance Consultants
Cost Consultant Gardiner & Theobald: Gary Faulkner
Total Area 62,770 m²

Signature Towers [188]
Dubai, UAE, 2006–
Mixed-use Development Competition
Client Dubai Properties
Design Zaha Hadid with Patrik Schumacher
Project Architect Chris Lepine
Project Director Lars Teichmann
Project Team Chris Lepine, Stephan Wurster, Eren Ciraci, Alessio Constantino, David Campos, Hoda Nobakhti, Chryssanthi Perpatidou, Bowornwan May Noradee, Nahed Jawad, Hussam Chakouf, Bassam Al Shiekh, Daniel Norell, Tomas Rabl, Chiara Ferrari, Erhan Patat, Inanc Eray, Ceyhun Baskin, Jose Lemos, Josias Hamid
Project Architect (Competition) Tiago Correia
Design Team (Competition) Ana M. Cajiao, Saleem Abdel-Jalil, Sophie Le Bienvenu, Hooman Talebi, Mathias Reisigl, Diego Rosales, Tyen Masten, DaeWha Kang, Renos Constantino, Graham Modlen
Total Area 500,000 m²

Masterplan and Podium [188]

Dubai, UAE, 2005–
Mixed-use Development Competition
Client Dubai Properties
Design Zaha Hadid with Patrik Schumacher
Project Architect Tyen Masten
Project Director Lars Teichmann
Project Team Tyen Masten, Michael Hill, Pia Habekost, Miron Mutyaba, Amalthea Leung, Rodrigo Baretto, Brandon Gehrke, Judith Wahle, Vincenzo Cocomero, Agata Kurzela
Landscape Architect Gross.Max: Bridget Baines, Eelco Hooftman
Project Architect (Landscape) Gross.Max: David Richards

Dubai Financial Market [189]

Dubai, UAE, 2007–
Client Dubai Properties
Design Zaha Hadid with Patrik Schumacher
Project Director Lars Teichmann
Project Architect Raymond Lau
Project Team Raymond Lau, Aturo Lyon, Aturo Revilla, Chikara Inamura, Bessy Tam, Renato Pimenta, Amalthea Leung
Project Leader (Concept Design) DaeWha Kang
Design Team DaeWha Kang, Simone Fuchs, Andrea Balducci Castè, Tariq Khayyat, Maria Eva Contesti, Jesse Chima
Landscape Architect Gross.Max: David Richards
Total Area 42,000 m²

Madrid Civil Courts of Justice [190]

Madrid, Spain, 2007–
Client Campus de la Justicia de Madrid
Design Zaha Hadid with Patrik Schumacher
Project Architect Juan Ignacio Aranguren
Competition Team Andrés Arias Madrid, Jimena Araiza Olivera Toro, Brian Dale, Amit Gupta, Ho-Ping Hsia, Sara Sheikh Akbari, Tomas Rabl, Paulo E. Flores
Structural Engineer Ove Arup & Partners
Mechanical and Electrical Engineer Ove Arup & Partners
Façade Consultant Emmer Pfenninger Partners AG
Total Area 74,448 m²; overground: 49,033 m²; underground: 25,415 m²

Bahrain International Circuit [191]

Sakhir, Bahrain, 2007
Mixed-use Development for a Race Circuit
Client The Bahrain International Circuit; MCC Project Partners
Design Zaha Hadid with Patrik Schumacher
Project Leader DaeWha Kang
Project Team Ceyhun Baskin, Andrea Balducci Castè, Jordan Darnell, Inanc Eray, Simone Fuchs, Tariq Khayyat, Mariagrazia Lanza, Fadi Mansour, Liat Muller, Daniel Widrig, Fulvio Wirz
Engineering Consultant Ove Arup & Partners
Total Area 10 million m²

Regium Waterfront [192]

Reggio, Italy, 2007–
Design Zaha Hadid with Patrik Schumacher
Project Architect Filippo Innocenti
Design Team Michele Salvi, Roberto Vangeli, Andrea Balducci Castè, Luciano Letteriello, Fabio Forconi, Giuseppe Morando, Johannes Weikert, Deepti Zachariah, Gonzalo Carbajo
Structural Engineer Adams Kara Taylor: Hanif Kara
M&E Engineer Max Fordham Partnership: Neil Smith
Cost Surveyor Building Consulting: Alba De Pascale, Edoardo Lima
Maritime Structures Studio Prima: Pietro Chiavaccini, Maurizio Verzoni

Dongdaemun World Design Park and Plaza [193]

Seoul, Korea, 2007–
Park and Design Complex
Design Zaha Hadid with Patrik Schumacher
Project Leaders Eddie Can, Chiu Fai
Project Manager Craig Kiner
Project Team Kaloyan Erevinov, Martin Self, Hooman Talebi, Carlos S. Martinez, Camiel Weijenberg, Florian Goscheff, Maaike Hawinkels, Aditya Chandra, Andy Chang, Arianna Russo, Ayat Fadaifard, Josias Hamid, Shuojiong Zhang, Natalie Koerner, Jae Yoon Lee
Competition Team Kaloyan Erevinov, Paloma Gormley, Hee Seung Lee, Kelly Lee, Andrés Arias Madrid, Deniz Manisali, Kevin McClellan, Claus Voigtmann, Maurits Fennis
Local Architect Samoo Architects & Engineers
Structural Engineer Ove Arup & Partners
Services Engineer Ove Arup & Partners
Acoustics Consultant Arup Acoustics
Lighting Consultant Arup Lighting
Landscape Architect Gross.Max
Façade Consultant Group 5F
Geometry Consultant Evolute
Quantity Surveyor Davis Langdon & Everest

Surfers Paradise Transit Centre Site [194]

Surfers Paradise, Queensland, Australia, 2007
Redevelopment of the Main Transit Centre
Client Sunland Group
Design Zaha Hadid with Patrik Schumacher
Project Director Charles Walker
Project Architects Elke Scheier, Federico Dunkelberg
Project Team Paulo E. Flores, Feng Xu, Elizabeth Bishop, Michael Powers
Total Area 119,100 m²; 346m (height)

Lilium Tower [195]

Warsaw, Poland, 2007–12
Residential and Mixed-use Development
Client Lilium Polska Sp. z o.o.
Design Zaha Hadid with Patrik Schumacher
Project Architect Markus Planteu
Competition Team Thomas Mathoy, Sophia Razzaque, Naomi Fritz, Daniel Widrig, Fulvio Wirz, Mariagrazia Lanza, Dennis Brezina
Structural Consultant Ove Arup & Partners
Services Engineer Ove Arup & Partners
Feasibility Estimate Davis Langdon & Everest
Total Area 101,205 m²

Bahrain Museum of Contemporary Art [196]

Al Muharraq, Bahrain, 2007–12
Client H.H. Shaikha Mai Mohammed Al Khalifa; Culture & National Heritage Sector, Bahrain
Design Zaha Hadid with Patrik Schumacher
Project Architect Elke Scheier
Project Team Gerhild Orthacker, Jimena Araiza Olivera Toro, Susanne Lettau, Hee Seung Lee, Alexander Janowsky
Lighting Consultant Arup Lighting: Andrew Sedgwick, Jeff Shaw
Visualization Moka-Studio
Total Area 10,000 m²

La Jolla Residence [197]

La Jolla, California, USA, 2003–
Private Villa
Design Zaha Hadid with Patrik Schumacher
Associate Director Christos Passas
Project Architect Ken Bostock
Lead Architect Marcela Spadaro
Design Team Theodora Ntatsopoulou, Barbara Pfenningstorff, Daniel Fiser, Eirini Fountoulaki
Structural and Systems Engineer Büro Happold
Façade Consultant Front Inc
AOR Public Architecture + Planning
Lighting Consultant Isometrix

EuskoTren Central Headquarters and Urban Planning [198]

Durango, Spain, 2004–
Client EuskoTren; ETS Red Ferroviaria Vasca, Department of Transport and Public Works of the Basque Government
Design Zaha Hadid with Patrik Schumacher
Project Architect Juan Ignacio Aranguren
Project Team Jimena Araiza Olivera Toro, Andrés Arias Madrid, Muriel Boselli, Daniel Dendra, Alejandro Díaz, Elena García, John D. Goater, DaeWha Kang, Kia Larsdotter, Sophie Le Bienvenu, Murat Mutlu, Mónica Noguero, Markus Nonn, Benjamin Pohlers, Aurora Santana, Guillermo Álvarez
Competition Team Alvin Huang, Yang Jingwen, Simon Kim, Graham Modlen, Sujit Nair, Annabelle Perdomo, Makakrai Suthadarat, Philipp Vogt
Project Manager MECSA
Local Architect IDOM UK Ltd Ltd
Structural Engineer Adams Kara Taylor
M&E Engineer/Local Structure IDOM UK Ltd
Cost Planning IDOM UK Ltd
Façade Consultant Emmer Pfenninger Partner AG
Acoustics Consultant Arup Acoustics
Lighting Consultant Architectural Lighting Solutions
Landscape Design Gross.Max
Total Area 7,291 m² (central headquarters); 9,576 m² (commercial and leisure centre); 9,536 m² (railway station)

Neues Stadt-Casino [199]

Basel, Switzerland, 2004
Concert Hall
Client Casino-Gesellschaft, with the Baudepartementes des Kanton Basel-Stadt, Hochbau- und Planungsamt and the Erziehungsdepartementes des Kantons Basel-Stadt
Design Zaha Hadid with Patrik Schumacher
Project Architect Jim Heverin
Project Director Helmut Kinzler
Project Team Daniel Baerlecken, Matthias Frei, Naomi Fritz, Rebecca Haines-Gadd, Paul Peyrer-Heimstaett, Helmut Kinzler, Judith Reitz, Patrik Schumacher
Competition Team Daniel Baerlecken, Ana M. Cajiao, Tiago Correia, Helen Floate, Matthias Frei, Jim Heverin, Patrik Schumacher, Caroline Krogh Andersen, Saffet Kaya Bekiroglu, Yael Brosilovski, Christine Chow, Gemma Douglas, Mariana Ibanez, Tyen Masten, Judith Reitz
Structural Engineer Adams Kara Taylor
Mechanical Engineer Max Fordham Partnership
Acoustics Consultant Arup Acoustics
Theatre Consultant Theatre Projects Consultants
Façade Engineer PPE Engineering
Partner Office Burkhardt + Partner AG
Total Area 13,723 m²

Zhivopisnaya Tower [200]

Moscow, Russia, 2004–
Residential Development
Client Capital Group Holding
Design Zaha Hadid with Patrik Schumacher
Project Architect Tiago Correia
Project Team Christina Beaumont, Achim Gergen, Nils-Peter Fischer, Feng Chen, Larissa Henke, Sujit Nair, Agnes Koltay, Makakrai Suthadarat, Atrey Chhaya, Ken Bostock
Sketch Design Team James Gayed, Daniel Baerlecken, Sujit Nair, Yang Jingwen, Li Zou
Engineering Consultant Ove Arup & Partners
Total Area 95,000 m²

Eleftheria Square Redesign [201]

Nicosia, Cyprus, 2005–
Client The City of Nicosia
Design Zaha Hadid with Patrik Schumacher
Project Architect Christos Passas
Project Team Anna Papachristoforou, Amina Hussein, Sylvia Georgiadou, Marilena Sophocleous, Sevil Yazici, Phivos Skroumbelos, Ta-Kang Hsu, Stella Nikolakaki, Georgios Maillis
Competition Team Christos Passas, Saffet Kaya Bekiroglu, Michele Pasca di Magliano, Viviana R. Muscettola, Daniel Baerlecken, Daniel Fiser, Gemma Douglas
Project Manager Nayia Savvidou
Structural Engineer Hyperstatic Engineering Design
M&E Planning Unemec Engineers Ltd
Lighting Consultant Kardoff Ingenieure
Cost Consultant MDA Consulting Ltd

West Beach Villa Dellis Cay [201]

Turks and Caicos Islands, 2005–
Client The O Property Collection
Design Zaha Hadid with Patrik Schumacher
Project Architect Saffet Kaya Bekiroglu
Project Team Melike Altinisik, Ceyhun Baskin, Inanc Eray

E.ON Energy Research Department [202]

Aachen, Germany, 2006–10
Offices and Laboratories
Client Building and Real Estate NRW
Design Zaha Hadid
Project Architect Philipp Vogt
Project Team Philipp Vogt, Gernot Finselbach, Nadeen Mirza, Stefan Rinnebach, Sebastian Arnold, Mingzhe Lu, Tom Finke
Competition Team Philipp Vogt, Gernot Finselbach, Britta Knobel, Arnoldo Rabago, Margarita Yordanova Valova, Graham Modlen, Nils-Peter Fischer, Sara Klomps, Helmut Kinzler
Consultant Architect Mayer Bährle Freie Architekten BDA
Structural Consultant Ingenieurbüro VSI
M&E Services Transsolar Energietechnik GmbH; BFT Planung GmbH
Façade Consultant Planungsbüro für Innovative Fassadentechnik
Total Area 6,900 m²

Zorrozaurre Masterplan [204]

Bilbao, Spain, 2003–
Mixed-use Development
Client Management Committee for the Urban Development of the Peninsula of Zorrozaurre, Bilbao
Design Zaha Hadid with Patrik Schumacher
Project Architects Manuela Gatto, Fabian Hecker
Project Team Juan Ignacio Aranguren, Daniel Baerlecken, Yael Brosilovski, Helen Floate, Marc Fornes, James Gayed, Steven Hatzellis, Alvin Huang, Yang Jingwen, Gunther Koppelhuber, Graham Modlen, Brigitta Lenz, Susanne Lettau, Fernando Pérez Vera, Judith Reitz, Marta Rodriguez, Jonathan Smith, Marcela Spadaro, Kim Thornton, Zhi Wang
Local Architect Arkitektura Eta Hirigintza Bulegoa S.A.
Engineer Ove Arup & Partners
Landscape Architect Gross.Max
Total Area 60 hectares

Design for Proposed Museum in Vilnius [206]

Vilnius, Lithuania, 2007–11
Museum and Cultural Centre
Client City of Vilnius
Design Zaha Hadid with Patrik Schumacher
Project Architects Thomas Vietzke, Jens Borstelmann
Project Team Kristof Crolla, Julian Breinersdorfer, Melodie Leung, Claudia Wulf, David Seeland
Structural Engineer Adams Kara Taylor
M&E Engineer Max Fordham Partnership
Cost Consultant Sense
Media Concept Checkpointmedia Multimediaproduktionen AG
Theatre Consultant Anne Minors Performance Consultants

Maldives Luxury Resort [208]

Munandhua Island, Maldives, 2007
Residence Prototype
Design Zaha Hadid with Patrik Schumacher
Project Director Nils-Peter Fischer
Project Architect Britta Knobel
Design Team Daniel Widrig, Melike Altinisik
M&E Engineer Transsolar Energietechnik GmbH: Matthias Schuler

Farrer Court Towers [209]

Singapore, 2007–
Client CapitaLand
Design Zaha Hadid with Patrik Schumacher
Project Architects Michele Pasca di Magliano, Viviana R. Muscettola
Project Manager Charles Walker
Project Team Edward Calver, Bianca Cheung, Dominiki Dadatsi, Loreto Flores, Hee Seung Lee, Helen Lee, Jeonghoon Lee, Feng Lin, Jee Seon Lim, Ludovico Lombardi, Clara Martins, Kutbuddin Nadiadi, Hoda Nobakhti, Annarita Papeschi, Line Rahbek, Hala Sheikh, Zhong Tian, Sevil Yazici, Effie Kuan, Sandra Riess, Eleni Pavlidou, Federico Dunkelberg, Evan Erlebacher, Gorka Blas, Bozana Komljenovic, Sophie Le Bienvenu, Kelly Lee, José M. Monfa, Selahattin Tuysuz, Ta-Kang Hsu, Emily Chang
Local Architect Raglan Squire & Partners
Structural Engineer Maunsell Structural Consultants Ltd
M&E Engineer (Concept) Max Fordham Partnership
M&E Engineer Beca Group
Acoustic Engineering Acviron Acoustics Consultants
Lighting Design Lighting Planners Associates
Landscape Architect (Concept) Gross.Max
Landscape Architect ICN Design International
Quantity Surveyor DLS Singapore
Total Area 220,000 m²; basement: 70,000 m²

Middle East Centre, St Antony's College [209]

University of Oxford, England, 2006–
New Academic Building
Client Middle East Centre, St Antony's College, University of Oxford
Design Zaha Hadid
Associate Director Jim Heverin
Project Architect Ken Bostock
Design Team Goswin Rothenthal, Theodora Ntatsopoulou, Saleem Abdel-Jalil
Structural Engineer Adams Kara Taylor
Mechanical Engineer Max Fordham Partnership
Lighting Design Arup Lighting
Façade Consultant Arup Façade Engineering
Cost Consultant Sense
Fire Engineer Arup Fire
Planning Supervision JPPC Oxford
Forestry and Arboriculture Consultant Sarah Venner
Access David Bonnet
Total Area 1,200 m²

Symbiotic Villa [210]

Taipei, Taiwan 2008–10
Client De-Nian International Co Inc
Design Zaha Hadid with Patrik Schumacher
Project Architect Wen-Yuan Peng
Project Designer Rafael Portillo
Project Team Amenah Benjasem, Shao-Wei Huang, Seda Zirek
Local Architect Ricky Liu & Associates
Structural Engineers Ove Arup & Partners; King-Le Chang & Associates
M&E Engineer Ove Arup & Partners
Lighting Consultant Chroma33 Architectural Lighting Design
Total Area 700 m²

Darat King Abdullah II [210]

Amman, Jordan, 2008–
Concert Theatres, Educational Centre and Galleries
Client The Greater Amman Municipality
Design Zaha Hadid with Patrik Schumacher
Project Director Charles Walker
Project Directors (Competition) Christos Passas, Nils-Peter Fischer
Project Architect Tariq Khayyat
Design Team Maria Araya, Melike Altinisik, Dominiki Dadatsi, Renata Dantas, Sylvia Georgiadou, Britta Knobel, Rashiq Muhamadali, Bence Pap, Eleni Pavlidou, Daniel Santos, Daniel Widrig, Sevil Yazici
Structural Engineer Ove Arup & Partners
M&E Engineer Ove Arup & Partners
Theatre and Acoustics Consultant Artec Inc

Capital Hill Residence [211]

Moscow, Russia, 2005–
Design Zaha Hadid with Patrik Schumacher
Project Architect Helmut Kinzler
Project Designer Daniel Fiser
Design Team (current) Anat Stern, Thomas Sonder, Muthahar Khan, Kristina Simkeviciute, Talenia Phua Gajardo
Initial Design Stage Leader Tetsuya Yamazaki
Design Team (previous) Mariana Ibanez, Marco Vanucci, Lourdes Sánchez, Ebru Simsek, Daniel Santos
Project Manager Capital Group: Natalia Savich
Local Architect Mar Mimarlik Ltd
Structural Engineer ENKA Engineering
M&E Engineer ENKA Engineering
Electrical Engineer HB Electric
Façade Engineer Group 5F
AV Sound Ideas UK Ltd
BMS/Security Siemens
Lighting Design Light Tecnica
Interior Design Candy & Candy Ltd
Pool Design Rainbow Pools Ltd
Landscape Panorama Landscape Design
Water Feature Design Invent Water Features Ltd
General Contractor ENKA Construction & Industry Co Inc
Façade Consultant Wagner Group

Deutsche Guggenheim [212]

Berlin, Germany, 2005
Exhibition Design
Client Deutsche Bank
Design Zaha Hadid with Patrik Schumacher
Lead Designer Helmut Kinzler
Design Team Tetsuya Yamazaki, Yael Brosilovski, Saleem Abdel-Jalil, Joris Pauwels, Manuela Gatto, Fabian Hecker, Gernot Finselbach, Judith Reitz, Daniel Baerlecken, Setsuko Nakamura

Urban Nebula [212]

London Design Festival, London, England, 2007
Client London Design Festival 2007
Design Zaha Hadid with Patrik Schumacher
Project Team Charles Walker, Daniel Dendra
Structural Engineer Adams Kara Taylor
Manufacturer Aggregate Industries
Size 240cm × 1,130cm × 460cm

Lilas [213]

Serpentine Gallery, London, England, 2007
Temporary Tensile Fabric Installation
Client Serpentine Gallery
Design Zaha Hadid with Patrik Schumacher
Project Architect Kevin McClellan
Structural Engineer Ove Arup & Partners
Steel Fabrication Sheetfabs Ltd
Membrane Fabrication Base Structures Ltd
Lighting Design Zumtobel Illuminazione s.r.l.
Furniture provided by Estabished & Sons, Kenny Schachter, Sawaya & Moroni, Serralunga, Max Protetch, Swarovski
Total Area 310 m²; 5.5m (height) × 22.5m (width) × 22.5m (length)

Heydar Aliyev Cultural Centre [214]

Baku, Azerbaijan, 2007–
Mixed-use Cultural Centre
Client The Republic of Azerbaijan
Design Zaha Hadid with Patrik Schumacher
Project Architect Saffet Kaya Bekiroglu
Design Team Liat Muller, Sara Sheikh Akbari, Deniz Manisali, Lillie Liu, Marc Boles, Shiqi Li, Jose Lemos, Jose Ramon Tramoyeres, Phil Soo Kim, Yelda Gin, Yu Du, Josef Glas, Michael Grau, Erhan Patat, Simone Fuchs, Deepti Zachariah, Fadi Mansour, Jaime Bartolomé, Tahmina Parvin, Ceyhun Baskin, Daniel Widrig, Helen Lee, Murat Mutlu
Total Area 170,000 m²; building: 76,500 m²

Next Gene Architecture Museum [214]

Taipei, Taiwan, 2008–10
Client De-Nian International Co Inc
Design Zaha Hadid with Patrik Schumacher
Project Architect Wen-Yuan Peng
Project Team Amenah Benjasem, Rafael Portillo, Shao-Wei Huang, Seda Zirek
Local Architect Ricky Liu & Associates
Structural Engineers Ove Arup & Partners; King-Le Chang & Associates
M&E Engineer Ove Arup & Partners
Lighting Design Chroma33 Architectural Lighting Design
Total Area 700 m²

New Passenger Terminal and Masterplan [215]

Zagreb, Croatia, 2008
Competition
Client Zracna Luka Zagreb (Zagreb Airport)
Design Zaha Hadid with Patrik Schumacher
Project Architect Tiago Correia
Project Team Victor Orive, Mónica Noguero, Fabiano Continanza, Alejandro Díaz, Goswin Rothenthal, Oihane Santiuste, Rafael Gonzalez, Irene Mennini, Maren Klasing, Martin Krcha, Andres Schenker
Aiport System Consultant Deerns Consulting Engineers BV
Structural Engineer Adams Kara Taylor
Sustainability Consultant Max Fordham Partnership
Transport Planning Consultant Savell Bird & Axon
Total Area 75,000 m² (terminal); 500,000 m² (masterplan)

Atelier Notify [216]

Paris, France, 2007–08
Client Crystal Denim
Design Zaha Hadid with Patrik Schumacher
Project Architect Ana M. Cajiao
Design Team Muthahar Khan, Hooman Talebi
Structural Engineer Adams Kara Taylor
MEP Engineer FirstQ Ltd
Local Architect Gilles Fourment Architecte

Tea and Coffee Set [220]

1995–96
Limited-Edition Tea and Coffee Service
Client Sawaya & Moroni
Design Zaha Hadid
Design Team Maha Kutay, Anne Save de Beaurecueil
Material Stainless steel

Tea and Coffee Piazza [221]

2003
Limited-Edition Tea and Coffee Service
Client Alessi
Design Zaha Hadid with Patrik Schumacher
Design Team Woody K.T. Yao, Thomas Vietzke

Z-Scape [222]

2000
Furniture
Client Sawaya & Moroni
Design Zaha Hadid
Design Team Caroline Voet, Woody K.T. Yao, Chris Dopheide, Eddie Can

Iceberg [223]

2003
Seating
Client Sawaya & Moroni
Design Zaha Hadid with Patrik Schumacher
Design Team Thomas Vietzke, Woody K.T. Yao

Ice Storm [224]

2003
Installation, Lounging Environment
Client Österreichisches Museum für Angewandte Kunst
Design Zaha Hadid with Patrik Schumacher
Project Architects Thomas Vietzke, Woody K.T. Yao

Belu Bench [226]

2005
Client Kenny Schachter
Design Zaha Hadid with Patrik Schumacher
Project Designer Saffet Kaya Bekiroglu
Project Team Maha Kutay, Tarek Shamma, Melissa Woolford

Zaha Hadid Bowls 60, 70 and Metacrylic [226]

2007
Client Sawaya & Moroni
Design Zaha Hadid with Patrik Schumacher
Lead Designer Saffet Kaya Bekiroglu
Design Team Maha Kutay, Melissa Woolford, Tarek Shamma
Size (Bowl 60) 600mm (width) × 275mm (depth) × 130mm (height)
Size (Bowl 70) 700mm (width) × 325mm (depth) × 130mm (height)
Size (Metacrylic) 700mm (width) × 325mm (depth) × 130mm (height)

Aqua Table [227]

2005
Client Established & Sons
Design Zaha Hadid with Patrik Schumacher
Project Designer Saffet Kaya Bekiroglu
Design Team Tarek Shamma
Size 420cm × 148.5cm × 72cm

Flow [227]

2006–07
Client Serralunga
Design Zaha Hadid with Patrik Schumacher
Lead Designers Michele Pasca di Magliano, Viviana R. Muscettola

Z-Car I and II [228]

2005–08
Design for a Concept Car
Client Kenny Schachter
Design Zaha Hadid with Patrik Schumacher
Project Designer Jens Borstelmann
Design Team David Seeland
Size 3.68m (length) × 1.7m (width) × 1.4m (height); wheelbase: 2.45m

Z-Island [229]

2005–06
Installation for the Salone del Mobile
Client DuPont Corian
Design Zaha Hadid with Patrik Schumacher
Project Architect Thomas Vietzke
Design Team Georgios Maillis, Maurice Martel, Katharina Neuhaus, Ariane Stracke
Manufacturer Hasenkopf
Size Exhibition space: 214 m²; main island: 4.5m (length) × 0.8m (width) × 1.8m (height); second island: 1.2m × 1.6m × 0.9m; wall panels: 100 pieces at 0.6m × 0.6m

The Seamless Collection [230]

2006
Client Established & Sons; Phillips de Pury & Company
Design Zaha Hadid with Patrik Schumacher
Design Team Saffet Kaya Bekiroglu, Melodie Leung, Helen Lee, Alvin Huang, Hannes Schafelner

Dune Formations [231]

2007
Installation for the Venice Biennale
Client David Gill Galleries
Design Zaha Hadid with Patrik Schumacher
Design Team Michele Pasca di Magliano, Viviana R. Muscettola
Materials Aluminium, resin
Size 24m × 13m

Crater Table [232]

2007
Client David Gill Galleries
Design Zaha Hadid with Patrik Schumacher
Project Designer Saffet Kaya Bekiroglu
Design Team Chikara Inamura, Chrysostomos Tsimourdagkas

Moon System [232]

2007
Client B&B Italia
Design Zaha Hadid with Patrik Schumacher
Design Lead Viviana R. Muscettola
Design Team Michele Pasca di Magliano

Mesa Table [233]

2007
Client Vitra
Design Zaha Hadid with Patrik Schumacher
Project Designer Saffet Kaya Bekiroglu
Project Team Chikara Inamura, Melike Altinisik

Zaha Hadid Chandelier [234]
2008
Client Swarovski Crystal Palace
Design Zaha Hadid with Patrik Schumacher
Project Designers Saffet Kaya Bekiroglu, Kevin McClellan
Project Team Jaime Bartolomé, Simon Koumjian, Amit Gupta
Engineering Consultant Arup AGU: Tristan Simmonds
Fabrication LDDE Vertriebs GmbH; Stainless Steel Solutions; Sheetfabs Ltd
Materials Swarovski crystal, aluminium, SS cabling, copper wire, microprinted LEDs
Size 6m (height) × 2.25m (width) × 10.5m (length)

Swarm Chandelier [234]
2006
Client Established & Sons
Design Zaha Hadid with Patrik Schumacher
Project Architect Saffet Kaya Bekiroglu
Manufacturer Established & Sons
Material Crystal

Vortexx Chandelier [235]
2005
Client Sawaya & Moroni
Design Zaha Hadid with Patrik Schumacher
Design Team Thomas Vietzke
Partners Sawaya & Moroni; Zumtobel Illuminazione s.r.l.
Material Fibreglass, car paint, acrylic, LED
Size 1.8m (diameter)

Crevasse Vase [236]
2005–08
Client Alessi Spa
Design Zaha Hadid with Patrik Schumacher
Design Team Woody K.T. Yao, Thomas Vietzke
Manufacturer Alessi Spa
Material Silver-plated stainless steel

WMF Cutlery [236]
2007
Client WMF
Design Zaha Hadid with Patrik Schumacher
Project Designer Jens Borstelmann
Material Mirror-polished stainless steel

Series ZH Door Handles [237]
2007
Client Valli & Valli
Design Zaha Hadid with Woody K.T. Yao
Material Nikrall Zamak alloy UNI 3717

Icone Bag [238]
2006
Product Design
Client Louis Vuitton
Design Zaha Hadid with Patrik Schumacher
Project Designer Ana M. Cajiao
Design Team Muthahar Khan

Melissa Shoe [238]
2008
Product Design
Client Melissa/Grendene S/A
Design Zaha Hadid with Patrik Schumacher
Lead Designer Ana M. Cajiao
Design Team Maria Araya, Muthahar Khan

Celeste Necklace and Cuff [239]
2008
Showpiece Jewelry
Client Swarovski
Design Zaha Hadid with Patrik Schumacher
Project Designer Swati Sharma
Project Team Kevin McClellan, Maha Kutay
Materials Blackened pure silver and precious stones: white topaz, smoky quartz and black spaniel
Size Necklace: 43cm (length) × 40cm (width); cuff: 45cm (length) × 10cm (width)

Lotus [240]
2008
Furniture
Client La Biennale di Venezia
Design Zaha Hadid with Patrik Schumacher
Design Team Melodie Leung, Gerhild Orthacker
Materials Glass-reinforced plastic and polyurethane with high-gloss lacquer paint finish, foam mattress, wood, printed fabric, synthetic rubber, and stretch fabric
Size Closed: 5.7m (length) × 5.7m (width) × 2.6m (height); Open: 10.2m (length) × 6.1m (width) × 2.6m (height)

Home Bar [241]
2008
Private Members' Club Interior
Client Home House Ltd
Design Zaha Hadid with Patrik Schumacher
Design Team Maha Kutay, Melissa Woolford, Woody K.T. Yao, Susanne Berggen, Sophie Le Bienvenue, Susu Xu, Gabriela Jimenez
Materials Fibreglass, resin, fabric
Total Area 158 m²

Aura [241]
2008
Client Fondazione La Malcontenta
Design Zaha Hadid with Patrik Schumacher
Design Team Fulvio Wirz, Mariagrazia Lanza
Lighting Designer Zumtobel Illuminazione s.r.l.
Manufacturer Idee & Design GmbH; The Art Factory
Core Material PU-Foam RG100 and Polystyrene EPS 20 milled parts; coated with PU-SB1
Installation Details Aura-L and Aura-S: lacquered fibreglass with embedded steel frame
Size 6m × 3m × 2.45m

Cirrus [242]
2008
Furniture
Client Lois & Richard Rosenthal Center for Contemporary Art
Design Zaha Hadid with Patrik Schumacher
Design Team Melodie Leung, Gerhild Orthacke
Materials Laminate by Formica®, colour Black (909-90) in polished finish stained medium-density fibreboard
Size 1.8m (diameter)

Seoul Desk and Table [242]
2008
Furniture
Client NY Projects
Design Zaha Hadid with Patrik Schumacher
Designer Daniel Widrig
Size 422cm × 125cm × 72cm

Neil Barrett Flagship Store [243]
2008
Client Neil Barrett
Design Zaha Hadid with Patrik Schumacher
Project Architects Claudia Wulf, Elke Presser, Torsten Broeder

PHOTO CREDITS